Volume II

PRISONER OF WAR SERIES

U. S. Naval Institute
Annapolis, Maryland

1977

PREFACE

This Volume II contains a transcript of several interviews with Rear Admiral Jeremiah A. Denton, Jr., USN and with Commander Everett Alvarez, Jr. USN.

The interviews with Admiral Denton were obtained at the Armed Forces Staff College in Norfolk, Virginia where Admiral Denton was Commandant (1976). The interviews with Commander Alvarez were obtained at the Post Graduate School in Monterey, California (1976). Admiral Denton's interviews are intended to supplement his book ("When Hell was in Session", Reader's Digest Press, 1976). He speaks frequently on national forums and elsewhere. An example of these speeches may be found in the appendix to this volume. Commander Alvarez has given a number of interviews. A most recent writing of his - "Sound: a POW's Weapon", was published in PROCEEDINGS for August, 1976.

Both officers have checked their transcripts and the transcripts have been re-typed and indexed for the convenience of users.

John T. Mason, Jr.
Director of Oral History
U. S. Naval Institute
Annapolis, Maryland

September 1977

DECLARATION OF TRUST

The undersigned does hereby appoint and designate as his (her) Trustee herein, the Secretary-Treasurer and Publisher of the United States Naval Institute to perform and discharge the following duties, powers, and privileges in connection with the possession and use of a certain taped interview between the undersigned and the Oral History Department of the United States Naval Institute.

1. Classification of Transcript.

   ( )a. If classified OPEN, the transcript(s) may be read or the recording(s) audited by the qualified personnel upon presentation of proper credentials, as determined by the Secretary-Treasurer of the U.S. Naval Institute.

   (✓)b. If classified PERMISSION REQUIRED TO CITE OR QUOTE, the user will be required to obtain permission in writing from the interviewee prior to quoting or citing from either the transcript(s) or the recording(s).

   ( )c. If classified PERMISSION REQUIRED, permission must be obtained in writing from the interviewee before the transcribed interview(s) can be examined or the tape recording(s) audited.

   ( )d. If classified CLOSED, the transcribed interview(s) and the tape recording(s) will be sealed until a time specified by the interviewee. This may be until the death of the interviewee or for any specified number of years.

2. It is expressly understood that in giving this authorization, I am in no way precluded from placing such restrictions as I may desire upon use of the interview at any time during my lifetime, nor does this authorization in any way affect my rights to the copyright of my literary expressions that may be contained in the interview.

Witness my hand and seal this 24 day of February 1977.

witnessed by: C. J. Martin

I hereby accept and consent to the foregoing Declaration of Trust and the powers therein conferred upon me as Trustee:

R. E. Bowler Jr.

Interview No. 1 with Rear Admiral Jeremiah A. Denton, U.S. Navy
Place: The Armed Forces Staff College, Norfolk, Virginia
Date: Tuesday afternoon, 5 October 1976
Subject: Prisoner of War Experiences
By: John T. Mason, Jr.

Q: This is a great occasion for me, the opportunity to talk with you. I've known about you for a very long time and I'm most happy to have this opportunity.

Would you, perhaps, give me the date on which you became a prisoner of war and then tell me in what way, as you reflect upon it, you were equipped to deal with the situation as you obviously did deal with it?

Adm. D.: As a preamble, I would say it's an honor to be interviewed by a representative of the Naval Institute. I feel somewhat self-conscious about being given that much attention because the Naval Institute does deal with the significance of naval history, and particularly with great personalities. A lot of us who were losers, prisoners, have received a disproportionate degree of attention. I, perhaps foremost in that category, by virtue and happenstance of having been the first ex-POW to come home in the normal release sequence, and the first spokesman for the first airplane got an overwhelming sympathetic reaction from Americans and even from people of other nationalities when I made my little off-the-plane speech, a speech that was not at all unique. The others after me gave very similar comments. But, by the goodness in people, I became the recipient and symbol of the expended relief. I don't really feel worthy of the special recognition that I have received. This interview is further evidence of that.

With that preamble, I was shot down on July 18, 1965. I believe that since the explosion, impact, and eventual total loss of control of the aircraft occurred coincident with my pushing the pickle (the bomb-release button), that perhaps one of my own bombs went off on its own due to malfunction or being hit by antiaircraft fire. The coincidence of damage was identical with that pushing of the pickle. It is possible that the N. Vietnamese were mechanically freezing their A/A bursts for our release altitudes which were pretty stereotyped at that time, and that they were concentrating on the lead aircraft since we were losing a lot of leads. At any rate, this occurred on an Alpha strike against what was called the Thanh Hoa port facility, located a mile or so east of the Thanh Hoa bridge, and the center of a good deal of anti-aircraft emplacement.

I'd flown over the area on many other occasions and this was only my twelfth combat mission in North Vietnam, all twelve of which I'd led and most of which were Alpha strikes (strikes against very important targets). This was during the time of accelerated Alpha strikes because President Johnson's attention was apparently diverted to the Dominican Republic crisis and his metering out of the punishment to North Vietnam had to some degree stopped. It became less centralized and our air commanders, Air Force and Navy, then took their long-awaited chance to hit them harder, one which I shared in joy.

Q: Admiral Sharp must have rejoiced at this change in emphasis!

Adm. D.: All of us did. It reached such a point that I think on the flight before I had led a flight in which we struck one Alpha (major) target and then climbed up from that rendezvous and split into two flights and each went out and struck another Alpha target, making a total of three. So it was an eventful time during the air war over Vietnam and one which we welcomed as progress. But it was a short-lived progress and we never came close to hitting them hard enough until December 1972.

Well, I found myself without controls, apparently due to lack of hydraulic fluid because my speed brakes promptly "bled in". In the book, it says the speed brakes weren't working. The speed brakes were working during the dive-bombing run, but at bomb release, when the impact came and the left wing came up, the speed brakes bled in in a matter of seconds so that the plane immediately oversped. Recognizing that I had a hydraulic leak and seeing through the mirror that I was losing hydraulic fluid, I flicked a switch that isolated the systems one from the other, leaving the flight-control system isolated perhaps from any hits

Denton #1 - 4

that may have been in the landing-gear flaps or simply in the speed-brake system.

It worked enough to get me pulled out but apparently we had hits all over in the hydraulic system, because very shortly the controls failed at which point I soon ejected. That was the genesis of the situation that brought me to the Hanoi prisons and, as far as my sources of preparation were concerned, I would put patriotism about on the same level as belief in God. I believe one flows from the other. I believe "Render unto Caesar what is Caesar's and unto God what is God's."

Q: The fifth commandment? (See note in index on Fifth Commandment.)

Adm. D.: As it were, that commandment is pretty much the key to the situation. In that some people had trouble with reconciling what was Caesar's and what was God's, and felt that the war was unjust and conscientiously objected or perhaps even evaded because of that feeling. I believe there's a lot of danger in being overly responsive to one's own ability to distinguish between that which is right and that which is wrong, if it is ordered by the head of state of a just nation. I think we should just go ahead and do our thing. I notice that Christ, in His lifetime, did not rail against colonization by Rome of His native land. He wasn't even railing against slavery and many other conditions we perceive to be injustices now and which I'm sure were. But, nevertheless, because of the necessity of viewing God as the supreme authority, and the state as a subordinate but important authority, and coming on down to the paternal and tutorial authorities -- I believe that hierarchy should be respected and one should be extremely conservative about taking exception to the orders of those authorities.

In any event, I had no problem with the intellectual resolution of the justification for that war. I believed we should have been there. I believe the techniques that we used were no particular person's fault. They were the wrong ones. I anticipated that we might choose the wrong ones at the beginning. I hoped that we would hit them rather hard early, get the attention of the mule by hitting him sharply on the head, attack the tiger at his heart or his throat rather than at his claws. But we chose to attack the claws for political as well as, in some cases I think, improper military-estimate reasons.

Q: Incidentally, had you read Admiral Joy's book?

Adm. D.: No, Sir, I had not. I have also tried to keep my mind clear after I came home of other people's impressions, not because I thought that mine were superior but I just wanted to remember what mine were and record them for what they were worth.

Q: He wrote about his experiences with the communists in Korea, and Admiral Moorer is always telling me that all these people had the book available on how to deal with communists, but nobody read it in Washington.

Adm. D.: I didn't read it. He was the peace negotiator, Turner Joy?

Q: Yes.

Adm. D.: No, I hadn't read that book before being shot down and refrained from reading other people's books on Vietnam after I came back. Westmoreland's actually came out before mine. General Westmoreland will be our graduation speaker this time, by the way.

I have talked at length with Mr. Dean Rusk, with Maxwell Taylor, and with various admirals. I identify with what I know of Admiral Moorer's view. I have also talked briefly with Mr. McNamara, and that, I think, from the Naval Institute's point of view, might be an interesting conversation to recount, having to do with the philosophical part of the war.

Q: Indeed, yes.

Adm. D.: I think we don't have that war in perspective yet. I think it will take some years, and I offer this for what it's worth.

I was a student at the Naval War College, Naval Warfare or Senior Course, from 1963 to 64, and while I was there the subject of commit or not to commit in South Vietnam was the uppermost issue for the class and the subject of many of the talks given by speakers. Dean Rusk was a speaker there during my Global Strategy Week at the end of that class. I'll never forget his talk. I'll never forget the debates that raged among the students and the faculty on the issue.

I remember that an Army colonel there, who taught me how to play badminton, had won an outstanding-thesis award. I also won one. They gave two awards to the Army, two to the Air Force, and two to the Navy. We in the Navy were in the vast majority. We had 250-odd students and they had only fifteen each. This colonel got one of those awards for a thesis opposing our entry into Vietnam and he not only was allowed to outline his thesis from the stage after it was considered one of the better ones, but he outlined to me in great detail in private his views on that subject; including his conception, after a number of years in Vietnam in the prewar stage, that the Vietnamese people (I'll use that term now, but I would formerly have said the South Vietnamese and the North Vietnamese) would come to perceive us as foreigners like the French. He thought it was too late now to stop that trend; we simply wouldn't get the unity of purpose among the South Vietnamese we wanted because of that innate feeling they all had. That was his principal thought.

At first, I was rather swayed by it. Then I listened to other points of view and changed my mind. A former editor of the Marine Corps Gazette was in my seminar and he felt very strongly that we should commit. But I disagreed with him regarding the manner in which we should commit. He thought we should go in there the way we did, a very metered piecemeal approach, graduated response. I thought that was the wrong way to go. I thought these barefooted guerrillas would have an advantage over the highly technical capabilities of our land, air, and sea forces, and that we should strike at the source of their strength in the north, rather than try to tackle them on the Ho Chih Minh

Trail logistically.

But he said, "Well, Jerry, do you want to kill babies over there? We have the technology to tackle them in the field and beat them with all of our amphibious vehicles and that sort of thing. We can handle them."

I remained unconvinced and thought that we should go in there with what the Army used to call "shock" when I was a student here at the Armed Forces Staff College. I had to ask an Army man to explain what they meant by shock and he explained it to me. I believe we failed to employ shock in North Vietnam and cost both sides many lives, resulting in the loss thereby of the freedom of tens of millions of people, to say nothing of the broken lives of many people and the divisiveness that still exists in this country. Had we employed shock earlier, I believe all of this would have been avoided. We'd still have a relatively bipartisan foreign policy, lot more political unity than we have right now, and a lot more moral integrity than we have right now, as long wars do demoralize sadly.

The conversation with Mr. McNamara in 1975 related to the way in which we did conduct that war, especially early in the game. Aside from the conversation with that Marine, I had had conversations with people in the Navy about what we could and could not do in that environment with given weapon systems, including the A-6, which I flew. And I thought that perhaps some of the "careerist" type military people, including some naval people, were acceding to the tendency to say to their superiors what their superiors wanted to hear, both within the military organization and from the military to the civilian hierarchy.

Q: A very human trait!

Adm. D.: Right, an occupational disease of a bureaucracy, if you will.

Mr. McNamara happened to encounter me at one of Vice President Rockefeller's famous six parties, or whatever number he gave about a year ago, and I was honored with an invitation. I went. General Brown, my immediate boss, was there. He brought Mr. McNamara over and introduced me. So Mr. McNamara knew who I was and, of course, I knew who he was. He very generously opened the conversation by saying that he wanted me to know that he felt very apologetic about the way the war had been conducted and he accepted full blame for not having seen right at the beginning that we should hit them hard. And I said:

"Well, Mr. McNamara, that's a very generous acknowledgment on your part, but I'd like to test a thought that I've had on that. I believe that some of the military upon whom you had to rely for expertise before that war was actually joined and in the early days of it, may have given you an overoptimistic estimate of what we could achieve in a given amount of time with a given expenditure of blood and treasure."

As I finished that sentence, I saw the expression in his eyes change and he said:

"Admiral, I am not going to dwell on that, but there is a

great deal in what you have just said, and I think that we should guard against that in the future because it has cost us many battles and many lives in the past."

If I had to put my finger on the one characteristic of a military officer in peacetime that is most valuable to his country, it would not be experience or expertise, it would be integrity. You have got to be totally honest in the national interest about the limitations as well as the capabilities of given weapon systems in given environments. You cannot let yourself be carried away by the positive thrust which the respective defense industries tend to forward; one which the respective branches within the given services tend to propel an officer toward. If we were to correct this, not at any cost to esprit, I believe we would win more battles and win more wars and fight fewer battles and fewer wars than we have.

Q: It would eliminate a Madison Avenue approach to military capabilities?

Adm. D.: Yes, exactly, which we are more or less forced into by the congressional budget arena by which the one who boasts the most gets the most in some cases. This is, as I say, sort of an occupational disease.

At any rate, that was Mr. McNamara's reaction to that.

This is not to gainsay the over-all truth that it was the military, the regular military establishment, which early on urged, not only perceived but urged, the need for the use of more shock. Maxwell Taylor, though he was a proponent of graduated escalation theoretically, did himself recognize early enough on that the graduation shouldn't be as gradual as it was. By that time, which was very early, the civilian leadership wanted to believe what they first heard but very shortly it became impossible, because of the political situation back in this country and the pacifist anti-war thing, to do what even they, the civilian leadership, began to recognize as necessary. I also believe some of the Army generals had an erroneous view of what constituted effective bombing, and an inadequate understanding of how effective bombing could be in resolving the issue early and favorably. So it became a political rather than a military war at great political and military cost.

Q: And would you not say that it was all aided and abetted by the ability of the television to project battle scenes into one's living room?

Adm. D.: I think if the television had existed in any of our other wars to the degree it existed in this one, they would probably all have ended unsatisfactorily, because the living room, with the child, mother, father, the family environment, is not the proper receptacle for the hell of war. You cannot have ordinary people just looking at the means which, as Sherman called it, constitute "hell." The citizenry should keep in mind the justice of the end and have only a general knowledge of the fact that sacrifice is required to achieve it. No one really likes to risk his life. No one really likes to suffer. But unless the soldier or the sailor or the airman is allowed to maintain his momentum of resolve of doing that which he doesn't want to do physically but wants to do morally, unless he is allowed to maintain that, you can't win a war. And if the citizenry loses its support morally for a war because they are repelled by blood and guts, there's no way to prevail over an enemy. The battle in essence is truly moral and once you lose the psychological resolve to persevere, you've had it. If you're simply going to present the gore without presenting the real issue, which was the preservation of freedoms for those people who wanted freedom, there was no way to win.

To me, the greatest travesty has been the televised and printed criticism of, the Diem regime, which in retrospect was not nearly that bad. Maxwell Taylor - I don't think he'd mind my quoting him on this - very courageously answered a question here at the Staff College, and, although nonattribution is one of our respected conventions, I'm sure he wouldn't mind this. A student, thinking he was going to get a given answer from Mr. Taylor, asked why we hadn't more expeditiously rid ourselves of Diem, why did we wait so long to permit his assassination, when he was obviously an unpopular and reactionary leader.

Taylor did not quail. He did not give in to what he knew was expected of him. He said: "My only comment on that is that, in retrospect, although I know we did not order the execution of Diem nor did we contrive to get it done, we certainly didn't take any pains to indicate that we would resist it. I consider that one of the greatest mistakes we made in the war, because after that it was chaos with one lesser leader after another taking over. Had we stayed with the Diem regime, which is something the public doesn't have in perspective yet, we would have been better off."

So there are a lot of little things about this war I'd rather not see remain shoved under the rug. I'd like to see us take it out from under the rug and look at it, dissect really what went on, rather than stick with the emotional thrust of what did go on in the media about the war. I consider the out-of-context, disproportionate emotional treatment of that war on television, although it was news and sensational, to have been one of the most unfortunate features of the war and one of the greatest factors leading toward what became a disastrous defeat.

Q: Admiral, since you've talked about the role of television in stirring up this thing, perhaps I could inject this question. Why did not our government, once we had prisoners of war in Hanoi and had some knowledge of how they were being treated, want to talk publicly about this and more or less counteract what the television was doing in terms of battle scenes?

Adm. D.: For a very good reason, in my opinion. The higher a value the United States evidenced as being placed on the lives of those prisoners, the higher the value the North Vietnamese placed upon us as hostages. In other words, we would become a blue chip that could be exchanged for a higher and higher price in terms of the settlement of that war. And, in cold-blooded terms, we were but a few hundred Americans for whose wellbeing our government should not have, and didn't, sacrifice the freedom of tens of millions of those in the south.

It was a logical time to bring the prisoner issue up, after the American withdrawal from Vietnam had been forced by political developments in this country. Then, in order to achieve what punch we were able to deliver in spite of the withdrawal and with Vietnamization inevitable, it was logical to place a value upon us because we would have been able to say, "OK", if you don't give us our prisoners forthwith and in reasonably good shape, we'll mash the hell out of you," which is eventually what we did. As you will see in my book, and I confirmed this with Mr. Nixon (I haven't talked about it with Dr. Kissinger) in 1972 we were split into two groups. Half of us were up by the Chinese border and the North Vietnamese settlement was going to be to let that half, generally the junior half, go home. The rest of us were going to be kept in Hanoi. The juniors near the Chinese border were to be released through Hong Kong. We were to be kept there until the Americans showed "sufficient goodwill" following the peace settlement for us to go home. If the U.S. had agreed to that it would have been an example of too much value being placed on our lives and wellbeing vis a vis the lives and wellbeing of those in the south, who numbered in the millions.

Nixon didn't allow that. He made what I considered to be a decision as difficult and as important as any made during the war.

He refused that kind of settlement. I think that his decision to bomb Hanoi, military targets around Hanoi, with B-52s is comparable directly to Truman's decision to use the nuclear weapon on Hiroshima and Nagasaki. I believe his decision to continue the bombing on December the 26th was an even more difficult decision because it had to pause for Christmas and take the full brunt of the peaceful, Christly Christmas anti-war movement, and I believe that Christ was on the side of bombing North Vietnam! The POW cause helped give Nixon a sense of enough soliderity of concensus to make up his mind to hit them some more. Had he not done that, I would not be sitting here talking to you right now.

So that gave him additional leverage, as did the North Vietnamese Tet offensive, to go down there - not the Tet offensive but the big tank push across the McNamara Line, when was that?

Q: That was in the spring of 1972.

Adm. D.: Yes, that offensive, plus the issue made by the wives at the behest of the administration. Free rein was first given to the wives, as stated in my book, through Secretary of Defense Laird who, I'm sure, was directed by the president to say ok, girls, go public. That group of girls, including my wife, had remained loyal and had remained silent up to that point but once they were given the go ahead, they went. That plus the leverage that he got from the undisguised North Vietnamese aggression in the south with armor afforded the president the feeling that he probably had enough concensus to go ahead and bash them, which we should have done in 1965. And he did it. He won the war by that deed. The loss of that war took place after that fact, and I have some interesting correspondence here (which I will show you and ask that it perhaps not be released at this time) with President Ford on that matter. I originated this correspondence in December of 1974 and it deals with what I thought was going to happen.

All the intelligence that we had, and I was reading intelligence at that time, classified intelligence, on this subject plus all of the public newspaper estimates by all of the strategists in the newspapers, were to the effect that there was not going to be a North Vietnamese push in 1975. I disagreed strongly with that assessment and sent the president a letter, which I will show you, dissenting and recommending that he do certain things: one, put the supplementary appropriation for South Vietnam on the front burner, instead of the back burner; and, two, instead of asking for $200,000,000 or $300,000,000 as a supplementary appropriation, go ahead and have Dr. Kissinger or he himself tell the American public that it's really going to take $5,000,000,000 or $6,000,000,000 over the next several years to do the job. It would be well invested because our previous war budget had been up near $30,000,000,000 and we'd expended 50,000 American lives. And don't tell me it wouldn't have been acceptable to the American people - if the media had not distorted it out of all proportion.

He wrote me a very nice letter back. He sent my letter over to the State Department. It was a fairly hot item over there.

They did end up putting the supplementary appropriation on the front burner. Dr. Kissinger did come out and ask for $5,000,000,000 or $6,000,000,000 to do it. In other words, lay it out the way it was, don't get into the pussyfooting procrastinating stuff that happened early in the Johnson administration, but lay it out and let the American people judge.

Well, the media and Congress never gave him a chance. It was already an issue emotionalized to the point where it was too late to be rational. But in a cool-headed media environment, Kissinger's explanation would have persuaded. Then we could have saved the situation. As you know, I believe that we not only lost that situation but I don't think we have yet seen the end of the erosion of our credibility in the minds of our allies, and in the minds of the third and fourth worlds. I don't believe the situation is tragic. I know that they believe that we would act in our basic national interest in the case of Western Europe. We're not in NATO because we like them; we're in NATO because we know that Western Europe must survive in order for us to survive, and when you involve the basic national interest of survival of this country and the basic wellbeing of this country, they know we'll act.

South Vietnam was not a survival issue in itself. It was not a vital national-interest issue in the short term. In my opinion, it was in the long term. I believe you can't have international security, therefore you can't have national security, and therefore you can't have national wellbeing, unless you have a compassion for and a willingness to commit proportionately in support of the preservation of the freedom of those in other parts of the world who otherwise would be simply scooped up by communist aggression.

I don't believe that that's an idealistic point of view. I believe that it's a long-range selfish point of view, and that was the context in which I saw South Vietnam. But it wasn't perceived as an immediate vital national interest.

Q: Well, Sir, shall we go back to what you started to talk about, which was your equipment to deal with your sudden state as a prisoner of war? You mentioned patriotism as being a terribly important factor. Patriotism was instilled in you as an individual where? In the home? In the Naval Academy?

Adm. D.: Well, yes. Let's talk about patriotism in a rather general context first. So many nations warring against one another had as mottoes "For God and Country" and that has brought them through many, many wars for thousands of years of recorded history. The infidels versus the Christians, they were both thinking about God and nationality, and on up through history from there. It's always that way, so patriotism isn't something unique to Americans or to me.

Q: It's somewhat unique today, however, isn't it?

Adm. D.: Yes, it's becoming increasingly so.

The point I want to make is that patriotism in jail does not grow. Its partner, love of God versus love of country (if I may use the word "versus") does grow. Patriotism has no reason to grow. You already have your ingrained idea of the goodness of your country. You already have whatever sense of dedication you have towards your country and willingness to sacrifice. That does not grow, from the genesis of patriotism. What happens is the same thing that happens to anyone who's confronted on a prolonged basis, perhaps more than minutes, sometimes a few seconds is all that's required, with the absolutes of life or death. When one gets confronted with that, then the accoutrements of affluence, the incidentals, luxury, the distractions of the non-basic but perceived needs that we have about automobiles and fancy homes -- all that drops away and man is confronted with what man is, a species superior to the animals, which in turn is superior to the plants. Plants have sustenance, growth, and reproduction as their capabilities. Animals have that plus sensitivity and instinct. And man above that has intellect.

Because of that intellect, he is accountable for it. He is given that intellect by his God. He's given a conscience from which he can discriminate right from wrong, and when you are confronted with death you suddenly get that sense of accountability. You are made aware of what you are as a being. Your identity drowns you in realization. From that love of God and the increased perception of what you are and what God is, you grasp toward Him for help. He's the only thing you have left. Your country can't help you. You don't even want your country to help you because you don't want them to over-value you because that hurts them; you're a hostage that they can trade.

But God does respond. There is a God. He does respond. Most of us felt Him respond, saw Him respond, in ways that will leave our lives more impressed than any other incident or set of incidents that occurred within our lives. That certainly was the case with me.

Q: As you cited several times in the book.

Adm. D.: Yes, Sir, and they were just samples, really. And, as I say, this is not something that is peculiar to prisoners of war who were in danger of death from their own bombers as well as from the enemy, from disease and so forth, but it's the case with people who are dying with illness or people who have lived with physical pain or disadvantages all their lives, automobile accidents, and this sort of thing. When I go to the Veterans Hospital and visit these people who have been paralyzed for thirty or forty years, I find the same kind of self-realization because they've either self-realized or they have expired from despair, and the same thing would have happened in this camp. So I don't want to make us unique. I just want to categorize the situation.

So it brings out that which is best in a man. If he survives, he has to share his nature with God and nurture that. And that is capable of growth and did grow in most of us. It was definitely the thing that was responsible for my being able to look at myself without revulsion during my time there and after I came home.

Q: How does it grow in a man who is a prisoner in a cell? Does it grow from his experience daily with his guards and his torturers, or does it grow through prayer, meditation?

Adm. D.: Both. The experience with the guards and the torturer, and the deprivation is that which drives the man to turn to God in prayer. And I believe that, in justice, God would not respond simply to helplessness or pain but He will respond to an appeal. A man will pray when he's in need and man gets his prayers answered when he's in need. And that encourages him. It confirms, it strengthens, and God gives you more power. The more you pray the more tendency He gives you to pray, and the more you pray the more you get. It's a geometric progression. And that is the story of the whole thing and is the story of any exposure survival situation I've ever read about. I pick up the paper and about every week I read a similar experience and I don't see how people can read it and not be brought up short and consider how apathetic they are about that kind of situation in their daily lives, as a result of affluence. Christ said it's more difficult for a rich man to reach heaven than it is for a camel to pass through the eye of a needle. That's our basic problem in the United States and in the Western World in general. Coping with affluence. That's what destroyed every society that's gone down the drain. It's our basic problem.

Our leadership doesn't want to talk about that much because it's a corny problem. To start with, it's not very popular, and number two, it begs an argument. You win presidential elections by talking about how much more you're *going* to get. "Things aren't good now, we don't have enough employment," although we're at the highest level of affluence in the history of this country. Right this instant, the issues are going to be employment and whether or not business can get better and whoever wins the argument about how this can be done is going to win the election. Democratic politics are not much lent to identification, much less resolution, of the problem of coping with affluence, which is our problem. You become very aware of that problem by other means when you're in a little country like North Vietnam and you watch men fight over an empty tin can, just for the utility that that tin can can afford them. To say nothing of a fight over food or water. Rationing was very strict up there and we used to see the guards stealing - racing to steal - the few pieces of fat that the authorities would sometimes put in our soup. They would pluck it all out and eat it before we got it. And if we told the officers about it, they, knowing that it took place, would not be able to admit it. They would say, "Of course, you're mistaken." But it happened, and when you see that kind of poverty, and as I went to the airport in Hanoi to leave and saw the kind of poverty those miserable refugees were living in outside of Hanoi, I wept and I resolved that I would never forget that.

I do believe that it's also in the long-range interest of the United States to share what it can proportionately of its largesse with the rest of the world. You can't take a short-term point of view toward that because we couldn't try to give away and equalize -- it's impossible, because by giving away our power we would give away our long-range wherewithal to perpetuate this fountain of bounty that comes from the validity of our system, the free-enterprise system. Free enterprise is something that my co-author didn't want to stress in our book very much for reasons of his own, but I wanted to put it in there. I believe that what is distinctive about democracy, particularly about the United States of America at the time of its Declaration of Independence and what it has evolved into since then, is free enterprise, on the one hand, and, on the other hand, almost constituting a **dichotomy**, love of God and neighbor. Because free enterprise was the answer that they found at Jamestown, that they found up in Massachusetts, after trying the equivalent of communism by which everybody works, more or less but everybody gets the same reward. They found out in Massachusetts, they found out in Jamestown that that wouldn't work, that you had to realize that people are human, with human failings, with human selfishness, with human laziness, and that the most reliable generator of economic, of material welfare for the whole group is to graduate the rewards according to the output and the excellence. That is our system.

Q: In spite of your co-author's attitude toward injecting that note of free enterprise, you did succeed, I believe, in some of the conversations you recorded with your captors and your tormentors, you did on one or two occasions argue with them.

Adm. D.: I hope you're right.

Q: That came through to me.

Adm. D.: Good, I'm glad to hear that because I don't remember making a specific issue over the free enterprise thing. I did mention that nationalistic versus communistic Russia would, as Eastern European nations had dreamed, end up draining North Vietnam twenty years down the pike, but I don't remember -

Q: That's what I read into it.

Adm. D.: Good, I'm glad to hear that it's there. I have always stressed this in talks that I've given, that those two things must go together. They are mutually indispensable. You can't do without the free enterprise and get the material wellbeing that we've developed. And you can't go without the governor, the moderator, on that which ran amok would not work: Namely, the concern for neighbor, which is basically in the ten commandments, but more specifically stated in Christ's summation of them, "Love thy neighbor as thyself."

If you love your neighbor as yourself and practice free enterprise, you've got a winner, and we're starting to overemphasize the latter of the two. We're hot on the free enterprise still, and we're even losing a little of that - profit's becoming a bad word - but we're still sounder on that than we are, in my opinion, on the other ingredient of essential Americana, namely, love of God and subsequent love of neighbor.

Q: That's where your love of materialism creeps in and takes over?

Adm. D.: That's right. That's why the real problem is coping with affluence.

Q: I would think that you had a wonderful opportunity to have a wonderful perspective on this. Not only seeing the lack of material comforts among the North Vietnamese, but in a much more limited scope that you had within yourself. You were deprived of practically everything.

Adm. D.: Yes, sir, and I found that a purifying experience, really. Previously, I didn't have enough guts ever to deprive myself voluntarily to that degree, but I finally came to realize, speaking of sources of strength, the validity of that which I heard going through my relatively religious exposure in school -- I'd heard during that exposure that the most elevated form of human life was that of the cloistered monk or nun where, in deliberate self-abnegation, one spent one's time in contemplation and prayer. Well, like Simon of Cyrene, who was forced to carry the cross against his will, we were jerked from the average in the crowd and forced to carry a cross and, in the deprivation, found ourselves and were able to develop our strengths, our spiritual strengths.

It's too bad that there are so few men - I do see men - who are able to live abstemiously, even in this affluent society. They are able to live that way. That, I think, is what Christ meant by "Blessed are the poor in spirit." Regardless of how much you have, you've earned, and you give to your family, you can yourself live above it and make yourself poor with respect to how you indulge yourself with respect to things that aren't even good for your body. There are men who live like that. I hope I can keep my waistline from growing further and stay reasonably abstemious, because I think the Spartans had something in that.

Q: You talk of the monastic life and of willingly shuffling off all the accoutrements of civilization in order to be with God and make that an enriching experience. I think of my favorite saint, St. John of the Cross. Did you experience in your cell something similar to what he experienced on occasion, The dark night of the soul," when God seemed to be not available?

Adm. D.: Yes. You're always tempted to drown yourself in despair, as the war looked to be interminable and the end further and further away. You were tempted that way. I managed to avoid it as a matter of daily living. I think I can say that I never lived in hopelessness. But there were moments. I can remember one.

In the book, we simply say I prayed to God, but it was more than that.

Q: After five days of torture?

Adm. D.: It was not that particular occasion where I had five days of torture followed by another five days of torture, but it was the occasion when they invented this rig which wouldn't allow me to simply pass out. I had developed a capability of taking pain until I passed out, and this rig defeated that. I describe it in the book. After going through that four or five times and knowing there was no way I could end this, I'd always heard again in school, in church, that the martyrs had this "out": "they could get unconsciousness - and always remember that, that you can be tortured so far and then you can become unconscious." I had finally developed this capability myself, and then they had this method of thwarting it. When I got through four or five times of that and saw there was nowhere I could go and I'd already been praying all I could, I finally got to about the same place as saying not only "God, why have you forsaken me?" which Christ said, "Father, Father, why hast thou forsaken me," but just despair. God's not going to answer, there's no way out of this. That was when I hoped to die, but I knew the odds were against that. I was really hoping to beat them because I'd beaten them on the last few occasions and I knew if they busted me this time that I would have lost the advantage of those precedents I had established.

That was the closest I ever came to dwelling in despair and that was the time in which I told Harry Jenkins, who was the next senior guy, that I thought they were very close to breaking me permanently and that if they ran me through the mill one more time I thought I would break permanently. And, incidentally, that was their aim, not only with respect to me but to all the prisoners. Their original aim was to break you so that you were permanently broken. They got absolutely no satisfaction out of breaking you once to get you to write "I hate Johnson" or "I hate Nixon," or whatever it was that they wanted you to write. They got no satisfaction out of that. They knew that they could do that to one another, they knew they could do it to you. Their plan was to get you broken by that torture once or twice to the point where, then, upon their bidding alone and by only the threat of torture, you would go ahead and walk the way they wanted you to walk and talk the way they wanted you to talk. In that sense, we won. They never got us that way. Very few.

Q: Stratton talks about that and says he was broken and that it sometimes took six months for a man to recover from being broken on a given occasion. And a man was able to do this because the community of prisoners held him up.

Adm. D.: That's right. And that was an important early lesson because two perfectly good officers, after having each been unconscious a number of hours after a session and then writing a confession, felt so much in despair that they were telling others, young officers, new prisoners, that looking back on their own experience it hadn't done them any good to resist. Not only had they written a confession but they had undergone torture to unconsciousness for a long period of time, so why have both? Why not just write the thing and let it done?

Q: Take the short cut?

Adm. D.: Yes, and I had to countermand that order. Later, they both apologized tearfully and I'm sure would have come out of it on their own in a few more months. But you also had to allow for the fact that it did take a man time to bounce back. For example, after that particular torture session I was referring to a moment ago, when I thought I had licked them by developing the capability to take it till I passed out, they asked me before they let me out if I would copy a Dr. Spock paper three times, and I said I would. I did copy that paper, although the actual copying took days for me to do. They made me do it over and over again and I did not require any further torture to do that. I did write it.

Q: What was the purpose of that particular passage?

Adm. D.: I never have figured that out. I didn't know whether they were going to use my handwriting to forge things, because they kept telling me to write it more carefully, don't scrawl, write carefully. They made me repeat it so many times that I don't know how many pages it took to write this article over and over again. Either that, or what the man was saying they thought was extremely persuasive. As you know, Dr. Spock had a rather psychologically persuasive anti-war thing there, and they may have naively thought that the simple repetition of my writing this and being conscious of what I'd written in my weakened physical and mental state would somehow have a major effect on me.

They took it as a thorn in their side that they were never able to get me down for very long. It was a matter of days, at the most, that they could even sort of cope with me. I think they may have thought that this would have persuaded me because some of the guys were beginning to shake a little bit, mentally, about the war. We'd been pounded for years about how unjust it was and what was going on back in the States.

At one camp I was the only one who held onto the belief that we hadn't been kicked out of KheSanh. Even my own comrades were telling me, aside from the North Vietnamese, that I was a fool not to believe that, or to believe as I did. The evidence was overwhelming, even reading through the propaganda. And I'm proud - this is a boast! - to say that I just did not believe it. I couldn't believe they'd kicked those Marines out of Khe Sanh.

Q: One more thought on Spock, and that is they must have known that what he said and what he wrote was quite unpopular with most of the prisoners?

Adm. D.: They did believe that. That might have been a punishment for me to have to write what he said. The last time I was threatened with torture and was a little bit confident that I wouldn't be tortured because the treatment had changed, they threatened to have me write like Senator Fulbright. That was a real sense-of-humor dig at me because they knew how I would like that!

Denton #1 - 31

Q: Going back to our original discussion about how you were equipped to deal with this situation in which you were thrust, would you say something about the value of your home and the value of the home in general as a supportive element?

Adm. D.: Surely. It's corny but -

Q: No, it's not so corny!

Adm. D.: One of the earliest things I can remember, before I even have remembrances of religious convictions, is my mother reading me a story out of something called the Bookhouse series. You're familiar with those. Most people had them when they were kids. I'll show them to you. I still have them at home, what's left of them, some of them are pretty well ripped up.

There was one story in there about knighthood and these magic shields. These guys would be sent out on quests and into battle and if they upheld their honor they would come back and their magic shields would be all shiny, and if they did badly or not too well they'd come back clouded up. If they did very dishonorably, they'd come back black. And, strangely enough, I thought about that a lot. Then, as I say, the God bit is even more important, in my opinion, especially in dealing with the communists or fighting atheistic communism. It's pretty easy to put yourself into the martyr role, as I did when I communicated with Stockdale when I was going into the confession torture. I told him I wouldn't come out and I believed that I would go to heaven directly because martyrs, by tradition in my church, do. So the lines are drawn.

Q: Was he able to counteract that in any way? Did he say anything to you?

Adm. D.: Stockdale? No, he was just respectfully listening to my last words, which included a message to my wife Jane, asking her to get married again and tell her that I loved her enough to love the man she would marry, and that I knew that that would in no way deprecate her feeling toward me. So he was, as I would have been listening to the same kind of thing - and I did listen to it a few times - just sort of quiet.

Q: Would you not have looked upon another man saying that as -

Adm. D.: Melodramatic?

Q: No, no, no, as weakening him in the face of a forthcoming ordeal?

Adm. D.: No. I knew that they had broken Risner. I just learned that before I left, and I respected Robby and I knew that if they had broken him, the only way out for me was death, that they would be able to impose enough pain to get me to do something. I saw death as the only way out. So that's the way that was.

The sources of strength? Okay, the way my mother raised me, she tried to instill in me that kind of stuff. Then the God bit in church and school. It was always in front of me. I went to Catholic schools in grammar school most of the time, and I learned from the example of those good nuns. My father and mother were not of the same religion and they allowed me to choose, so I went around and looked in libraries and read books on religion, and I ended up consciously choosing the one I finally embraced. I embraced it fairly firmly. I believed in it, all the things I believe in now I believed in before I was a prisoner. I didn't have the strength of belief or conviction to keep me living a life that was consistent with that which I perceived to be virtuous. I lived an imperfect life, I think a reasonably good life, but not a perfect life. There were times when I did things that I'm very ashamed of, plain old bad sins. The problem now with our society, to me, and I don't mean to jump this far ahead, is that we're starting to try to do away with the idea of there being any difference between right and wrong.

I don't condemn sinners. I condemn the idea that there is no difference between right and wrong. I'm more concerned with that as an issue in our society as it relates to the essence of what America is ("Love God, love thy neighbor" and free enterprise) than I am with the outside threat to the United States of America by communism. I believe that if communism weren't there and we didn't have any outside threat, we could still decay and fall by self-destruction. It's that coping with wealth thing that bugs me, and I see many evidences of its advanced development. And that has to do with the possibility that if the Navy is not able to use me in a way that I can continue to concentrate on that aspect of national security, then I will have to change my suit.

I regard the naval profession as noble as any, but I regard the threat now, the _immediate_ threat, as non-naval, even non-military.

I believe that were we to increase our budget by $10 billion -- yes, we would have more wherewithal for fighting and thereby have a more favorable balance of physical power vis a vis our adversaries, but I don't think that's where the main problem is. I believe that the problem is that we, with a tremendous inheritance of spiritual strength which is responsible for our greatness and for our physical power, are beginning and are well on the way toward discarding the values of that spirituality and thus destroying ourselves.

Q: Why do we want to destroy our standards? Is it all attributable to affluence and an easy way of life? Or is it something else? Is it involved with more education? What is it?

Adm. D.: The basic issue which affluence bears upon it is the one which, if there is any truth to the myth or tradition about it, concerns the fallen angel who was banished from heaven when he became so proud that he was thrown out. This is the same problem that beset Adam and Eve when they had everything that they could conceive of as being desirable, but for the sake of asserting pride, asserting ego, chose to bite an apple, the one thing they were told not to do. That is what is involved.

It's not a matter of really thinking you _need_ any more, although that's a minor feeling; it's a problem like in the sexuality thing today, the new permissiveness, the new morality on that. The problem isn't that man has become any more sexual or woman has become any more sexual. The problem is that we want to do something that is wrong. If we were simply more sexual, we would just be having that much more intercourse with our wives. But that's not it. It's got to be forbidden. The guy who formerly was faithful or occasionally unfaithful to his wife under circumstances maybe involving booze or extreme temptation, would now under this set-up, be more tempted to take on a mistress. The abuse of pride is to do something that's wrong, because, what the hell, you're not dependent upon God or anything, get your kicks, be free, do your own thing. The guy who previously had a mistress would try some other kick, say, homosexuality. The guy who was into that would get into sadism and masochism.

That's the way I see things going. I see them going that way to a degree that is absolutely unprecedented in American history, but not absolutely unprecdented in the history of the world. It happened in Persia, Greece, and Rome. It happened in medieval Europe. I don't know why we have to learn the same lesson again. I believe the identification of this problem is so important that it transcends even the material strength, the physical strength, the military strength question. Because in our selfishness to possess our goods, I think we will maintain a reasonable degree of military strength for awhile at least. But the decay that comes about, started by affluence in which ego, pride, becomes transcendant over self-subordination to God. That is where it all is. And that decay in its early stages, while not causing a great decrease in national defense appropriations, does affect what the national concensus permits in allowing the President to do with military forces in regard to their use or threatened use. This adversely affects national security.

Q: What happens when we eradicate the sense of doing something wrong? I mean being daring and doing something that's forbidden. Because we're erasing that feeling that it's forbidden and anything is possible.

Adm. D.: That's right. I'm not naive and I'm not idealistic enough to think that we're ever going to have an ideal society. I don't believe that the good old days were days without plenty of wickedness and so forth. I'm not capable of conceiving that kind of a situation here on earth, but I believe that when we erase the inhibitions against infidelity in marriage or against total sex before marriage or outside of marriage, as soon as you achieve that -- which is very easy to achieve and has been achieved in other societies -- when you achieve that in the societal sense, when the mores come down to the point where they are now, as you say, we are erasing that difference, then the glue that holds a marriage together gets weak. That glue has to counteract the vicissitudes, the boredom, the way the wife looks after she's had a hell of a day at home, and you've had a hell of a day at work. You come home and you've got to see each other as attractive and somehow be happy rather than think about that babe next door, so-and-so's wife, when you get to the point where you're neighing after your neighbor's wife like a well-fed stallion, which is the way the Bible puts it, then the family has gone, because a wife can't stand a man being unfaithful to her. That's what caused the women's liberation movement -- the double standard. Those women resent that. If it's flaunted, they're going to do their own thing. You've come a long way, baby: you can go round and have yours, too, on the side and outside of marriage.

As soon as you do that, the family is on the way down the drain, and we've got one marriage in three or four ending in divorce right now. Forecasts now say one in two will fail during the next few years. When you destroy the family as an institution in a nation, you destroy the basic building block of a nation. If we could keep our family, we could keep our nation, and under atheistic communism, which is very, very young, they can't keep theirs. Their society would fall apart if we had had the resolution in South Vietnam to go ahead and win it when we had it won. They would be a hell of a lot worse off over there in the Soviet Union than they are right now. They can point with great pride in North Vietnam and Russia at the way we copped out on our own stated position -- for a decade we stated what our objectives and commitments were and we abandoned them. They can say to themselves, "Ah, ha, look." To the whole population they can say convincingly, "They don't have the character, they don't have the guts." If we'd hung in there, then people like Sakarov and Solzhenitsyn wouldn't be going around having to bleat, the way they do, about, "for God's sake, hold on to what you are, because that's the only thing our people have to hope for, the fact that you will outlast this system, which is rotten and will die on its own vine if you will just live long enough to let it happen. Be true to yourselves that long."

Q: In the book you mentioned several occasions when your captors threw at you, or at one of your colleages in prison, the offer of a woman and implied that it was never accepted by any of the prisoners of war. Does this say that the men who were incarcerated there had a strong loyalty, a strong feeling of loyalty, to their homes?

Adm. D.: Well, to make a generalization, I would say that 80 per cent - maybe that's an exaggeration, but certainly a large proportion of those people, if they were back home or in a foreign port, would have had irresistible temptations to be unfaithful to their wives at one time or another when the woman wasn't forced on them. "The grass is greener. I've got my own choice, I take it." It was the confrontation with the moral opposite of what we are that caused us to be conscious of the need to be true to what we are. Therefore, we could, with very little temptation, tell them to take the girl and throw her in the well, we don't want her. No problem.

I don't know anybody, even the couple of guys who finked out on the anti-war bit, who, in their hearts were not trying to justify to themselves what they were doing. Even they wouldn't have taken that route because it wouldn't have been consistent with their so-called moralizing about the war. Basically man is a moral animal. And when he gets down to the guts of life and death and his own sense of self-integrity, even the guys who were able to fink out on patriotism weren't able to fink out in that manner whereas practically all of us would have finked out on it back here under normal circumstances. We would have been tempted and not felt any direct, general moral confrontation on the issue. At times, on a long deployment we might have rationalized, well, my wife's not here and _she_ is, and, man, she smells good and I'm a little drunk and let's go to bed.

Q: Yes.

Adm. D.: But over there it was an entirely different presentation that you were confronted with, and it was in context with all of the other goodies they were offering: you got better food than your buddy got, or you go home early, or you go home now. If the American public will just get one thing out of my book, and that is dissuasion from any possible suspicion in anybody's mind that there was a big line of people over in the North waiting to come home, which is the impression they tried to give, come home on any basis, like some of the guys did early -

Q: Not many. You could count them on the fingers of two hands.

Adm. D.: Not many, that's right, and I don't want to name any of them. Some of them came home with permission, as you know. Do I make the distinction clear that the sex bit is put in context with all of the other perceived evils of the opposite of belief in God, and you just can't handle that? You see things in black and white and you won't accept that.

Q: Yes.

Adm. D.: And that was true of some guys whose lives before that had been totally promiscuous.

Q: Yes. What was the real objective of the captors in dealing with their prisoners?

Adm. D.: It went in phases. The first, in my opinion - and all this has to be personal impressions but from my experience - from July 65 to October 65 their aim was persuasion, enticement for privilege, propagandizing with the end of converting us to their point of view so that we would write, act, beseeching our government to desist and condemning our president.

In October they realized that wasn't going to work and they started the torture program. From October of 65, with torture, until December of 66, with torture and with increasing torture (including the Hanoi march and the preface and the aftermath of that, which was an orgy of torture) their end was unique, their aim was unique and they dropped it. The aim during that time frame was, by torture and cajoling, the stick and carrot, to subjugate <u>totally</u> the <u>entire</u> <u>mass</u> of prisoners to the point where the entire mass of prisoners would line up and do their will. That's one aim.

They changed that aim. They came off of that aim and started feeding us better, seeing that wasn't going to work, and we were all literally proceeding toward death. We were dying. George Coker didn't even recognize me, because of my skeletal appearance, although he'd known me for years, when he saw me through a crack. They saw that that wasn't going to work. Yes, they could torture a guy to make him sign something, and they could torture him again to make him sign something else, but instead of making progress they were making the guy even more stubborn and they had to torture him even harder the next time to get him to do the same thing. Or maybe they couldn't get him to at all. That was about the time when I was getting to the point where I could take it to unconsciousness and took it to unconsciousness during that time.

They were beginning to wonder and guys were probably beginning to die off, and all of us were near death. They came off it.

The aim then changed to get "spot" propaganda advantages. In other words, take a limited group, given individuals, for various reasons, usually if you were relatively senior, relatively well known back in the United States, or giving them a great deal of trouble, and using the "crimes" that you committed, such as communicating or exhorting others to resist, that sort of thing, torture those individuals. They would also break an individual by extra torture, extra solitary confinement, to get him to stop affecting their efforts toward the rest of the prisoners.

Q: Because of his intrinsic value among the group?

Adm. D.: That's right. That was one factor in the concentration of torture on given individuals and on solitary confinement.

But they did abandon the idea of mass subjugation by simple torture, one after another, which is what was happening in both the Briar Patch, which I forgot to mention in my book, and at the Zoo, as well as back at the Hanoi Hilton. They were doing it at all three places. I only gave it from the perspective of the Zoo, but the same kinds of torture devices and strategies were being employed at the Briar Patch, which was another camp, and at the Zoo, as I described in the book. They did come off of that mass subjugation thing and did go toward just groups after that.

Indeed, they would punish a whole camp, for example, for an escape effort. They would try to deter you from another effort by a two- or three-month torture purge. The objective was no longer mass subjugation. They had determined that that was an unrealistic objective. It was just to hurt you enough to make you decide that it wasn't worthwhile to try another escape. Or, if you had tricked them in any big way, something like what Nelson Tanner did when he wrote his biography, including Clark Kent for Superman, and other names like that in there. They tortured him for that and then they tortured men for military information. But they did not retain the unrealistic objective - they didn't consider it realistic to try to subjugate the whole bunch of us by massive torture, campwide, prisoner-program-wide, to subjugate us. They came off of that and went for spot-purpose purges. That's the main difference. Of course, they tortured newly shot down men for "confessions" at times in order to warm them up to give military information, and at times they went straight for the military info with no disguise.

Q: Did you gain any insight as to who dictated these policies?

Adm. D.: Yes. Cat, you know, was obviously enough - when I say "obviously enough," I mean it was apparent enough to us, and I had as much time person-to-person with Cat as anybody -- that he was actually originating the strategy and he was relying on his much-boasted-of experience with the French in the previous war with them, to set the pattern.

It was he, and if you read this carefully, we do bring out it was he who after Ho Chi Minh's death apologized to me as the leader of that camp, and I happened to be the acting leader, as I brought out in the book. But there were some people senior to me there who weren't running it - Stockdale was one but it wasn't his fault because his roommate was a psychopath (we can't ever print that), and wouldn't let him communicate. But there were some Air Force guys who were there and they just weren't piping up.

Cat knew I would run the camp. I did run the camp. He called me in and said that Ho Chi Minh had died - no, he said that from now on we would be able to follow the code of conduct, that he, Cat, had been required to make public apology, public criticism before the people, because he and other North Vietnamese

Denton #1 - 44

officer and guards had violated the 2,000- or 4,000-year-old policy of Vietnamese leniency towards their prisoners. They had, against the rules of the state, treated us unfairly and brutally. He had been required to make public apology for that, and from now on -

Q: This was after Ho's death?

Adm. D.: Yes. When he called me in there it was late December 1969, and I had already noted, having been caught twice communicating at Alcatraz just before this, in October and not being tortured for it for the first time, that the treatment had changed. I relate that in the book.

Q: Yes, you indicate that.

Adm. D.: The Cat's scene with me, which went on for about three weeks, three or four hours a day with a French dictionary, French-Vietnamese, French-English, and Vietnamese-French dictionary, that's the way we had to go, and we really discussed this thoroughly. My helper in the book did not make clear that the key point was that they wanted us to take home the perception that Ho Chi Minh had been responsible for the torture purge. And that only a few North Vietnamese culprits, such as Cat who was running the show at the operational level, were responsible. Also they wanted us to know that the bad thing (that would have been the cause of war crimes trial for them, had the war ended the way it should have ended) was buried with

Ho Chi Minh. Only Cat and a few others were responsible. This would have cleared all of the other North Vietnamese officers and men from any reprisals by the United States government. That was why he told me this.

He also told it to Howard Rutledge in about five minutes. He spent days telling me. He told it to Howard a little later. And Cat couldn't keep his dirty paws out. They, I'm sure, had told him to come off the torture, come off the pressure, get these guys fattened up and ready to go home in good shape some day.

Well, he, as described in the book, couldn't resist trying certain things like keeping some men in solitary and keeping one group of relatively collaborative prisoners segregated from the others and conspicuously favored by his treatment. When I protested this, because he was making inroads on our morale and unity -

Q: Devastating, wasn't it?

Adm. D.: Yes - he came back with, "Well, you're all my nephews. I am your uncle. Some of my nephews I treat differently from others and you cannot tell me what to do about that."

Without ever admitting to him how much trouble he was causing us, I said, "You keep that up and I'm going to give you real trouble." I told him that three times, and when he didn't come off it, that's when I called this fast, that John McCain wrote about in the Newsweek thing, that was very unpopular in the camp. There was no way I could explain to everybody in a tiny piece of paper what I was doing, but I knew that Cat wanted us fat and that Cat was doing things against the orders of his superiors. They wanted peace with us at that point, but he was still hung up on trying by devious means to split us up and exploit some. The big shots weren't really interested in that any more and I knew that. I knew the biggest thing they wanted was to keep us healthy.

So I laid on this fast and said voluntary participation, sick people don't have to join - I mean are forbidden to join. John Dramesi jumps on me about that fast in his book, but it worked. They took their usual face-saving period and, then, in a couple of months everybody got cellmates. Cat, we think, was ostracized and maybe kicked out. We know he was demoted. He lost his star. Cat left the camp and the next camp commander, three days after he was there, called me in and said, "Denton, I want you to know from now on all of you will be treated equally." And never again did they flaunt a difference in treatment. They tried secretly to work on a few guys, but what Cat had been doing was openly flaunting to us, "Now, these guys are cooperating. They're going to be allowed to eat outside, they have free run, they can walk from their cells to the latrine, they can walk outside and play. The others of you are bad guys and you can't."

This was resulting in a murderous state of mind, literally murderous state of mind, in the camp. Guys would have killed one another over this.

So they officially came off of this. They did later segregate some people, they thought we didn't know about, and treat them a little better than the others. But they did not plan or try to flaunt this thing in a way that was harmful to our morale.

Q: Why did they not adopt this policy from the very beginning?

Adm. D.: That is the dumbest thing they did, because with the French and with the North Korean experience that the Chinese and North Koreans had had, they thought their other thing would work. They thought that the massive torture program would work, and eventually they'd have everybody pretty well kicked down.

Q: It seems to me they did have the key to nullifying your whole unit?

Adm. D.: Correct. If they had done that from the beginning, if instead of choosing the obvious, which was to humiliate myself and other seniors in front of the others, like they didn't give me any shoes for a long time and the others all had shoes, and they wouldn't treat my foot which was infected from the irons and I was limping around, and they wouldn't do other things, they just treated me with great disdain, which was dumb. And they kept on doing that.

The first big confession torture was for Risner and then the next one was for me. Well, that was exactly counterproductive for them. They tortured a whole lot of guys between Risner and me for confessions, but they published Risner's and mine first. That's the dumbest thing they could have done because the guys knew that Robby and I were fairly tough.

Q: They weren't very well versed in human psychology, were they?

Adm. D.: In that one particular instance they weren't. They'd come up with a thing of meat and start shoving it in my cell and then say, "Oh, no, no, sorry" and then pretend to give it to another cell. They tried all that stuff.

Had they started early on offering girls, booze, and stuff like that, they'd have made a lot more money. But they waited until they had confronted us with a challenge to our individual and group integrity and we solidified, and then they tried it but it was too late.

Q: You indicate three or four times, as I recall, in the book, evidence of a humanitarian streak among some of the guards and some of the attendants. What can you say about that? I mean how does that tie in with the Vietnamese character, as you came to know it?

Adm. D.: I don't find the Vietnamese character to be repulsive. The only thing repulsive about the Vietnamese behavior was the poisonous influence of totalitarian communism. The same kinds of things that Solzhenitsyn writes about with respect to Gulag Archipelago, to the camps that he knows about and was in, the same kinds of things that Cardinal Mindszenty wrote about, the things that Sakarov writes about -- that was introduced into the North Vietnamese strain and they tried to practice it. Early in the game, in 1965, you could almost see the man reading the textbook about how the Russians and the Chinese were telling them to apply the stick and carrot, and then they would go and do it by rote. It was childish to watch this happen.

For example, after my torture for the confession when I told Stockdale I wasn't coming out and so forth and giving my final messages, they thought they had me down because I had had a pretty good go in that room. They tortured me all day and I was unconscious for a pretty long time. So they needed somebody reasonably presentable to get before the press, and they felt while they had me down from that pretty rigorous session, they would get me to spout some stuff to a newsman, a Japanese newsman.

So for three days and nights they kept me up -

Q: He was a sympathetic - ?

Adm. D.: No, he wasn't. He turned out to have more reporter blood in him than he had communist blood, that's all. He wasn't sympathetic. That wasn't described too well in the book. Anyway, Mickey Mouse kept me up three nights, telling me the "truth" about the war. Well, the "truth" about the war went all the way back to World War II, and he would go into things about how the Russians won World War II. If he had told me that the Russians had a lot to do with the defeat of the Germans, that would have registered all right.

Q: That's the way you read the history books!

Adm. D.: Sure, but he told me they defeated the Japanese. He said, "You poor guys have been brainwashed by your government to believe that you beat the Japanese, and actually what happened was a decisive land engagement up there between the Red Army and the Japanese Army –

Q: At the last minute!

Adm. D.: Yes, when the thing was over. This was childish and this was the kind of stuff I was expected to say to the Japanese reporter! Well, there was no way I was going to do that. The question in my own mind was whether I was going to be tortured again to get me to the interview but they thought I was down far enough to go in and perform because that's how far they had gotten me already. Risner and I talked it over and we decided I'd go in to the Japanese reporter and just blow it wide open by saying the opposite of what they wanted.

But was the Japanese reporter sympathetic? No. They set me up in front of a table full of goodies, beer, lemonade, cookies, candy.

Q: Which you were supposed to be enjoying?

Adm. D.: Oh, of course, routine fare! And I was sat on a nice chair in front of that and right outside the back door, on the porch, is the guard Pig eye with his rope and a pistol and handcuffs –

Q: The threat?

Adm. D.: Yes - and I'm still weak and in pretty bad shape from what they had done less than a week ago. And the Japanese guy was not sympathetic at all. He wanted to play the act. I mean he was on their side. He came in and did all the smiling and tried to say things to get me to smile. "Oh, have some beer," and all this stuff. Then, when none of that worked, he started in on the long tirade about - and he sounded just like they sounded, except he was a little more articulate and he made fewer grammatical and rhetorical errors - about what the United States was doing to North Vietnam with the bombing. How they were deliberately homing in on the schools and the hospitals and the churches and all that sort of thing, and how could I approve of that. The way he was asking me the questions, he was putting me in the position of either saying I enjoyed cutting up and eating little children for breakfast or I condemned my government, one or the other. So he was not sympathetic.

But when he got his sensational story, and I don't think the Vietnamese fully understood what he had -

Q: But he did"

Adm. D.: Yes, he did - and I think that they couldn't stand the loss of face of telling him after they'd set this big deal up weeks ahead of time, probably a week ahead of time, with him knowing that they'd just finished torturing and thought they had me -- so they couldn't tell him, well, we're going to take the tape away from you. That would lose face because he's

Japanese and he was a socialist, a pinky, but not a full communist. But he was cooperating with them on this thing. He ends up, as Ed Brandt points out, selling that thing to some network in the United States. He wasn't welcome, I think, back in the country after that because after he released the tape he was probably looked upon -

Q: As persona non grata!

Adm. D.: Right. Before that time, he had appeared in many, many issues of their daily newspaper, interviewing captured American "air pirates" and relating their confessions, taking them down and that sort of thing.

Q: Of what importance was what we usually hear as ascribed to the oriental as lack of concern for the value of the individual? Of what importance was that in your whole situation?

Adm. D.: Well, as Mark Twain said, "East is east and West is west and never the twain shall meet," and as the New Yorker says "the inscrutable Orient." I don't consider myself qualified to analyze the oriental mind. I don't even consider myself qualified, after living among them for almost eight years and dealing almost exclusively with them, since I was in solitary confinement for four years, to give a really learned appraisal, but I would give an answer to you.

Some of this amounts to my lack of ability to make a conclusion. How could you reconcile their lack of concern for human life with these deeds, these facts, these practices, that they did employ in front of me? And before I give these, let me state that there is no question that when you introduce communism, communistic totalitarianism, into it, there is no regard for human life or human mentality if they're not able to make that human being conform to the system. They have absolutely no regard for a life. They will wipe it out. They will wipe out the mind. They will do what the Russians do in their psychiatric wards and that sort of thing.

Q: Look what Mao did.

Adm. D.: Yes, what Mao did and what Ho Chi Minh undoubtedly did. Once, early on, I had a North Vietnamese civilian in a cell next to me and I learned enough Vietnamese and could read enough into tones of voice to know what the argument was. This man was a political dissident. He thought he was a communist. He was treated very well. His wife was allowed to visit him alone. I could tell what was going on in the cell. It was his wife obviously because she was his age and not very attractive and she talked to him like a wife. They would come in there, the head of the camp, and talk to him in Vietnamese and you could tell that they were arguing about the course of the war, whether or not they should be this heavy-handed in their foreign policy to take on the United States. He would always end up his argument by saying, "Boooom" and then the guy would slap him in the face and walk out and slam the door. What he was saying was we were going to drop an atomic bomb up there on Hanoi. That was his point of view: "My God, you're pulling the hair of a giant."

So they had that up there and I watched them torturing that man one time when I passed the cell and they were engaged. They had either steel rods or sticks that they were inserting into his eyelids and the blood was running down his face. And we heard other North Vietnamese prisoners that they had in the camp early in the game. The camp that became known as Camp Unity later was used only for civilian North Vietnamese prisoners. We heard from DAT (nickname MAX), the South Vietnamese prisoner who was with us, about conversations he heard between the prisoners and the captors, and what they wanted them to do politically and so forth, and the courage these people had. All over the latrine area, for example, in New Guy Village, was written "Ky," Nguyen Cao Ky. The dissidents up there - this is not even in the book, why, I don't know, I told it. I used to swap cigarettes with them. When I'd go to the head I'd find a little hole and swap cigarettes with these young Vietnamese who were hanging in there against communism. You could see them subjected to more and more pressure and finally you'd hear them screaming in torture. Occasionally they would at least pretend to be convinced.

Stockdale told me a story about a woman who was in there for a long period of time. She needed "correction," and she was a lady, very beautifully dressed. She was at first very haughty and wouldn't have anything to do with them. They slowly treated her ignobly and demoralized her to the point where she finally started at least pretending to go along with the indoctrination that they'd given her, and they had a big party for her when they let her out and that sort of thing.

So they'll work on you with a concern for human life that, from my perception, was as if they were treating human beings as a natural resource and if they could, with a reasonable dollar-effective treatment, get them to conform sufficiently to get them out and be productive. They would do that. Otherwise, they would wipe them out. But some of the practices that were counter to the theories we have about Orientals were these. One, I watched them manufacture (when I climbed up in my window) these big concrete manholes, as it were, concrete tubes about six-feet deep with a concrete cover, and they were dug all over Hanoi. I saw them leave the assembly point on tractor pulled dollies. I did see that mostly officers used those. They bragged on the radio of making so many hundreds of thousands of these things and tried to impress us that they were trying to protect the individual, and they did have bomb shelters for the soldiers. They did have a lot of assistant doctors, as it were, and I've got to believe some of these statistics about health because of what we learned about North Korea. They did put in a considerably good medical setup there. I'm not sure that they didn't do reasonably well with extending life expectancy in North Vietnam.

It's done, though, with the materialistic, communistic idea of a natural resource. As a contribution to the state, the human being is no more important than an animal or a plant, but they do want to preserve it. They will work on it. The Russians will then bleed it, but the North Vietnamese hadn't gotten to the stage of seeing that bleeding. They'd never been an industrialized power like Czechoslovakia.

That was the most amusing incident I had in jail, when I predicted that Czechoslovakia would revolt some day and they had revolted about four days before, unbeknownst to me. That guy would have bet his life that I had a radio, and they came in there and searched my ears, they searched every crevice in my body. And my little cell they went over it over and over again. They were positive I had a radio. "The voice you heard was on Voice of America"! It was the funniest thing that ever happened to me.

And they actually started believing my international relations staff. I got some credibility with that guy, and when I was talking to the two enlisted men, they told me that never again could I talk to enlisted men on political matters. They enforced that later, which I mentioned in the book. So they're not all that inhuman or invulnerable to persuasive argument.

Q: Was the situation in North Vietnam alleviated in any way by the presence of Christianity?

Adm. D.: Yes. Again, it's not mentioned in the book, but a number of North Vietnamese, particularly a number of Vietnamese water girls, made the sign of the cross when I could see them and the guard couldn't. The girl I called Greta would do this when standing behind the guard who was abusing me. Most of the

Christians in North Vietnam were Catholic.

Q: Introduced by the French?

Adm. D.: Yes, and the weird setup was that most of the Catholics were in North Vietnam and it was the south that was fighting against the thing. Only a few million of the Catholics got out of North Vietnam. A great many others were left up there. I described the encounter with the old priest, Father Jean Baptiste, and he is in the same category with many of the middle European priests who had to decide whether to go the Mindszenty route and get locked up and kicked out, or to stay with their flocks.

Q: And lose their effectiveness.

Adm. D.: Yes, that's right -- to a degree. The pope has a lot of trouble figuring out how to handle that thing.

Q: The only one who's done it successfully, I think, is the former cardinal in Poland who was really effective for so long.

Adm. D.: Wyszynski, or something like that.

Q: Yes.

Adm. D.: That's a hard tightrope to walk, and that man's face was the archaeology, the fossilized history of that effort to walk that tight rope. The crinkles, the wrinkles, the lines, the expression. We had seen many pictures of him and movies of him walking in the streets and clutching his fist and condemning

American imperialist aggressors. So when I got with him alone it was interesting to watch the way he was. There's as much compassion for a human being in North Vietnam as there is in Antarctica or in Australia or in the United States, except for the difference between the occidental and the oriental.

The other thing I wanted to mention that goes against my preconceived belief that they don't care about human life or about the other individual the way you put it, is the extreme formality and deference which even the lowest class show to one another -- the bow, the extreme politeness, much less informality. They're getting this way, probably from associating with us, but the guards were generally familiar with each other and there was a lot of homosexuality and some of the arm in arm and that sort of thing. But a lot more deference shown man to man. Now the women - I wish some of the women's lib people could see the way those women over there are treated. They're just like beasts of burden.

Q: That surprised me, the presence of homosexuality among the guards?

Adm. D.: There's a great deal of that, some of it manifested toward the prisoners.

Q: How do you account for that?

Adm. D.: The same route that we are going, except their departure from morality is not a result of a failure to cope with affluence, which is a psychological problem. Their resort to homosexuality and kicks like that and the deterioration of their family life is a result of a political order. There is no god. And the Russians have had a lot of trouble playing that game. You may know the history of that. They first came on with promiscuity as the way to go. Then they had to change the law and say, oh, no, if you have four kids you're a blue-star mother, if you have five you're a red-star, and if you have seven or more you're a gold-star.

Q: First it was if I don't like my wife I'll divorce her.

Adm. D.: That's right. Then they found out that didn't work, and they're trying to cope now with their gangs of teenagers running amok in the streets of their metropolitan districts, and they've got their beatniks and dropouts, too.

So it's a question of whether or not the threat of physical violence upon them to keep them lined up will outlast our fear of God. That's what it amounts to, because our government has nothing whatever to do with imposing moral dictums in so-called victimless crimes, and in my belief victimless crimes are sins according to the Ten Commandments and are not victimless. I believe that the growing number of disoriented children, psychologically fouled-up kids, the crowded orphanages, the increased degree of juvenile crime, those are the victims of the victimless crime of promiscuity, if you will.

Q: And, in a broader sense, society as a whole.

Adm. D.: Absolutely. To me, as I said before, if you don't have respect for God's laws, why should you have it for the state's laws, and if not for the state's laws, then why for the parents' or the teacher's? I believe that's where it is and I think it's folly to go on asking these inane questions about solutions: should we make more jails, should we make the jails easier, should we go back to capital punishment? None of that is addressing the problem. Let's identify the problem.

The problem is we're getting away from that which we were and that which is responsible for making us great. We came here in a desire for freedom and a desire to practice religion the way we saw it. That's the way this continent was settled. It was settled in a fervor for religion, in a fervor of love for freedom, and the fortuitous dichotomy, as it were, was established: "Love God, love thy neighbor, but also free enterprise." And, slowly, the originally segregated religious sects, the Quakers and the Mennonites and the Catholics and the different ones warring with one another (and Roger Williams having to flee down to Providence to escape the puritan narrow-mindedness) - all of that pretty much got reconciled.

Just at the foundation of the country, George Washington wrote a beautiful letter (that I have in this speech delivered at West Point) to a Jewish friend, which for the first time included Jews in the Christian benevolence that was going on. For example, in Maryland they give the Maryland Catholics a great deal of credit for being the most tolerant colony, and you read their law, the famous Maryland Toleration thing, and it says that no one will ever be punished by virtue of his choice of practice of religion. That meant any Christian. The penalty under that Maryland law for not being a Christian was death, and it was all the way up to George Washington's time, before he wrote that letter to that Jewish friend, that that was squared away.

The guys who wrote that Declaration of Independence and said all men were created equal and are endowed by their creator with certain unalienable rights -- those guys knew when they wrote that that we had black slaves, but they knew we were going to work toward that ideal. They knew that blacks were men. It took a hundred years by civil war, and I'm from Alabama, before we got that squared away. We're still squaring away, but it's within our system only that it can be squared away, and systems like it, Western European democracy.

Eldridge Cleaver knows this now and he's been around.

Q: Yes, he came back, didn't he?

Adm. D.: That's right. And for God's sake, if we don't stick to that system and the ethic that makes it not only noble and not only makes its practitioners eligible for heaven in the religious sense, but it provides the system by which, and the only system within which, man can coexist societally on this earth in a happy manner. Because that's what God's laws are all about. And it's amazing the similarity between Islam, Judaism, Christianity, Buddhism, Confucianism on these behavioral conscientous perceptions.

One guy may say the Virgin Mary ain't a virgin, there ain't no such thing as the pope's infallibility, or you shouldn't call him God you ought to call him Allah, or there ain't no god but Buddha's got a lot of rules like God's. But as far as behavioral rules, the built-in conscience, that some God gave us - I've got my perception of God and I respect another man's perception of his - those are in common. And when you start saying there ain't no religion, the conscience isn't to be listened to, the state is; and just as the state allocates resources and prime commodities, we will also assess what your behavioral characteristics are supposed to be -- you're getting just as screwed up in the moral and political sense as you are in the economic sense, because that system of economics won't work for the same reason that the state's getting into the moral sphere won't work.

Back here we had superimposed on and underlaid our entire political process with religious principles. These principles underlie national interest, the definition and choice of national objectives of policies and commitments in pursuit of those objectives. Those things are all affected by our principles, and we're starting to throw our principles away. And when you do that you destroy the United States of America as a philosophy and you destroy its strength, not only its present material strength but, perhaps even more importantly, its potential for growth, for continued growth and sustenance. That's why we've got where we are, and that's the main problem I see about national security and everything else. I believe that if we were to look at that problem we would have less trouble with seeing that, on the one hand, there's atheistic communism, and, on the other hand, there's what we've got over here.

When we have an educational system and some media, which have as much to do with education as school does, which are willing to see that the perception of that distinction is the first requisite for effective exercise of citizenship; and when the media, instead of concentrating on sensational criticisms of governmental figures or of debunking how good George Washington and Thomas Jefferson were, keep the thing in proportion. Then we'll be rid of a cancer. We need to know that George Washington was infinitely better than Joseph Stalin, that he was an imperfect but well-meant man, that he sacrificed a great deal for his God and country; and that Thomas Jefferson, although he couldn't bring himself to free his own slaves, worried himself to death about it. He had the drive to do it. He just couldn't quite get himself to do it. It's not whether a man is good or bad, it's whether he's trying to be good or not. That's where the infinite difference is. And this country has tried to do good and it has done good.

Q: You speak of all men being created equal, and it suggests to me the idea that the captors in Vietnam attempted, when they were going to break the will of all the men, to apply this principle erroneously in that they didn't take into consideration the fact that men have different abilities.

Adm. D.: Oh, Yes.

Q: They first went ahead with the idea that everyone could be broken.

Adm. D.: Yes, that's right. They didn't treat each one the same. The average guy was tortured once. The average guy had a matter of less than six months of solitary confinement, and the ones that they chose to put in solitary confinement for four years or more could be numbered on the fingers of one hand.

Q: Yes, you make that point when you say that eleven of you were sent to Alcatraz, was it?

Adm. D.: Yes. I did express a qualification in the book, but that doesn't mean necessarily the eleven most-repugnant-to-them guys, the eleven toughest guys. There were other people -

Q: But you were eleven who had given them a lot of trouble?

Adm. D.: Oh, yes, we were among those who'd given them the most trouble. One thing we all agreed on, Stockdale and I and many others, was the way to measure how tough you were to them: our fitness report was written by the North Vietnamese. That's the only one that really counts. The bullshit that takes place after we get home is after the fact and there's a lot of politics in it and everything else. My fitness report was written by them and what they gave me to suffer were my good marks. The same thing is true of the other guys. Not all of them had seniority like I did, which kind of gave them an excuse to do that to me anyway. Some of the junior men were that much better than I was, that much stronger themselves, to merit that kind of extra torture and extra solitary. Those were our brownie points, and in this life, no matter when I die and no matter when the rest of the guys do, I know and respect all that they did, and that's what we're going to consider our fitness reports, not the ones that we got after we came home.

Interview No. 2 with Rear Admiral Jeremiah A. Denton, U.S. Navy
Place: His office at the Armed Forces Staff College, Norfolk, Va.
Subject: Prisoner-of-War Experiences
Date: 23 November 1976
By: John T. Mason, Jr.

Q: Today, I imagine you're going to continue your remarks on the general subject of how you were able to endure through all these years and what were the elements that constituted a kind of a saving grace for you?

Adm. D. All right, Sir. "Continue" might be an over-optimistic word because I don't recall precisely where we began, what was in the middle, and where we left off the last time, but I have tried to organize rather sketchily a perhaps more direct approach to the kind of answer you want, and I can launch that or else you will review to me what we've already covered and I could continue in the sense that you suggest.

Q: All right.

Adm. D.: I will try to consolidate a little bit more briefly what I put into loose construction the last time and say that religious faith was a big part of the kind of strength needed because the confrontation was principally moral and war is really an effort to break the enemy's will, and will has a great deal to do with morality. So the political or patriotic part of it was actually, in my opinion, rather secondary to the contrast in principles that they represented vis a vis the Americans and myself in particular. So religion has some part to play in it and I will go into that. The faith that I derived from observation of my comrades had a part to play. The familial faith I had in my wife and children had a part to play. And my education had a part to play.

But the part that I would like to develop the most today would be the morality aspect of it. I was raised in circumstances which resulted in exposure to religion, most specifically a Catholic education in grammar school in most grades, all the way through high school, one year of college, and in the Naval Academy there was a good mixture of professional and religious indoctrination. We went to church on Sunday, not by necessity - no, I believe we were required either to attend chapel or go to church -

Q: You were, indeed. That has been true until a couple of years ago.

Adm. D.: Yes. Well, I hope that they will, if not reinstitute the obligatory aspect, then continue to at least encourage it because one of the things I intend to address as a professional matter before I leave the service, or as I continue, depending on shortly seeing Admiral Holloway. He's coming down here to talk. He says he wants to see me alone for a while. I don't know whether he's going to give me what we used to call at the Naval Academy a CIS or he's just going to tell me that maybe he'll continue me as an officer! But in either case, I shall mention General Order No. 21, which came out under President Eisenhower, and was generally reflected in writing in General Order 21 of the Navy in May of 1963 and was even being practiced within the Navy by executive order prior to that time. That has fallen into disuse and I find that the paragraphs referred to in Navy Regs are no longer relevant to the subject. It's not pushed any more.

I have talked with people who are involved in this process of de-moralizing, a hyphenated word, the Navy Regs and so forth. That was a result of the kind of permissive and amoral developments that took place in our society in the late sixties. So Navy Regs were sort of cleaned of that, and I'm sorry to see that. In many cases the changes were good, eliminating unnecessary administrative junk from Navy Regs that didn't belong there, but I'm sorry they took out the responsibilities of a commanding officer toward a moral responsibility in his men. That should be emphasized rather than de-emphasized.

It was emphasized in my naval career and that was part of my preparation. So basically I had, to begin with, what I had experienced already, and then developed that considerably in prison due to nothing that should be credited to me. I extrapolated on that from having been placed in extremis and forced to ask for help and forced to take recourse in sources other than my own present capabilities. I had to pray, and the very first act of most of the prisoners was to try to organize their time because the first shock really for most of us, particularly at the time I was shot down since they weren't torturing at that particular time - it was several months before they began it - was simply having to deal with being in isolation. Almost everyone was in solitary confinement upon their introduction to prison life. I ended up with over four years of that.

Q: What's the rationale for that?

Adm. D.: They thought it was going to be demoralizing. I believe they drew a good bit on the Korean experience and, as I may have pointed out last time, they found that to be a misconception on their part. In my case, isolation unquestionably depressed me, but also in my case, it led to a strengthening of my ability to resist them because I was forced to pray more intensely, and it's an understatement to say there's no doubt in my mind that many of those prayers were answered. It's a fact that I was strengthened, and as time went by and as the prayers increased in number and as answers flowed back, transcending the requests in each case, I became stronger. I was able to withstand more physical punishment. I was able to accept with more equanimity the prospect of never getting out of there, the prospect of death. I used to prepare myself for torture periods after the first few, as the others did who were tortured a number of times, by long days of prayer. We usually had enough warning to give you plenty of time to "think deeply," as they called it.

I used that time to prepare myself and I would consider myself prepared when I got to the point at which I could find myself capable of walking into a machine that would shred my body. When I got to that point, I knew I was ready. Then I would go ahead and commence my normal communications with my next-door neighbor, if I had one. All of us out there at Alcatraz if a guy said, "I'm getting ready," having been threatened with torture and knowing that he was going to get it in a day or two, you always respected that and, unless you had something really urgent to talk to him about, you didn't interrupt him and he'd let you know when he had completed his preparation. I did the same thing.

Q: This was a point that the captors missed, was it? I mean the inner strength, the spiritual strength.

Adm. D.: I think so. There are those who disagree with me, who think that isolation was the worst aspect of confinement, then there are those who agree with me. So it just varied from person to person.

In my case, I found that in that isolation I was able to reach an awareness, as I may have said the last time, of a thought I'd heard in the past that the highest form of life is the contemplative life.

Q: Yes, you did say that.

Adm. D.: And I did experience the joy and the serenity that comes from reaching that kind of life.

Q: In your association with the other prisoners of war, what percentage of them responded in that way? You're all social animals, yet deprived of the social aspect of your lives some of you went on to strengthen the spiritual. What percentage would you say?

Adm. D.: Of course, I couldn't state it with any definitive authenticity, but from what I observed of the way the prisoners behaved while I was there and the way they have behaved since they came home, I would say that percentage is related to several identifiable variables, one of which would be the degree to which they were mistreated by the enemy. In other words, the degree of deprivation, the degree of torture, the degree of brutality inflicted upon them. That would be the first variable. The more you got of that, the more prayerful you were going to become. That is about 100 per cent true, in every case I know of.

And secondly the amount of solitary confinement to which you were subjected. In other words, the degree to which you were forced to go to God would be the key to finding the percentage of men who became more devout. There are men who are going into the Chaplain Corps, having been aviators, for example. That's more of an outward proof than what I'm doing. My life is sort of mixed with the old and a new thrust in that direction, but some have made the complete switch like that. And in each case those men were among those most badly treated. So those would be two definitive factors, the degree of mistreatment and the degree of solitary confinement.

You will find, I believe, from rough memory of the statistics, that something less than 5 per cent of the prisoners were in solitary confinement for over one year. In fact, it's a very small percentage who had solitary confinement for over six months. There are only five of us who had it for over four years, and I would like to boast that I was the first military prisoner to reach four years. And I might be the only one who had four years' solitary confinement during the time in which efforts to communicate were punished invariably by torture or long periods in irons.

So that solitary confinement that came after that time, when they were not very strict in enforcing punishment for efforts to communicate, I like to regard that as a less difficult kind of solitary confinement. I didn't have much. I only had a week or ten days like that, which was like standing on air. I could take a couple of years more of that. But a week when you were going to be tortured if you were caught communicating was a tough really enforced type of isolation.

We did make a distinction between total isolation in which there was no possibility, by virtue of physical separation by hundreds of yards from your comrades, and solitary confinement in which you were adjacent to a man and could surreptitiously communicate.

Q: Stockdale was an example of that?

Adm. D.: Stockdale had some of that. Risner had the most of it. I had some, too. But Stockdale does make a big point of the difference between isolation and solitary confinement. In my case, as I say, when I was isolated I didn't find it that demoralizing.

Q: Because you had another life?

Adm. D.: Because I did live that particular life. I think Jim (Stockdale) would say this, I perhaps a little more than he, probably by virtue of our conditioning before we got into the experience. I in no way mean to imply that Jim doesn't have tremendous spiritual faith, it's just of a slightly different kind. Nor do I mean to imply that I would compare myself favorably with him with respect to strength or resistance or anything like that. No. Only that we agree with one another that the spirituality aspect of it, in isolation with him - he didn't consider it as great a resource as I did. It seemed to buttress me for everything that hurt me.

But as I was saying, right after you were captured, you had to figure out how to deal with time on your hands, and most of us did that with efforts to communicate. I blocked out the day in planned phases - escape plans, singing either mentally or physically, other kinds of plans. Particularly when you're senior, you're trying to figure out how to cope with, anticipate, what the enemy's going to do or cope with what he's already done and establish the line, exercise of some kind. And then you were left with a great abundance of extra time, which I organized into prayer as did others to a greater or lesser degree.

My prayer was organized into formal prayer, examples of which would be my morning prayers in which I said something that Catholics used to call the Morning Offering. I think in this age they've come off of much of the formality of prayer, but in that particular prayer you offer all the prayers, works, joys, and sufferings of that day to God. It's a very brief prayer.

Q: Of the day which is before you?

Adm. D.: Yes. I used to do that, and then I said a little childish prayer to my guardian angel! That would be asking protection for me from the angels of God. It was in the singular when you prayed for yourself, but I always prayed for my family, so I'd say:

"Angels of God, our guardians dear,

To whom God's love commits us here,

Ever this day and night be at our side

To light, to guard, to rule and guide."

The "day" and "night" took care of the fact that there was a twelve-hour difference between where I was and where my family was! If they were in day, I'd say "day" first.

I'd get that one off and after the routine of the day began, dumping buckets or whatever, and I would be returned to my cell. Unless there was something hairy going on for which I'd prepare myself - I'd either say a Mass as if I were in church, and I could do this pretty much —

Q: From memory?

Adm. D.: Oh, yes, 98 per cent of the English and probably 85 per cent of the Latin I was able to go through. I would also do at least one rosary, and I won't bore you with what a rosary is.

Q: I know.

Adm. D.: Roughly, it's five Hail Marys — five decades of Hail Mary's — interspersed with the Lord's Prayer and a Glory Be to the Father, Son, and Holy Spirit, as it was in the beginning, is now, and ever shall be, world without end, Amen, in the middle of those five decades. And you have three sorts of flavors of rosary. You can contemplate upon either of three sets of so-called mysteries, the Joyful Mysteries, the Sorrowful Mysteries, or the Glorious Mysteries. The Sorrowful Mysteries dealt principally with the Crucifixion and the things that happened in and around that. The Joyful Mysteries dealt with such non-miraculous things as just the Birth of Christ, the Finding of the Lord Jesus in the temple, when Mary and Joseph couldn't find Him that time, and that sort of thing. And the Glorious Mysteries were the great miracles associated with Christ, such as His Resurrection from the dead and his mother's assumption into heaven, which is an article of faith of the Catholic Church, and so forth.

So you could choose to say one rosary or more than one rosary. I mentioned to you, I think, that one night in a rig I just kept saying rosaries over and over again all night long, in a rig that was fairly painful and I found myself toward the end pretty distracted and rapid in the way I was saying it. I tried to control myself and think of each word and each thought. Then I had a five, five, and five thing - five Our Fathers, five Hail Marys, and five Glory be to the Father - that I said every day, and I had my night prayers, which consisted of the act of contrition, in which I asked forgiveness for my sins, and some special prayers that I said for my family and little things that are called aspirations.

That was my sort of daily routine of prayer. I had it broken up into four or five times during the day, which were sort of built around efforts to communicate, escape plans, plans against the enemy, and exercise.

Q: I gather that as you approached these periods for prayer this was almost a joyous moment, was it not?

Adm. D.: It was. One thing that might be worth noting is that the Sorrowful Mysteries, when you go through five decades of the rosary, I was told once by Brother Charles, who is mentioned in the book and was my main freshman high-school teacher, that the Sorrowful Mysteries, although they're sorrowful and can make you cry, at the end of them you always feel a tremendous sense of relief and gratitude and triumph. And, gradually, as I developed more and more intensity in applying myself to meditating on the events which that set of mysteries commemorates, I found that to be quite true. At the end of the Sorrowful Mysteries, although my face felt as though it were being entrenched with tears, I always felt as if I was a lot less pressured. I mean, after all, that was the greatest suffering a human being ever went through. Little things that you meditate on during that time - I remember being told that one of the greatest pains that Christ underwent, one which I couldn't understand or fully believe until I got in jail, was the fact that as He walked around during Holy Thursday night and the early hours of Good Friday morning for his trial before the state and religious authorities of the Jews. He was in irons, He was in chains. I was told that that was one of the most painful things He had to endure. I didn't know until I put traveling irons on and walked in them how true that was, the regular set of traveling irons. I could only imagine what it would be like with very rough-hewn, sharp bands around one's ankles, dragging chains which catch on obstructions and jerk the steel or the iron - sharp iron - against bone and flesh and nerve. Having experienced a little of that, I really felt for what He was feeling. And this before the real passion began, the scourging and that sort of thing, which we got with the fan belts but not to the degree He had it. He was subjected to a scourging that would have killed an ordinary man. He withstood that.

The carrying of the cross after He was crowned with thorns, the long carrying of the cross, as tired as He must have been after all of that, and the compassionate way in which he greeted the Holy Women of Jerusalem along the way and said, "Weep not for me but for your children."

Q: But then, as you emphasize, the greatest agony on the cross, and then the victory.

Adm. D.: Yes, that's right, but even before He got on the cross, after He got up there (on the hill), the ripping-off of the clothes after He had been scourged and they put those robes on Him. Having been told previously in my education that the pain was a tremendous - you know how it is with a football player or an athlete when if you don't shave your legs when you pull off the tape binding your weak ankles or knee or whatever, it's fairly painful. And when you pull off a bandage where you have a good scab, it's quite painful, and His body was covered with scabs, and when they pulled those clothes off of Him, it was a pretty rugged experience.

Then when Jesus is nailed to the cross in the Stations of the Cross, that's another thing I used to do, when you think about the hand being laid down on that wood and the first blow on that nail and the inevitable occasional missing of the nail and smashing into the bone and flesh with the hammer, and that sort of thing. And then the same thing for the feet. And, of course, meditating on the hanging on the cross, the impossibility of getting into a comfortable position, the cross being vertical, the whole body is thrust forward, and even with a little bit of wood down there cut at a diagonal, if that was the case on the cross, the whole body was thrust forward. It was off balance, pulling against the nails and finding no way to get comfortable.

Of course, the thing was supposed to result in bleeding to death or some kind of strangulation from blood, it's an involved thing, but a heck of a lot of pain. That was a more merciful death than being tied to the cross. You think about pain a lot over there, so that's a more merciful death than that which the two thieves were enduring alongside Him, because crucifixtion normally resulted in death in much less time than three hours, which Christ traditionally is supposed to have hung up there. But the thieves who were tied to the cross, that was the worst death the Romans were using in that day because they hung there for days, and that was the same kind of punishment they were giving to us. The rope trick, that's what it was. Those guys would just hang there until they died. They were tied very tightly, and they often did that to us.

There's a part in my book that I might have talked to you about when I found myself tied to a tree. It was hurting a little bit. It was after the Hanoi march, and about three o'clock in the morning I was gagged and handcuffed to a tree with my arms behind me around the tree. I had the thought, well, here I am, a sinful man and it's like it ought to be. Like that thief tied alongside Christ, I belong here and I would like, like that thief, to ask His forgiveness. So I prayed, Lord, forgive me, just as you forgave that thief and you said to him, "Such faith I have not seem in all of Israel. This day thou shalt be with Me in paradise." I made a little prayer like that, kind of almost laughing about how ridiculous it was. Then I coughed out my initials, JD, through my gag. It was very quiet, in the pre-dawn. And the man next to me coughed his out, JC! I thought, holy mackerel. It was Jerry Coffee, and I do tell about that in the book.

That was one kind of a funny little incident. But, yes, meditating about sad things ends up after you've finished going as far as you can with, that you feel better somehow and very grateful. As you say, the triumph of it, and that's what one of the poems I wrote for the guys was about, the fact that one of the saddest moments in history in the Pieta, with Mary holding her son in her arms, is a worldwide famous symbol of tragedy. And I tried to use that in the deepest part of our pessimism as a key to optimism. Because really, as you so aptly pointed out, it was a triumph. Even at that time Mary had faith in the divinity of her son and may have realized that although only John had stayed with her and all the people who had been offering Him alms and strewing palms in His way on the previous Sunday had fled, that somehow something good was going to come out of all that.

I think that I said something before about "even now she might suppose His thorns could somehow yield a rose," meaning the thorns in the crown that they put on Him.

So thoughts about things like that were pretty intense and I believe that God is pleased when we try to think in those terms. I think Christ is pleased when we try to become mindful of what He did to redeem the sins of man, and we tend to forget it.

Q: That was the purpose of His coming!

Adm. D.: That's right.

Q: Did you have an opportunity ever to talk with any of your colleagues who also endured tortue and who were men without faith? How did they fill their time, how did they fill their thoughts?

Adm. D.: Well, a man, whom I'll just call Man A, was one of the toughest men physically I know and he was relatively junior. They didn't spend a whole lot of time on him because he didn't meet any of the three criteria that normally drew their attention; seniority, notoriety for having a famous father like John McCain, or inciting others to resist. This particular guy didn't communicate, he just took it all upon himself. Although he was very strong about the Code of Conduct himself, he didn't communicate with others until after the torture had gone, but he was extremely tough. He resisted them tremendously, and he used to advertise that he was an atheist. But when I actually checked with that man, and I lived in the same building with him for four weeks, the only communal living that I did experience, except for nine days before release, I was curious about the same question. He told me that he could not describe himself really as an atheist any more. He could only describe himself as an agnostic, and the more I got into it the more I realized that he was by no means doubtful of the existence of a god. He was simply puzzled by the nature of the god. He wasn't able to conceive of God as a personal being, but he had no doubts about the fact that there was a god and that he was worth going to for help and that sort of thing.

I don't know really anyone who still claimed to be an atheist after his experience if he had considerable mistreatment. The only fellow I know of who called himself an atheist had almost none, and he may not be an atheist now. He might not say he was.

So the vast majority - I believe the percentage was 98 per cent - of the Korean prisoners and the same or more for us - credited God with being by far their main source of strength. So prayer itself - unknown to me, or at least unfelt by me in any dramatic way - I'm sure resulted in a slow accumulation and increased reservoir of ability to resist, ability to persevere. I'm not bragging. I'm simply stating the way it was. In fact, to avoid the impression of bragging, I would say that once I was reintroduced to something like normal prison life, after I came out of my four years in solitary confinement and was given a cellmate for a good period of time and then actually got into a situation, somewhat later, the last year or so, I was actually able to talk face to face with as many as eight other people, I found myself praying less, able to meditate less because of the distraction of other human beings, and the opportunity to exchange with them. I believe that my strength dropped measurably as a result of getting away from meditation and prayer.

In other words, I believe that after, say, the first couple of times I was tortured, or maybe even the first time, my ability to withstand physical pain and to accommodate the inevitability of another application of torture, I believe that that grew continually up through the last time that I was in solitary confinement, which was also the last time I was tortured. I wasn't tortured any more after I came out of Alcatraz. I was beaten around a little bit, but not tortured. I believe that I measurably weakened and had I been thrust back into that inferno of pain again, and the environment of the certainty of pain every month or so, extreme pain, I would have retrogressed to, say, phase three after my third torture or something. Had I kept going I believe I would have gotten stronger and stronger.

This is not to say that I wasn't suffering some kind of distortion mentally. I'm sure that I was.

Q: Because of your separation?

Adm. D.: Right. I'm sure that I was becoming more short-tempered and less capable of associating with human beings who didnot feel the same as I and so forth! I think I still have a problem that way.

Q: Since you returned to normal life, have you been able to maintain a certain intensity in the spiritual life?

Adm. D.: Yes, Sir. Every time I do speak anywhere, and I am not a compulsive speaker in the sense that I do not try to take advantage of all opportunities to speak. Actually, on the other hand, I try to fend off invitations, unless I see that they're a major thing. Like just a couple of weeks ago I was the principal speaker when such notable speakers as Bob Froehike, former Secretary of the Army, was a subordinate speaker - I'm not boasting, I'm just telling you the kind of things I accept - at the National Fraternal Congress of America's annual convention down in Florida. They, as do all the other groups, thought I was going to talk about my prison experiences. I don't. I always talk about morality, the need to get back to basic national principles which made the country great and try to expound upon the subject.

Although the level of our arms and our proficiency in their use remains my immediate professional concern, my over-all belief now, and this has changed from the way it was before I was captured, is that that is not the biggest factor that we should be concerned about in respect to national security. I believe that the erosion of national principles, adherence to our basic national principles, the ones that brought us to our present level of material and spiritual greatness, is the greatest threat to our national security. I believe that that concern has a need for expression not only to civilians or to clergymen, but also within the military. I believe that as we become less principled in rhythm with the rest of society, further away from a rather rigid effort to adhere to the Ten Commandments, for example, more permissive, the new sexual morality, and so forth, that that reflects in integrity at every level, including the willingness to sacrifice oneself for any cause bigger than self.

So I believe it's an extremely important factor in military life. I find myself having to suppress my desire to talk about it within the military, because I would come on distortedly again, and when I do address my own students here I couch the organization of my talk around the conventional terms involved in national security, starting with the basic national interest of survival, which has a duality, really.

National security, I define, cornily, as the effort to protect what you have, your life and your possessions and your way of life against other human beings who would take them away from you. The wellbeing aspect of the duality in survival is defined, again cornily, as more or less economic in nature: the acquisition of, the preservation of, means to protect you against exposure, disease, starvation, and that sort of thing. And wellbeing can become perceived as vital in the national interest sense for the protection of such things as our communications and transportation systems; luxuries to which we have become accustomed and regard as necessities now. I have no absolute criticism of that.

Starting from that, I then go on through the national strategy triangle and talk about national objectives which we choose to forward the attainment of those interests, the policies that we develop to reach those objectives, and the commitments that we then choose, the actual commitments. Then I read the bottom line which involves such things as willingness to sacrifice life by those in the service, to sacrifice life even in situations like the charge of the Light Brigade, in which you might have 98 per cent certainty is a mistake. Nevertheless, you follow through because you recognize the integrity of commitment of a platoon or of an individual is absolutely essential to the over-all success of any battle plan and the winning of any war.

I believe that national principle not only undergirds that entire structure of factors in national strategy, but it also helps define your choices of objectives. It even helps you define what your national interest is, especially in the wellbeing context. For instance, it's laboring the obvious to show that the growth of a materialistic philosophy in this country within the last fifteen years or so, as opposed to a more spiritualistic philosophy going back to the principles of the Founding Fathers and so forth, is reflected in such things as how long do you persevere in a commitment, as in Vietnam, which, in my belief, was won militarily in December 1972 and lost afterwards by just such a factor. We didn't have the perseverance and the patience. I believe that had we gone ahead and supported the four-power agreement and given them $5 million or $6 million, as Dr. Kissinger asked, they would have been able to protect themselves without any further major involvement on the part of the United States. And North Vietnam, if they had perceived that we were going to do that, that would have been the end of it.

I have a number of reasons for believing that. I've corresponded with the president of the United States on that in December of 1974. I recommended certain steps. He took the steps. I recommended that he put the supplementary appropriation request on the front burner, which he did. I recommended that, instead of underestimating the cost, as we had early in the war under President Johnson - probably not entirely his fault, possibly because of some military estimates that were over-optimistic and then voiced by Mr. McNamara and so forth - go ahead and lay it on the line, it'll take five or six million bucks. That's what generals who were coming back were telling me was needed. That's what majors and sergeants were telling me. They said with that the South Vietnamese alone could handle it no matter what Russia and Red China gave to the North.

And from my conversations with the North Vietnamese before I left, I knew that they had no thought of getting their slimy fingers back into South Vietnam. They thought it was over and there was going to be a permanent peace, and that we were going to follow through on the four-power agreement - they would try to cheat but we would check those efforts. Then when they saw that the whole country wanted to put it behind them so much, the whole Vietnam issue, they knew that they could become more adventurous. This is what I wrote the president about. I said I thought that his intelligence, the intelligence I was reading and he was reading and the newspapers and the television saying that there was not any prospect of a North Vietnamese push in 1975; I said that in my humble, but very firm, opinion, that was wrong. It was an incorrect estimate. I told him what I thought the estimate should be.

Unfortunately, I turned out to be right in detail and I suffered considerably during that spring and summer. That's what was behind my submission of a resignation. I just didn't feel that the military was even relevant to the damned problem. I thought the problem that had to be addressed was the consensus of the citizenry.

I still believe that is the major problem in national security right now, in the maintenance of national security. I believe it affects not only our prospects for economic advance, the maintenance of our present standard of living, but it is actually threatening our survival.

Q: You brought out some of these points and did it beautifully, I thought, in two speeches you gave me and which I would like to attach to the transcript. The one you gave before the Knights of Columbus and the one you gave at Yorktown. Excellent presentation.

Adm. D.: My National Fraternal congress thing was extrapolated somewhat from the Knights of Columbus speech and perhaps you'd be interested in getting that one. The recent address I made at Pensacola attacked it more or less along the lines that I use when I talk to the class here; the strategy lines that I just used.

You're right, in the Knights of Columbus thing I did use that structure generally, didn't I?

Q: Yes, you did.

Adm. D.: I made it a little more specific.

Q: How do the students here react to this kind of presentation?

Adm. D.: Quite favorably. I'm usually in the upper 5 per cent of the grades they give. The first time I gave the talk they were required to identify themselves in their critiques, and I told them for my lecture I didn't want an identity attached. I wanted it to be anonymous, so that I wouldn't be able to get back at them! Since that time they've all been anonymous, and I do OK.

I didn't give it this time because I thought the two presidential candidates were going to address for this entire year preceding November, the issue of national principles in a rather large way, which I think both did. I think this was a unique feature of this particular election. At least in my lifetime I have never seen morality made such a big issue as the two of them made it and as the public sort of required them to do. I was encouraged in that.

Q: With Watergate as the backdrop to the whole thing, I suppose?

Adm. D.: To a degree. I believe, though, that Watergate in perspective is less of an immoral monstrosity than we now have it. I believe that it's already been brought out but not emphasized sufficiently that the misdeeds involved were less in magnitude than the same kinds of misdeeds, the same category of misdeeds, for example, wire-tapping for political purposes, and the use of the CIA for improper purposes. That sort of thing was done worse by both the Johnson and Kennedy administrations, and I admired both of those men. I think Mr. Nixon has been unnecessarily castigated. I don't believe that Watergate is as bad, as we now look at it. I think history will bear that out.

But, yes, using that as a backdrop, we have sprung forward in another kind of new morality to demand of our leaders and politicians a new vogue of moral behavior. How we will fare in that with the particular system we have, I'm somewhat skeptical about. In other words, I believe there's a good bit of moral compromise pretty much built into the pork-barrel aspects of going for support for measures which congressmen or presidents perceive to be necessary. I believe that they have to make justifications of compromises that are often, within our system, inevitable in the sense of trying to wrestle with facts. In other words, it's pointless to wrestle with facts.

They take those actions knowing that there are gray areas and even some black areas involved in some of the smaller things they do in order to achieve what they talk themselves into believing are the more important accomplishments or aims for which they're working. I believe usually they're right, but it does involve some "wrongdoing," and that, to me, is one of the built-in occupational diseases of democracy and human nature. I believe we can improve in that respect but I don't think we're going to be able to eliminate that kind of thing.

Q: I think I heartily agree with you!

Tell me about the importance of the command structure within the prisoner-of-war camp. You haven't said anything much about that.

Adm. D.: It was essential to reinstitute that structure in the minds and habits of people who were taken away from a very rigid military life style, if I may use that word, in which they were a wingman following someone else, and the whole flight following the flight leader, and all of them under the command of the captain of the ship and the air group commander, and that sort of thing. Then they find themselves individuals split apart in a prison with time on their hands and all sorts of choices and questions and options available to them with respect to a myriad of issues, such as whether or not to accept a cup of tea or whether not to accept a banana when you didn't know whether the other guy did - a lot of minor and somewhat incidental things. This went all the way up to such major questions as whether or not to collaborate with the enemy, which some people chose to do in order to come home early.

To reinstitute in the minds of all of us there the fact that the first sentence of the Code of Conduct is the most important. I used to wonder why it was. Admirals used to inspect us when I was a commander and lieutenant commander in a squadron and they'd say, "What do you know about the Code of Conduct?" and the word that went around was "All you have to say to the old guy is 'I am an American fighting man,' and that will satisfy him." Although

I thought that was kind of stupid at the time, I realize in retrospect and I realized in jail in retrospect that that wasn't so stupid after all.

The primary thing a man has to remember when he gets into the hands of the enemy while his country is engaged in hostilities is that he remain an American fighting man - American - fighting - man. If you start presenting him with the familiar structure of the military organization such as "the senior man in your building is my deputy and if you lose communications with me, you do what he says. In the meantime, you do what I say. I'm running it. He'll take care of other details in which he doesn't feel it necessary to consult me. All of us will follow the Code of Conduct, we'll all be loyal to the president of the United States." That kind of thing, looking to the senior officer for answers to questions on borderline issues such as what do we do if. When that becomes a habit and when the senior officers lay it on the line and, by example, show that there is no happy answer in most cases -- there's no way to skirt around being hurt. Being hurt was the name of the game. You weren't doing your job unless you got hurt. There was no way to outsmart the enemy, as they told us in SERE school, which is quite correct. There were going to be times when you had to look him in the eye and say no, and it was very difficult to do this because they would set up psychological bugaboos to keep you from saying no. They would try to introduce the whole subject in such a way that it would be better to handle it in some other way than just plain no.

But sooner or later you were going to have to come to that instant when you were going to have to say no when you knew damned well that it was going to result in your getting painfully handled.

So, once the example is given and you've got the structure set up, you've got a bunch of heroes. You can take them out of any service. You can take them out of any rank. You can just take any cross section and put them in that situation, with their integrity directly challenged by the enemy, and get a little bit of a military organization established where it's "we" and "they," and not just "they" and "I." It's "we" against them. It's a team thing. There's a tremendous psychological victory right there, and that was the big thing.

At first, the organization, of course, when they were really cracking down on communications and the torture program was really rugged, the organization had to be relatively simple. The kind of organization I've just described to you was the kind we had. There's one SRO, one senior officer for the camp. My way of doing it was to appoint each building senior as responsible for his building if and when we lost communication. This was early in the game because Robby got pulled out of that camp and I was at the Zoo really the first one under siege with torture. I had to set that up and it was the best I could do.

I'm the boss. Robby's gone. I'm sorry because everybody knows Robby and looks up to him. You don't know who the hell I am, but I've got it. Then the question of: OK, if you lose communications with my building and me, then the senior guy in your building has it. And if I get pulled out of here, the senior guy underneath me has the whole camp, will follow my past orders but has leeway to change the line as conditions change according to his judgment.

Those things I laid out and I tried to address the answers to the questions that came to me, like write or don't write, and that sort of thing, as did the others. And when we did get back together in sort of a community living thing, and communications were not under the threat of torture, we were able to maintain relatively sophisticated communications, then the organization became extremely sophisticated and we set up Pentagon Southeast over there. Everybody had a job. Some people had three or four jobs. That was good. John Flynn was quite adept at realizing that he had better administratively get squared away because people like Stockdale and myself and Risner, who had been involved and habituated in more primitive circumstances were unable even to address such a dream as setting up an extremely elaborate organization, it was kind of fortunate that he was the man who got it.

Risner and Jim and Larry Guarino and the others who had to hack it while it was a burning trial, more or less, did it about the same way. The organization was skeletal but effective. What it lacked in sophistication it made up for in steel.

Q: That's the most powerful explanation of the value that I've heard or read and I'm very grateful for it.

It seems to me, Sir, that you've mentioned several things

that are basic in human existence, I mean for a Christian. You mentioned the significance of the crucifixion of Christ and you mentioned the military code of ethics, the basic things in your life, and it seems to me, as a prisoner of war, you gained a rather unique understanding of these things, unique in the sense that ordinary citizens don't achieve. Therefore, now, you should have the greatest value as a military man!

Adm. D.: Well, I said I didn't have a compulsion to speak, I mean I don't have a compulsion to waste myself speaking too many times. I do have a compulsion to address the issue you just brought up. I do have a compulsion now to talk about the significance of moral principles, which I didn't have before I was captured. I feel a responsibility to do it, even a responsibility as a professional.

To say that I have achieved a unique understanding of those things, yes, with a great qualification. To say that ordinary citizens don't would be too exclusive a statement because the only folks that I felt that I could really communicate with and empathize with when I first came home were people who had spent much of their lives in pain, mental or physical. In other words, they're lying in a hospital bed paralyzed, in pain, and with all of their relatives - usually their wives desert them after, say, fifteen years or so for obvious reasons, and all they have is that little book sitting over there on their table, and every one of them has it. Every one of them who lives has the Bible sitting on his end table, and he either reads it himself through a very involved contraption with mirrors, or he has a nurse or an orderly read it to him. They aren't ordinary citizens in the sense that I was, but they were ordinary citizens in that they weren't military. They could have had this happen in an automobile accident or as a result of a sickness or any kind of an injury. And the families of those men who do rise to the occasion of sticking with them, as many of them did, they have undergone a pressurized purification, if you will, in which distractions of optional things don't exist and the most basic things: life, death, love. Those things totally occupy their minds.

Under those circumstances, when that person goes to God, I can't believe God gives them a whole lot of credit because it's the most natural thing in the world. It's an inevitable thing. So I don't take any credit for that.

Q: Well, I modify what I say, although my intention was a broader application of you than simply you, Admiral Denton. But those of you who underwent this terrible experience as prisoners of war and thought about it have come back as unique individuals with a greater and deeper understanding of the basics in life than most people.

Adm. D.: Yes, and in that sense I agree with you. And, again, the ones who have come back and felt a revulsion toward the new morality, the new permissiveness, are the ones who suffered the most in jail. The ones who have come back and embraced it with admitted acknowledged joy are the ones who suffered the least. That is an almost ironclad rule. I can think of scores of people whom I've checked out this way, and that is the case.

So I guess whether it's considered a unique understanding or a grotesque monasticization (but I think that would be unfair), I do believe that we have learned the hard way the reality of God, the degree to which he responds, and gratitude toward Him for all the little miracles that go on all the time: like the growth of grass and the birth of human beings and the ability of the eye to water when it gets something in it, and veins being built on the inside of the arm rather than the outside so that you won't hemorrhage if you bump up against something. All of those things plus the reality that we tend to lose sight of. Now, H. G. Wells, he's a historian, but a better man than I because I don't know of any particular agonizing experience he went through to say this, but with his intellect alone - I would have to be crunched to get this way - he said: "I'm an historian, not a believer, but only a fool could fail to recognize that the birth of the poor carpenter of Nazareth is the centerpiece of all history." That's an historian. I'm a professional military man. He sees that as the centerpiece of history. I see it as the soul of service to country. I believe patriotism flows from love of God. The word "patriotism" has "pater" in it, father, the father land. "Honor Thy Father and Thy Mother." "Render unto Caesar what is Caesar's and unto God what is God's." He said it.

We forgot that in Vietnam. A lot of people in this country did. We can't have a country in which each individual makes up his mind about the advisability of a given direction issued by the person in supreme political authority of the nation. You won't have any national security when you have that. Right now we have a condition in which the press, the media, the educational system have "confirmed" that the draft-evaders, resistors, protesters were the right ones and the government was wrong about Vietnam.

What kind of position does that place us in vis a vis a future similarly mixed emergency in which we might have to say mobilize? Add to that the problem of the volunteer-force concept - I don't mean to say "problem" the fact of the volunteer-force concept, which without draft the citizenry is conditioned to the idea that a professional cadre handles fighting for the country. And add to that the fact that service to country is equated even by the Department of Defense to service in other fields, such as industry. And that the wages are set up to entice people based on that. I think we've gone too far in that direction. You cannot pay a man enough to sacrifice his life, because you can't take it with you. You can't pay a man enough to risk his life. You can pay a man to entice him to come into the service and lead a dignified professional life, but I'd rather have half the pay and twice the recognition of what my service means in terms of, say, not having to pay taxes, because my tax is my life, of not having to do without certain prerogatives and perquisites which were traditionally afforded senior military people, or even junior military people.

I find that that is hard to take because it represents a lack of appreciation on the part of the citizenry for what you're involved in. It's not new. Rudyard Kipling wrote about it when he talked about Tommy and how the people appreciated him when they were at war. But it's unfortunate and I think we've developed it now in connection with those other situations that I've mentioned: the war being looked at as having been wrong, the protesters as having been right. I think we're in a confused state right now and we should identify our problem and try to find our way out of it in the interests of national security.

As Wells addressed it as a historian, as a point of history, I address it not as a mystic, monastic pseudo-clergyman, but as a deeply interested and, to some degree, informed student of international affairs, and a servant of my country with my profession concerned with national security.

Q: Tell me about the change in attitude toward the captives, the prisoners, that came about with the development of the military situation.

Adm. D.: There were many changes. They used to boast over and over on the radio - they weren't boasting, they were trying to insist that there was no connection between our treatment and the progress of the war. Of course, the converse was the case and we used to laugh about it. You can go back to the initiation of the torture program and relate it directly to the build-up in intensity of the bombing, for example. The more they were hurt, the more they hurt us, and they tried to show that to the United States by publicizing the "confessions" of Risner and myself and others. They knew that our government would know we had been crunched to make those statements. No one in the Navy believed that I or any of the other guys who had confessions wrenched from us would have given them voluntarily. So they were using that as a lever.

They tried to use the whole bunch of us as hostages and they would treat us worse as we had more success in the war. And I thank God for the fact that during the Johnson administration and early Nixon administration we didn't let the wives go public and start protesting our treatment, or make a big issue of it because then they would have been successful in making the return of the prisoners a big pawn in the settlement of the war, in which we could have traded that off for the freedom of the South Vietnamese people, which is a ridiculous thing to do. There are tens of millions of souls involved there, and 354 of us. It was absurd.

So there was that all the way through. If I may complete that thought, which is a little tangential, I do think it was wise once it became politically inevitable to start withdrawing American troops, the de-Americanization, as Johnson called it, Vietnamization, as Nixon called it. Then, seeing that air strikes and blocade would be about our only recourse, it was found desirable to try to develop a little leverage for application of considerable force in those air strikes by raising the issue of the POWs' plight and making people dislike the North Vietnamese for that. It was used strategically, in my opinion. It came at a fortunate time for us. We were as a group, particularly ones who were being especially ill treated, nearing death. We were starting to die off.

We were not only in bad physical state but, although our wills were even stronger and we were more stubborn in our resistance, we were also in a very deteriorated mental state by the summer of 1969. Ron Stor (Storz) in my camp was dying and the rest of us were getting pretty nutty. We were in very poor physical shape. McKnight probably would have died, had he continued with the lung problem he had. All of us were down around 100 pounds, and that sort of thing.

President Nixon through Mel Laird (according to Ed Brandt, the guy who helped me write my book) announced that the wives could go ahead with this program to publicize our plight. That announcement, I think, was made in the late spring of 1969, and it got rolling sufficiently that year, although it hadn't really taken sufficient form for us to perceive it or for much of the American public to perceive it, to be perceived by the North Vietnamese as being the monster that it would become. They're very sensitive to public opinion, and they saw that growing in the summer of 1969, and in the fall of 1969, in my analysis, that wives' campaign was at least partly responsible for the huge change that took place - the change from night to day - in our treatment. Ho Chi Minh died 3 September 1969, and I believe they seized upon that as a fortuitous milestone upon which to base an explanation for changing our treatment, burying the bad treatment, as far as the free world was concerned, with Ho Chi Minh and such advisers as were popular and operable during his particular lifetime. Because the change in treatment occurred in the very next month.

I'm sorry that this book, POW, leaves out what I have reported in detail in my own book, the long series of exchanges I had with Cat, the man in charge of their torture program. He knew I was running that camp and when he moved us from Alcatraz back to Little Vegas (where almost all the seniors were and what I would call the notables like John McCain and the guy who was recently killed, Gary Anderson, whose father was big in the government, CIA or something, and escapees, people like that, or great resisters like Jack Fellowes, Bud Day, and that Air Force Academy guy (Ben Pollard) - I keep forgetting his name, I didn't put it in my book, I wish I had - people like that, the toughest guys were there in that jail, and it ended up that I was running that camp. He knew I was going to interfere with his program to fatten everybody up, and he was trying to tell me "cool it, don't have these guys continue to cause sufficient trouble like food strikes and that kind of thing, fasts, because the treatment is going to change, has changed."

And he told me formally that he had been required to make self-criticism before the people for his mistakes; mistakes in the form of cruelty to American prisoners, which was in violation of the 4,000-year-old tradition of North Vietnamese leniency toward their prisoners. He had been required to make self-criticism of that, and the fact that he and certain other officers and certain guards had been unable to restrain their anger against us for what we were doing to their country, and that they had violated the official policy of the country.

Q: Was there no sincerity in this, when he said it?

Adm. D.: Well, he was trying to appear sincere. I don't think he thought that that was going to have much conviction with me. I didn't even try to look polite when he told me that. I knew it was bullshit, and I immediately saw what they were trying to do. They were going to make a few scapegoats like Cat, as if it were a minority involved, that it wasn't a governmental policy. They took this line because they believed then that President Nixon was going to go through with the successful prosecution of that war, and they did not want, all of them, including the politicians, to be subjected to a Nuremburg-type trial.

That was the whole thing, in my view, and there are a number who agree with me.

Cat gave the same kind of little pitch in a few minutes to Howard Rutledge, but I was the one whom he had in there with a Vietnamese-French dictionary on one side and a French-English dictionary on the other. He couldn't go from English to Vietnamese, except through that way. He said he wanted to make it perfectly clear, he wanted me to understand. This took about three weeks, the whole thing, and that was essentially his message. This was in exchange for what he said would be permitting us to follow the Code of Conduct without torture. He wanted me to get the guys to kind of cool it, as far as we Alcatraz types were concerned, because we were still pretty much out of our heads. We were starting fights with guards and things like that because we were so damned mad and we knew the treatment had changed and we could probably get away with it.

I wasn't in favor of going that way, but some of the guys were so damned mad they were all enthused by it.

He asked me to do that and not communicate with the rest of the camp. I looked him in the eye and said, "You know this is ridiculous. If I can communicate I'm going to communicate, especially since I've learned that you're not going to torture me if you catch me. You know I communicated during the times when you were torturing me."

My insistence was that he stop trying to afford some better treatment than others. We had three major divisions in that camp then. The Thunderbird cell block which had guys like Bill Lawrence, Byron Fuller, guys who had hung in there and tried to do their best during a very difficult time. In the center of the camp was the Desert Inn, where a number of the people were being given very special tratement, where Wilbur and Miller were, who were totally overtly forthcoming to the enemy, and many of the others weren't doing a whole lot. The North Vietnamese were sort of weaning them along by nonpunitive methods to try to develop them. Stardust was the third section, where he put the old Alcatraz inmates.

So what Cat was doing was trying to tear our morale apart by treating the center section of the camp better than the others, letting them eat outside, giving them special food, giving them the run of the camp, letting them go out by themselves to the head any time they wanted to. All this while some of the others were kept in solitary confinement.

So I said: "OK, if you want us to act reasonably, you'll have to give everybody in this camp the same treatment." He wasn't able to come off of this. I don't think he had official OK to do it. I believe he was still trying to use what he told me was his great psychological skill with the prisoners, that he'd learned from the French. He was still trying to do some things on his own.

I believe that his order from above had been this: when Ho Chi Minh died: "OK, we're going to cool the torture program, but whatever you can get out of them by hook or crook, short of torture, go ahead." They didn't want him to push us to the point where he pushed me, into calling a camp-wide fast. I called it because over a period of months, he wouldn't come through and give guys roommates, he had two or three still in solo. He had banished 90 per cent of solitary confinement, but he was still trying this big deal of showing contrast in treatment between his "good nephews," as he called them, and people like me, his "bad nephews," with whom he would have to deal a little differently.

I said, "You'd better treat all your nephews the same or you're going to have hell to pay." He procrastinated. He was slowly doing this. It wasn't fast enough and certain guys were saying, "Well, Goddam, I'm still in solo," so for morale it was very unpopular. And I called for the hunger strike which, after a face-saving gesture, a waiting period, caused them to come off of it entirely and the next camp commander within two months told me from now on everyone will be treated the same. Cat was demoted. We never saw him again. He left. A new camp commander, quite fair by their standards, came on and told me from now on everybody's going to be the same.

They did try to use discriminatory treatment after that, but not in the way that they had been using it. In other words, not flaunting it. They didn't know we knew about the difference in treatment. We had some secret ways to learn later. But they weren't parading the Desert Inn people out to eat outside and play around in front of the rest of us, which was making our guys murderously mad. There would have been people killed.

Q: Yes, naturally.

Adm. D.: So they stopped that entirely and they didn't try to use that, which was the main thing that was bugging me as the acting SRO of the camp, because it was tearing up morale. Once they started treating them apparently the same, that's all I wanted. And it was the same for all practical purposes. Later, they did isolate one group down at the Zoo and give them better treatment, but we couldn't see that, so it wasn't hurting the morale. We learned about that after the fact.

And he had another little group at Camp Unity in 1971 and 72 who were getting a little bit better treatment, but he thought that they had them isolated so that we couldn't see it, and that's all I was concerned about. I just didn't want them to flaunt it in front of the other guys so they'd get so damned mad. There was no way I could change Wilbur and Miller. We tried, but we couldn't. But they did come off the torture, and that was the biggest change in the treatment. October was when it began and it was not announced until December of 1969, when Cat really came to me. I've described previously how I was the first one to suspect that treatment change had taken place, at least in my camp, because I was caught communicating and, for the first time, they didn't torture me.

It was the Soft Soap Fairy from the Zoo, as some people called him, or Slick, as we called him, who had me in there and said: "Denton, you were just caught communicating," and I immediately went into my "get ready" mechanism, "you're going to get tortured," to myself, "better get ready." And he said, "But you will not be punished." I couldn't really believe him at first, and he said, "As long as I'm camp commander, anyone who is caught communicating, although they will be admonished because they have broken the regulations, will not be punished."

When I went back to my cell and tapped that information out to the guys and said, "I think something really big has happened," since I was generally optimistic anyway, the guys had a little trouble believing that.

The next day, in the rain, they caught me again and took me in there. And while I was sitting there, it was Slick and he was telling me the same thing again, a guard came in, saluted, presented arms, and garbled some stuff out in Vietnamese, and he said: "See, the guard is reporting that Johnson has been caught communicating. He will not be punished either." Then he let me go back to my cell. I tapped out, "Boys, was Sam just caught communicating?" They said yes, so I said they had just told me he wasn't going to be punished. Then they believed that the treatment change had taken place. That was in October.

It was December when Cat started having me in back at the next camp where we moved on December the 8th or 9th. He called me in formally and announced that he knew I knew he was the runner of the torture program the whole time we were there. He had been discredited, his friends who had done the same thing had been discredited, and that there was going to be a complete change.

My interpretation of all that was that they were going to make a few scapegoats or pretend that those guys were punished, and then the whole government would get off scot-free after the war.

My last quiz in Hanoi was on that subject. They called me in in February 1973 and asked me what was I going to say when I got home. I said, "Why do you want to know?" And they said, after much deliberation among themselves and consultation because they didn't want to stoop to telling you why they wanted to know anything. I said, "I haven't been answering any questions about that, why should I answer now? If you'll tell me why you want to know I'll consider answering you." We knew we were leaving in the next day or two. They talked it over and said, "We want to know because we think that when you get home your stories about your treatment are going to cause Mr. Nixon" - <u>Mr.</u> Nixon, they called him for the first time - "to have to abandon his plan for the development of the Mekong and aid to North Vietnam."

I said, "OK, that's fair." I believed them. I know that what they were telling me was true. I'd played poker with them for almost eight years. They were hanging on every word I said and it was a big deal for them to tell me that. So I said:

"Well, I'll tell you. I'm going to say you treated us like animals prior to October 1969." I told them all the things that they'd done to me and all the things they'd done to everybody else. They didn't bat an eye, and when I'd finished that, they said: "Yes, but what else are you going to say?"

What they wanted to hear is what I said next. I said, "I'm going to say that in October the treatment changed as from night to day and, although you never gave us treatment in conformance with the Geneva Conventions, you did treat us infinitely better than you had before then." That's all they wanted to hear, because they thought that that would establish their point that after the end of the Ho Chi Minh administration they took out the few people who were responsible for executing his policies and the rest of them would be OK (not punished for war crimes).

That's all now a matter of no consequence. But had we gone ahead and sustained the victory, which we won militarily, it would have been a matter of consequence, and I would have testified that I did not believe for a minute that it was only Ho Chi Minh or only Cat and a few other guys. They were all involved in it and, where they could prove that someone was accidentally or deliberately killed or where you could find out who originated the brutality of policies, those guys would have been war criminals. But now it doesn't matter.

Q: Tell me about the whole process of coming home.

Adm. D.: Well, even at the time it was almost like a dream.

The announcement that we would come home was made in accordance with the cease-fire agreement. It was scrupulously observed, but it was an anticlimax to us, especially to me. Because in my optimism when the bombing started on the 18th of December 1972, as I may have told you, I bet Jim Stockdale a hundred bucks that peace would come by Christmas. It didn't. Christmas came, and then I said, "OK, I'll bet another hundred that if "(- they were giving us all this stuff on the radio about the antiwar stuff about resuming the bombing after Christmas, I knew there'd be a bombing pause for Christmas, and the question was whether it would be resumed - I said) "it's resumed on the 26th, I'll bet you another hundred we'll have peace by the 1st of January."

I had a taker on that. Jim took me up on it. Well, I didn't miss it by far. Mr. Nixon came up with the bombing decision himself. I've talked to him about it. On the 26th it was reinstituted and by the time a few more days and nights had gone by and they had nothing left in the way of air defenses. We could have bombed them with impunity. The <u>Milwaukee Journal</u> made a big to do about what I said about that. They reported that in my book I said we should have bombed them more with B-52s. I didn't say that at all. We bombed them enough with B-52s to win it. All we had to do was abide by the four-power agreement and supply them proportionately relative to what the Chinese and Russians gave the North, which would have been well within our means and would have avoided the invasion.

Anyway, the end came as an anticlimax. We knew they were finished. The guards were obviously jelly. The officers were jelly. They started acceding to our demands. They started catering to our goodwill, and sort of "you remember me, I wasn't bad" and that type attitude. And as the release sequence came along, they asked us how many feet from us would we tolerate photographers? Could photographers come with us on the bus? And we would tell them yes, no, maybe, and this sort of thing? For the first time, rather than giving the kiss of death on something as a senior officer, the senior officers were actually telling the North Vietnamese what to do, and they did it.

So going through with it was, in a way, an anticlimax and, in another way, a test of restraint because you didn't want to go mad with joy. You just didn't want to go insane with joy. You had to try to keep telling yourself, "Now, come on, twenty years from now this won't be a real big deal"!

Q: Or maybe something will happen to prevent it?

Adm. D.: True, I was hanging on that. You didn't want to doubt that either. But there was a time in the first release sequence in which I was involved, we were on our way to the airport and they told us when the plane was supposed to land and we were supposed to leave, and it didn't happen that way. They were delayed. I've forgotten now the actual cause of the delay, but we began to worry. I tried not to show this to my buddies. I was the senior officer in the first release group.

I tried not to show them how worried I was, but, boy, my stomach. I just about lost it when I saw that it was getting late and I didn't know what the hell had happened. But finally the plane did land and when I saw that C-41 out there it was the most beautiful sight I've ever seen in my life. It was so clean and all new and the Air Force guys with all these fancy flight suits and the nurses all crisp and clean. It was the first time we'd seen any physical evidence of American power recognized by the North Vietnamese. They were awed. The crowd out there was awed by that airplane, awed by the military smartness of the people that came out of there. They were probably very favorably impressed by the demeanor of Mr. Seiverts, of the State Department, a very dapper, very dignified gentleman, and Roger Shields of the Department of Defense, crew-cut hair, honest face that they could sense the integrity of, and the colonel, who is now a civilian working for CinCPac both under Guyler and now under Weisner, was on the plane. He was the senior officer involved. There was a lieutenant colonel (Abel), now back out at the Air Academy. There was a couple of other junior guys that I don't remember.

Mr. Seiverts and Mr. Shields both greeted me and told me what a great job my wife had done. That made me happy.

And getting in the plane, I was just trying to suppress my own excitement. I was also very painfully aware that on that first plane we had Wilbur and Miller, who were traitors, and I didn't know how they would spoil the arrival, if they chose to.

Q: How did the other boys treat them on the plane?

Adm. D.: Just ignored them. They were too much caught up in the elation of getting there. It was my sack to worry about it. I was the senior guy. They let me worry about that, and I did. I worried about it quite a bit.

I went up to either Seiverts or Shields and told them that we had those two creeps aboard and I wanted to know what the hell they were doing there because we were supposed to come out in order of shoot-down and the sick and wounded first. That was our insisted policy, which the North Vietnamese agreed to honor.

A: And these two men were later shoot-downs?

Adm. D.: Yes, but I was later told by the prisoners who were on the airplane who knew who was where over in the New Guy Village sector, - that's where Wilbur and Miller were (it was a sort of sick bay part) - that they had apparently been ill and that they were coming out as sick. I didn't know whether that was true or not and I didn't trust the two gentlemen enough to ask them, but at least I didn't have to stand on ceremony. They were coming out as sick men and they had been in the sick bay, and the guys who had been with them said they did believe they had been ill, and these were loyal men who said that. So I didn't have to say, OK, the plane can't take off, and cause an international incident there, but I did have to cope with what the hell am I going to do with them.

So I told Shields and Seiverts about it and Shields said, "Well, what do you want to do?" First, Shields came to me and said: "Jerry, there's probably going to be some kind of an opportunity to say something when we get off the airplane and there will probably be a good many people watching." That just went right over my head. All I knew was he said, "CinCPac will be there," and I thought that's a big deal, but we already had for years, probably the first year, developed the policy that the senior officer on the returning airplane, ship, or bus would be the spokesman for the group, and he was responsible for getting the men further transportation. We had all that already laid out, so that was expected of me, and I'd been thinking about what I was going to say for five or six years if I happened to be senior, so that was no probelm for the general sentiments.

I thought the main threat was whether Wilbur and Miller were going to get off the plane and make an anti-war statement of some kind and kind of mess the thing up. That was his concern, too, and he asked me what I thought we ought to do, so I said, "Let me go have a chat with them." I've forgotten whether they said it would be a good idea for me instead of them to talk to them, or whether I suggested I do it. I think we sort of talked it over and I said, "Let me see if I can do it."

There was a man sitting between Wilbur and Miller and I asked him to swap seats with me and he did. Wilbur and Miller looked at me with what I would consider controlled expressions and, as I recall, the general tenor of what I said to them went like this: I know who you are. As you know, I tried to contact you myself and you didn't respond and later when you had people with you and Admiral Stockdale called down, the other guys answered and he gave you a word-for-word order to come back over to our side and you said you wouldn't. You were going to continue to support them. This is a matter for your conscience and for the government to handle. I'm not interested in that right at the moment. What I am interested in is what you're doing on the plane and what your intentions are when you land at the field. I don't feel empowered on my authority to prevent you from saying whatever it is you choose to say."

In my mind I knew that Mr. Shields - Dr. Shields - and Mr. Seiverts didn't want to impose themselves in any way. They were leaning over backwards not to affect what I was going to say or what those fellows might say.

So I made it clear that I didn't want to bully them around and I respected their right to their points of view and it was going to be, as I say, the government's and their consciences that would rule when they got home. But I was interested, since we, the main body of prisoners, had planned for the senior officer to be the spokesman, and I wanted to know was that all right with them. I told then generally what I was going to say. I told them I was going to generally say that we were honored to serve there and give the impression that we were conscious that we had been continually members of the U.S. armed forces, and that we were grateful for what the country and the president had done to get us out of there. And I wanted to know if they objected to that or felt that they had to say something at that time.

They said no, they didn't. They preferred to remain completely low profile and they didn't want to make any kind of public demonstration at all or manifestation at that time. Then I had to check with them on the way they wanted to depart the aircraft. There were two ways to leave, one out the regular ramp and one out the rear ramp, which was for the sick and wounded. I didn't want it to appear that those creeps had been allowed to come out of there out of turn as well men, since they were aboard as sick and wounded.

So I gave my opinion that since they were listed as sick and wounded on the flight, I thought they might choose to go out with the rest of the sick and wounded. They immediately acceeded to that, so that was the end of that problem. They weren't visible, they just went out with the other guys, the other sick and wounded, some of whom were quite recently shot down, B-52 crewmen and so forth.

That was a crisis that got over and then I made up my little thing. I asked the guys to give me a thumbs up if they liked what I had said. I didn't have the "God bless America" in the prepared part, and to give me a thumbs down if they didn't like it, and give me a hand up if they wanted to ask questions, or add or subtract. I wanted them all to have an input because it was something that represented them all and, since I had time, I wanted to make sure that I tapped all their opinions.

Q: This was the flight over to the Philippines?

Adm. D.: Yes, Sir, Clark Field. They all gave me a thumbs up and were pretty cheerful, so that's the way it went.

I peeked out of the airplane to try to see what the set-up was. I didn't see. I kind of stumbled going down the ramp, and I saw Admiral Gayler. I reported back to him: "Admiral Gayler, Commander Jeremiah A. Denton, Jr." and I gave him my old file number, 485087 USN, "reporting back for duty in the Navy," or some words that allowed for the fact that I had been on duty, but now I was coming back for regular assignment. I believe he mumbled something about - he didn't know what I was going to say either - "would you like to," and he pointed at the mike. I said, "Yes, Sir," and I walked over there and said my little saying.

I had instructed the guys as they came out that I would make those remarks and then I would proceed past the flag, which we heard would be there, that we would all stop and even though we were uncovered, since the Army and the Air Force salute uncovered, the Navy - there's a stipulation that says Navy officers can also salute to avoid embarrassment when uncovered - and we would all stop, do a left-face salute to the flag, and then proceed to the bus. I said, "In accordance with our plan, I will do that and then stay outside the bus until all of you are aboard, then I will get on the bus. We'll go from there and when we get to the hospital, you're detached from my command." And that's what we did.

Q: It's interesting that these two dissenters didn't raise any objections, but what you were about to say and what you did say apparently was not in keeping with their own sentiments?

Adm. D.: Well, I thought about that a lot. I didn't consider them when I made up my thing, but as I recall the words, "We are honored to have had the opportunity to serve our country under difficult circumstances. We are profoundly grateful to our commander-in-chief and to our nation for this day." Even with what they did, if they thought that what they did was serving their country - we had quite a little discussion even among some very tough guys. Some of these things are not discussed in the POW book or in my book either. They never will be discussed openly, but issues like when the propaganda got hammered at some people enough, they began to wonder whether or not the war was really legal. It wasn't ever declared. Are we supporting the Constitution as we swore to do, or are we supporting a president who has misstepped. I really made up, and it turned out to be correct, a statement to the effect that we swore to follow the orders of the president of the United States as well as to uphold the Constitution. Some of them didn't remember that. They remembered having said that they were sworn to defend the Constitution of the United States.

But in this swearing-in ceremony that we took originally as ensigns, and this one is for rear admiral, it does say - it's signed by the Secretary of the Navy and Vice Admiral Bagley, "And I do strictly charge and require those officers and other personnel of lesser rank to render such obedience as is due an officer of this grade and position, and this officer is to observe and follow such orders and directions from time to time as may be given by me, or the future president of the United States of America, or other superior officers acting in accordance with the laws of the United States of America." Although it's signed only by those two people, it says "By the President," so they signed for him.

So we are sworn and, believe it or not, many O5s, of which I was one, couldn't recall that that was actually in the wording. We all remembered "support the Constitution of the United States." That's the oath of the president. So it was a fine but very important point. You'd be surprised what great men were a little confused on that point for a while and gave us a little trouble at times.

But 87 per cent of us hung in there with Johnson and Nixon and I think, were all to be known, our country would still be proud of the performance of most everybody.

Q: Do you want to say something more about the reception you received when you came back to the States? And would you say something in particular about the way the Navy treated its own men?

Adm. D.: If you hadn't said that I would have anyway because that is what I'd like to say about the release sequence.

From the President of the United States on down, and I know because he did take some personal hand in this, and all of the people who were concerned with this in DOD and in the State Department and the executive staff of the president all along, there was an almost infinite compassion involved in the way they were going to handle us. It was simply tender. I know of no other word. For example, if I had decided to get off that airplane and say "hooray for Ho Chi Minh" they would have let me do it. They were not giving the slightest clue as to what they wanted us to do, because they didn't know really what to expect.

I think Seiverts and Shields probably had some idea of how various individuals had behaved there, but had Wilbur and Miller wanted to do something they would have been allowed to do it. There was a guy on The New York Times who accused me of having been briefed on what to say. I didn't even respond, and the next day somebody asked me at a news conference what I thought of it and I said, "My only response is I'm sorry for the gentleman." And that man two days later retracted his charge and said that he had thought that the United States was an apathetic nation, but he received 27,000 letters in a twenty-four-hour period condemning him for that inference.

Q: <u>The Times</u> can be wrong, can it not!

Adm. D.: Yes, very frequently it is, I'm afraid.

But the compassion shown to our families, the tenderness and consideration shown to them, leaning over backwards even to allow for bursts of temperament, which they perceived as understandable, all of that is deeply appreciated. The CACO arrangement, by which our families were assisted in temporal matters of all kinds, is undyingly appreciated. The financial advice, all that kind of thing that they got, was just infinite pains, and the whole release sequence as we came home was in the same vein.

One thing that did take place in the Navy especially, I believe, there are specific examples of this, was more, in my opinion, compassionate than the other services. They did much more than the others, from what I have learned. I'm not an authority on this, but I went once to the Chief of Staff of the Air Force about a family problem that wasn't being attended to because the husband and wife had been divorced after the man's return. I reminded the Chief of Staff of the Air Force that the Navy was providing psychological help to women in that condition, whereas the Air Force wasn't. And I said, "If the Navy is leaning over further than the law allows, please don't put them on report, but if you can find it within your means or interpretation of the rules to duplicate what the Navy's doing, I strongly recommend you do so in this particular case." I won't go into whose case it was.

The Navy stretched the point to make it a beautiful thing.

I guess there's no way to pay enough tribute to the Navy for that. I tried in the epilogue of my book to make it a vehicle for that as well as a vehicle for a few other expressions that were expunged. My epilogue was emasculated.

Q: Why would that be?

Adm. D.: Print costs money, for one thing, and some of the things I said in the draft of the epilogue about television were considered to be counterproductive to support for the book. They thought that the critics would murder me if I said what I wanted to say, and I said, "Those critics are out of tune with the body of American feeling. You guys up here in New York City are living in a walled prison of thought which is not the same as that which exists in the rest of the country." They didn't buy that. They said, "We're the publishers, we know how to sell books."

I said, "I don't care if this book doesn't sell any except to my wife and my mother. I want it in there."

They wouldn't do it and they took out a lot of stuff I had in there about the media and some of the stuff I had in, praising the Navy. Not because they were being vicious but simply because they wanted to save money on the print, on the pages.

But I think I had enough in there to express that gratitude. I talked about the names of the people in the hospital and that sort of stuff.

Q: Yes.

Adm. D.: But I didn't have all that I drafted up kept in the book. That was one of the compromises. I finally had to decide whether to say to print it or let it go the way it is, and it went.

Q: You had a so-called debriefing process, didn't you?

Adm. D.: Yes, Sir, we did, and that in itself was handled with tenderness. That is the only way to say it. Two fellows debriefed me with compassion, and in the hospital there we had other debriefers. At Clark there was an Air Force doctor who was sort of a pacifist with whom I had no empathy, but other than that it went very smoothly. The debriefing back in Portsmouth hospital was complete. It was traumatic to have to go back into the detail of things that happened to you, but it was necessary, and I must say that that Reader's Digest book, POW, by John Hubbell, contains probably a better picture in one set of covers than does any volume now existing within the intelligence establishments. So it's a damned good book that John Hubbell wrote.

Q: He had access to all the debriefing, I suppose?

Adm. D.: He had access to us. I don't know whether he had access to the debriefing material, but he and his colleagues did interview over a hundred POWs, so it's a rather comprehensive file. I wish he hadn't left out 1970 at Little Vegas but he couldn't put everything in there. That was when the Cat made the announcement, which I thought was somehow significant.

Q: This is sort of an addendum to what you've been saying, but would you give me some examples of the kind of prayer you engaged in and the answers that came to you?

Adm. D.: Well, I covered the general prayer scheme that I had developed, but there were prayers offered that had special reason for offering and special responses. I have outlined one in my recounting in the book, my book, of a rather sensational one, which to me was the most significant event of my life. I had been in the rig four or five days and nights and it was rather painful.

Q: The rig being the rope?

Adm. D.: No, Sir. This one was a special deal which involved the light set of traveling irons, the bar that they used for that, they had that under my ankles and they had the ankles encased in the two shackles so that two holes in the bed in this wooden pallet they wrapped a rope up over this bar upon which my Achilles' tendons were resting. They twined the rope through that and then up over the shackles that was over, say first the right leg and back down to and around the bar, then up over the shackle on the left leg, then back down to and around the bar, then through a hole in the bed and up to a pulley arrangement. When the guards pulled on that pulley the shackles forced my leg, as it turned out with all the vectors involved, forced the Achilles' tendon down onto the round iron bar slowly and over a period of days into the flesh. So that about three-eighths inch of the bar, at the end of the ten days in which I went through this, a three-eighths inch radius hole was made by this bar in the back of my leg. I still have two scars from that, one for the first five days and a second from the second five days. They moved the rig at the end of 5 days when I tried to satisfy them by giving them something they already knew. They didn't take it and put me back in. So I have two sets of scars from that.

It hurt pretty bad. They had my feet flat against the wall so that I could not bend my legs. The shackles were forced down in the front of my shins so that I couldn't bend my knees. My legs were held flat against the bed, the pallet, and I was sitting up straight because I had hell cuffs, we called them. They were wrist irons, attached to my wrists behind me. You can't lie down in that arrangement. They also had me far enough away from the wall so that I couldn't get my shoulder on the wall, even to lean over. So I'd been sitting up like that for five days and five nights. I tried to tell them what they already knew about communications hoping that that would let them save face and let me out.

I tried to tell them that we hollered under the doors, and that when the guards were marching us to quiz, we'd pretend to be talking to the guards and actually be giving out names. Well, hell, they knew all that and didn't accept it, so they put me back in. They really wanted to know how we were communicating, and we had some rather ingenious ways at that time.

I had prayed myself pretty much out and I also lasted as

long as I could. This was the second series of five days and nights sitting there. That night I just said or thought words to the effect, "God, I've prayed and You have responded many times. I'm not getting any response now that is going to be effective. I'm afraid that I am going to be broken to the point of having to give these guys something useful and I just can't do that, so I'm turning myself over to You without any further articulation of prayer. You've just got it."

At the instant I articulated or thought that prayer, which was the most intense I have ever made, the only analogy I can make is it was like a cloak. I was in chills. I was having alternating chills and fever. I was having a chill at that particular moment and it was like a cloak of warmth came over me. The most pain I was feeling was in my back. My legs had pretty well gone numb by then and my wrists were numb. But my back, from sitting up for 240 hours or whatever it was in that position, was not entirely numb and there was quite a bit of pain.

That cloak was one of warmth, total physical comfort and total psychological comfort; a feeling of physical and psychological comfort that I never felt before in my life and have never felt since.

About ten minutes after that happened - it happened instantly that I got that comfort and I knew that I could stay there for the rest of my life, and if I were going to die I would die like drinking a glass of water, nothing -- about ten minutes after that feeling was achieved, I heard footsteps outside the door and the guard Happy, who had been reported weeping as he would go from me after pulling on the pulley each day to pull the thing further into my Achilles' tendons. (He would go to Mulligan's cell two doors down and he would be weeping. Mulligan tapped this to me and I could hear him. He would tell me "Happy's crying again, he must be really messing you up.")

Then they would give me beatings and I would notice that he had tears in his eyes when he beat me.

Well, Happy came to the door with another guard and with someone whom I didn't see but whose voice I recognized. I finally saw through the crack in the door when it was opened. He tried to remain invisible, but it was a guy we called The Lump who had a tumor on the front of his head but otherwise was a very handsome man; extremely articulate, eloquent. He had perfect control of the English language, very little accent, and boasted, I think quite truly, and he represented North Vietnam frequently at trade discussions with East Germany and Czechoslovakia and so forth. He was running the psychological and torture program at that camp and he succeeded in getting some guys to think he was a pretty good guy. I knew he was our most deadly enemy.

Anyway, he was now exposing himself as a torturer because he had always told us that he was against the torture program. But he was outside the door and sent Happy and the other guard in there to pull on the rig, both of them pulling on the rig through the pulley until I gave in. I guess they thought I'd die because I was in pretty bad shape. I hadn't been eating deliberately because there was no way to get it down, or to eliminate; and I'd stopped drinking.

They came in and started pulling on the thing and Happy looked in my face and I felt absolutely no pain. I looked at him with a tranquil expression and one which I'm sure showed the total composure I felt. Then something occurred to me. Why not give him a look like "What the hell are you doing, Happy? How can you treat another human being like this? And you know damned well I'n not going to break. It's just stupid." I tried to impart that in a look. He broke up instantly. His face contorted, tears ran down his cheeks, he pushed the other guard away from the rope, and he ran outside and started screaming at the top of his voice at The Lump.

Lump tried to interrupt him because you could hear it all over the camp. It was like ten or eleven at night, I imagine. Happy wouldn't stop screaming and finally when he ran out of breath, Lump must have said things like, "Don't be a fool. Go back in there and pull some more. He'll give up." Happy screamed some more at him and it got pretty loud. It went on for ten or fifteen minutes and finally Happy won his point. He came in and loosened the rig, loosened the hell cuffs, left me in the position, but it wasn't forcing in any way, and I didn't feel any pain. I went through the rest of that night not feeling any pain, perfectly composed, and the next morning Happy came in and, avoiding my eyes, he wouldn't look at me, he roughly but with obvious inner relief applied medicine to the gaping holes in my Achilles' tendons and took the irons off very tenderly.

The normal way they would pull irons off in a situation like that would be..."swish"...like that, to rip them loose, slashing them along the wounds, to emphasize that further pain was coming, but he didn't. He took them off tenderly and then, when he saw I couldn't walk, he and the other guard helped me move. He did do one ironical thing. He pretended that he was going to move me in with another guy. He knew I knew where people lived and he took me across the campus as if to take me in where, I think, Jim Stockdale was and next to him were Lamar and Johnson. He made as if to lead me in that direction, but I knew he was not going to put me there. I knew he was going to isolate me at the gate because I'd been out there before. I knew they weren't going to let me tell anybody that I had gotten away without even giving them anything after long torture.

I had managed already to tap out to the guys that they'd loosened me. I tapped it on my bed and they heard me. I had nothing to lose if they caught me. So they did get the word that I hadn't broken. All they knew was that I was leaving. They didn't know what they were going to do to me.

They took me out to the gate and tried to put - I don't know whether this is too subtle or not - he was trying to guide me in an ironical jest toward one of these buildings where there were occupants, as if I was going to get a roommate. I shrugged and pulled myself toward where I knew they were going to put me.

Q: This is where I belong!

Adm. D.: I knew they were going to put me in isolation. He had this little triumphant smile. He was going to tease me, but he lost that gambit and then got impatient, so they shuffled me on in an isolated gate cell and tried to put the irons on my legs but they were so swollen they couldn't do it. They put ropes on.

Anyway, that was one of the three times I beat them altogether and it was the most sensational answer to a prayer I ever got.

That was October and they gave me a rope trick in December, and I took that rope trick to where they knew I was going to pass out and they wouldn't bug me. Again, Happy was arguing with Pierre, who had given me the rope. They'd just had me in there about forty-five minutes and I'd already gone to where - as I say, I got a little stronger about this, and the rope trick normally was effective, but all it was was a pure rope trick - and I got to where I could take pain to passing out. So with my cuffs and the rope I had caved in (fallen over backward) and they know when you do that that you can't feel anything because the cuffs are tearing your hands up when your body is resting. It's hard to explain, but they're twisted and they know that you can't feel any pain when you can take that. Your fingers are all folded up and frequently dislocated when you get in that position.

So they came in and Happy was saying "I told you so, Pierre," and they took the rope off me!

They did get twenty-seven confessions that night, but they didn't get mine that night. So that was two times in a row I beat them. I counted three. The first five days in irons in that rig, and the second five, and that. Those are the three times. Later I was stupid enough to brag in writing when they were going to break me again. I reminded them. I said, "The last three times you tried, you had to give up. You'll never break me. You'll have to torture me to death."

Well, they proved I was wrong. They got me to sign something else with a few bonus little things thrown in. I wish I hadn't written that.

That was one answer. Another answer was in that same place, out at the gate, George Coker moved in later by me. This was a time, like Stockdale, that I was totally isolated. He had some times like this. I don't know how long his times were. I was there from October until December before Coker showed up and I had no problem. I was praying away and having a hell of a good time in these light ropes on my legs and except for the rope trick, while they only gave me for that hour, I had no problem out there at the gate. I couldn't see. They had the lights out, but there was a little hole in my door through which I could look around. I was having a pretty good time. I never felt better in my whole time.

Q: It was cold, though, was it not?

Adm. D.: Oh, yes, it was cold all right, but I'd already been through the winter before that with less clothes on. By this time I had a sweat shirt, a blue sweat shirt, which was the only thing we had. It was a better winter than the winter before. I also had a blanket, so it wasn't all that bad. It was cold, no socks, but you got to where you could handle that.

I said a particularly hard rosary while I was up there and Coker was next door. Now they had freed my hands and I had only this loose thing on my legs, so we had a good chance to escape because I knew I could untie that damned thing. Coker was next door and we were right near the gate. They only had two guards on duty at night plus the guard at the gate. So I deliberately said a rosary for the specific intention of being granted an insight into how the hell to get out of that cell.

At the instant I said amen at the end of the rosary, which took about twenty minutes, my eyes unconsciously happened to be looking at the door, and at the instant I said amen I saw how to open that door. I described it to Coker. He didn't understand me and it took me a couple of days to convince him that I indeed knew how to open the door and that he could open his door the same way. It turned out that his door made a lot of noise when it was opened, so he wanted me to come out of my cell and come over to his and open his door. Well, I didn't have enough strength to lift his door up to keep that noise from happening, with the guard only fifteen feet away at the gate. He was looking in the opposite direction but he had a cut-out place where if he just turned his head he could see me.

So I said, "George, that's a little wild. It's concrete out there and he's going to hear the God-damned door." So I told him how to come over to my cell. I called, "Get up in your attic" -

they had barbed wire - it was a very low-security situation because they had us in loose restraint and thought that would do it, and I knew it was a chance of a lifetime - "come on over to my cell through the roof. You can get in the attic, then you could remove the tiles and come right down into my attic." And I had made a big enough hole for him to come into my cell. "You could use your pallet as a ladder," because the back of the pallet had these horizontal boards holding the other boards together.

He saw that we could get out that way but he thought I was trying to commit honorable suicide because if we got out of there we wouldn't get far and they'd catch us.

It took me weeks to convince him. He wouldn't buy the things that I was really going to do. There were bicycles next door. I wanted to steal a bicycle and on a rainy night we could get out of our cells that way. My door didn't make any noise opening. The guard was half-asleep. He was looking in the opposite direction. And I had stayed up all night for a month timing these other guards as the two made their rounds. I knew how long different guards took to get around and what their habits were.

Well, George finally agreed to go but he said we were too weak. He told me he didn't recognize me when he saw me because I was so skinny, and I was. He'd known me for quite some time before. When I got outside finally and saw what I looked like under that sweat shirt, I understood what he meant. My skin was hanging like a chicken off of this bone, off of that arm. There was nothing except bone and hanging skin. So he convinced me that I wasn't strong enough to get far enough away. Our plan involved going on that bicycle or running for as many miles as we could that night, then taking to the fields. He knew enough about the geography from having been up there on a few raids to know where the mountain range was, and we were going to get into that and go.

We settled on waiting until Tet when the guards would be drunk. Then they changed the treatment. They took everybody out of irons on the 8th or 9th of December. That time I watched twenty-six sets of irons coming back. I forget whether it was the bombing pause or what, then I knew it would be all right for Christmas. Then they'd wait for Tet, which was all true, and they started giving me exercise outside for the first time like everybody was given. So I agreed. "OK, George, we'll be all right by Tet and then we're going. Right?"

"Right."

Tet was about the 1st of February. On the 23rd of January they moved me out of that damned cell and moved me in with Mulligan for three days and then over to Little Vegas into solitary again. I never again got in a cell that had low security like that door. But George did, and that book by John Hubbell tells how George got in exactly the same kind of cell again and used the method I told him of opening that door. He and George McKnight had the same kind and he explained to George how to do it and they got out. And they had a happy little seven or eight hours!

Q: But they got caught?

Adm. D.: They got caught on the bank of the river after swimming all night.

Q: That's almost inevitable, isn't it, it would have been inevitable?

Adm. D.: Yes, Sir, but I considered the answer to that prayer, to say the least, sensational. I won't apply another adjective that I'm tempted to apply!

Another time, and this only makes sense to a Catholic, they have devotion in the Catholic Church to the Sacred Heart of Jesus. Mulligan and I, this was now in Little Vegas in 1967, were in irons and pretty philosophical about it, I in particular. I accurately predicted. We would get out of irons on the 2nd of September, their National Day. The way we got in them on that particular occasion, it was in the summer of 67, a guard had come to the door, opened the hatch, and one of our faces was there, namely Mulligan's, and he spat in it. Jim immediately spat back in the guard's face. He told me what had happened. Jim hadn't been through quite the mill that I had, probably principally because his arm had been hurt and he was a living skeleton. He was even then as thin as I was in 66, which was pretty thin. He was the thinnest man in the place. I was second thinnest at the Zoo. So they probably didn't feel like they could do much to him or he'd die.

After Jim spat in the guard's face, since he hadn't had a whole lot of experience of going into irons and I had, I'd been through the mill about five times at that point, not counting irons, I'm talking about torture - I was in irons an awful lot, I said: "Jim, we're going to be punished in irons, at least, so you'd better take a crap." And he said, "Ah, come on, he spat in my face, I spat in his. They're not going to do anything."

I said, "Jim, if you can, take a crap because in irons, you know it's kind of hard."

I sat down on my can and I finally got him to sit on his bucket, and sure enough, just as we finished that they came and put us in irons.

We could hear guys being tortured. They were having a purge then, as a result of increased bombing, and they had found out about Stockdale's "Back U.S." policy which smacked of a great deep conspiracy because it had a code word type thing and that really intrigued them.

Jim was running that camp very, very well and we had lost communications because a guard was stationed right at our door. We couldn't do anything, and that's when I conceived the idea of this voice tap code that I got later, where you just cough and sneeze, because that was the only way we could have communicated. I wanted to do it so badly because we couldn't tap. You could hear a tap, no matter how soft, and we were in a cell that was on the edge and we weren't adjacent to anybody.

We were getting kind of low in spirits. We were hearing these guys screaming. They killed one guy and shortly after that they were beating up George McKnight and Ron Storz, who later died. That was the night they jumped on George's stomach and he evacuated into his shorts and they gagged him with the shorts. It was a bad night. We were all screaming out "Torture, torture," which we had agreed to do. I'd suggested this to Jim and he agreed. So we were doing that and we got beat up a little bit that night, so the next day we were feeling kind of low, and the war news wasn't too good even the way we read it on the radio.

It began to occur to me that the war was going to go a pretty long time. It was getting bad. I got to a pretty low point. I was in the upper bunk, Jim was in the lower bunk because he couldn't climb to the upper one. I never got out to dump my bucket. Jim did it for me. My legs got paralyzed. I was in there from early August to the 2nd of September without moving my legs.

In the third week or so of that I was feeling pretty low and again I said, "Lord, I'm just about at the end of the old rope." We're both awake, Jim and I, and I said, "You've got to come in here and help some way. I don't know how to phrase any further prayers. I'm getting pretty near despair." I was in no great pain or anything, simply in irons. I wasn't even in cuffs. I had my back propped up with my blanket, as did Jim, and we were in no great pain but our morale was low.

So, in the quiet of this nap time which was going on, their siesta time, probably 1:15 in the afternoon, I heard a voice as distinctly as I hear yours when you speak to me, and I was sure Mulligan heard it. It was a beautifully modulated voice, rather on the deep side, but not too much so, and the words that were said were: "Say, Sacred Heart of Jesus, I give myself to Thee!" I was startled, to say the least, and I waited about twenty seconds to kind of compose myself, then I said, "Jim, what do you think of that?" And Jim said, "What do I think of what?"

We'd both been wide awake. I wasn't dozing, neither was he. In fact, we had been talking about a minute before it happened. I told him about the voice and he was totally convinced. He could tell from my expression, the expression in my voice, that there was no question about what I had heard.

Q: You had heard it but he had not?

Adm. D.: That's right. So I said that many, many times after that. Then when I got home it was almost like a miracle because I received a letter from someone with a very fancy card and medal and it was almost exactly the same words: "Sacred Heart of Jesus, I place my trust in Thee." That was the motto of whatever this little religious organization is within the church. I was quite taken aback. I was rather strongly reminded of that.

Then there's a story that I mention in the book. Ed Davis - this was before torture had begun in October 65, in fact it was September or August, I believe, when we were in New Guy Village, in cells, one removed from each other. We were whistling in code and stuff and he told me he had left a present for me in the latrine area. He told me where to look for it under such and such brick and I looked for it. It was a cross that he had woven - you're familiar with the story. He'd woven it very well and I prized it, cherished it. It was the only thing that was mine and I thanked him for it profusely. He said he had been pretty good at handcrafts when he was in the Boy Scouts and it certainly reflected that.

I kept it with me in a little propaganda pamphlet which they must have wondered about, why I kept it. I had in that same propaganda pamphlet a list of names of POWs which I hoped they would find if they ever searched because I thought there was some mutual protection involved. I thought torture would begin sooner or later, and I would have told them that everybody had those names and they'd better now feel that they could not just with impunity torture somebody to death without our reporting it - the survivors reporting it.

I was in another cell at the Zoo when they wanted to plug up my ventilation holes, which consisted of three bricks at the top of my cell wall where it intersected with the ceiling. These walls are higher than ours. Ours are normally nine feet. They were French style. For hot weather they had high ceilings. But I was able to get up to that hole and whistle over to Ed Davis, who was then in an adjacent building, and give him names and information as I got it during the night. I did this by placing my pallet up against the wall and using it as a ladder, and getting up there and whistling.

Q: And this they understood, did they?

Adm. D.: Yes, they figured it out over a period of time, and so they were going to stop up two of the three bricks. They didn't know that I was climbing up there. They thought I was whistling from within the cell, and they thought that by putting two more up there not enough sound would get out and I'd still get some air. That was my only source of air.

To do that, they got these civilian workers, five of them. I think there were two women and three men, and the man in charge of it was wearing good shoes and a leather jacket and a little leather cap. He reminded me of a teacher I had in school, Brother Charles. Of course, they didn't want these civilian employees to have any chance to directly contact me in any way for reasons that become evident. They couldn't trust their own people. So they had them wait outside the cell. They also didn't want there to be any chance for me to leave anything for those workers, any kind of a message or anything, apparently, because they came and stood me up against the wall. The regular guard with the bayonet held me up there while the "key" guard, the man in charge of the cell block, searched my goods. He conducted a better search than any they'd conducted up to that point. Searches became very efficient after that, but this was the first good search they conducted.

He found the propaganda pamphlet and went through that. I heard him snarl. He had found the cross. He decided to make a spectacle of this for reasons that might be apparent. He had the guard take me outside in front of the workers who were waiting to come in the cell. He turned me around, showed me the cross, slapped me in the face with the cross, tore it up as best he could with his hands, threw it on the concrete, and mashed it with his boots. Then he picked up the remains and threw them in an open sewer.

This hurt me quite a bit because it was the only thing I had that was not given to me by them, and, of course, I didn't like the desecration of it, either. But the bayonet was in my back. Having done that, they took me a couple of hundred yards away, put me in another cell while the workers went in there and did the patch work with the two bricks. When that was finished they took me back to my cell and closed the door behind me, and I immediately went over to see had they found the prisoner-of-war list that I had in the book. I reached under my pallet where they had left the book —

Q: Oh, they didn't take the propaganda book?

Adm. D.: No, they left it there. I had kept the list on the second or third page. I looked in there and it was gone, so I started to tear the book up, having no further use for it and somewhat venting what rage I felt. As I got about an inch into the book, tearing it, I was conscious of feeling a bulge in the book and sure enough, there was another cross. The workers had made it and left it for me, and they had done it at the risk of their lives. It was much better made than the one Ed made. He had used bamboo from a bamboo broom. They had used straw, thick straw, from a straw broom in there. They must have had lookouts and everything going.

Later I was able to exchange a glance of thanks to them and got a slight nod and a little smile back from one of them. We were very careful not to let the guard see this.

I use that at the end of most of my speeches when I'm talking about the erosion of national principles in this country, what television is doing to the family, what it's doing to the desecration of God, magazines like National Lampoon which show the apostles masturbating one another at the Last Supper and things like that. I say that I feel compulsion now to try to right things that I see going wrong in my country because I have been in a country when I was totally helpless, as the story of the cross indicates, and where those people who are still subjugated by a horrible system - the people are not bad - they are just not free. They're helpless.

And I say to my audience that I'm not helpless, you're not helpless, and I believe God will consider us culpable if we don't, while we are still a majority or possess a majority of power, do what we can to counter the same kind of desecration taking place in this free country. It's usually a pretty effective way of getting them going, and that's the way I got the Knights of Columbus going on that project I've got going on TV and the way I got the National Fraternal Congress of America turned on.

Those men have been here. They were in my office two weeks ago, the president, the vice president who will be the president next year, their vice president in charge of communications, and another gentleman who is a lawyer, and we are going to prosecute that program to teach television that they'd better get off of it and stop tearing the family apart and stop trying to tear up the principles that made us great and upon which we depend for survival.

Don't make this public yet but you will see us go public on this within the next year and a half. We've got to get it all together, the communications systems and everything. All the Fraternals are agreed to do it. The Knights of Columbus is one of 98 organizations in this. The Lutheran Aid Association. The Lutherans are the biggest ones in it. There are some Baptist organizations in it. The Southern Baptists we're going to get in it, as a group. We've got the Woodmen of the World, the Foresters of the World, all in that 98-organization umbrella, already committed, and we are proceeding not in a theoretical but in a very practical way to get this done. We have to be careful in the legal sense that it is not defined in a boycott way because that's illegal, but we can do this. We can choose to. Their motto for the next two years is "Fraternalism is a family affair."

They let me word the objective. That's what they wanted me to do. They came to me and said they thought I had a talent for simplicity and I suggested the wording, which is something like - first give their motto "Fraternalism is a family affair," and they will have a number of programs to promote and enhance the family. The television aspect will have just two objectives: one, encourage the television industry to support the preservation and enhancement of the family by their programing policy; two, discourage the television industry from subverting the family by showing a cause-and-effect relationship between profit and programing policy.

That's the way I think we're going to word it. That's the way it's proceeding so far.

We already have 50 million - you don't need but about 5 million - people, and we're going to let the teenagers be the ones who judge the morality of the programs, so we won't be pontificating down from on high over their heads.

Q: Yes, the generation gap. A smart move.

Adm. D.: That was their idea. I had a mental block on it. I didn't know how we were going to do it without being perceived as imposing morality. This is going to be with the kids themselves doing it.

OK, I don't know how I got into that.

The cross example was one. Another example of an answer to prayer was I got the camp to pray that Jim Stockdale would be removed from Heartbreak Hotel, where he had been for almost a year, out to the Zoo, where the concentration on him would be less intense because he would be one of seventy instead one of seven or eight in there at that place.

Q: He had got in that particular camp because he was a leader?

Adm. D.: Well, they were keeping him there for reasons of their own. For one thing, they kept people there who were hurt. He had a leg twisted sideways before he got to jail and they were still messing around with that.

But, yes, there's no question about it, he got all kinds of extra attention because he was a good leader. And at that time I got the camp to pray. I said, "I've already seen evidence of the power of group prayer here in jail and I'm asking you guys to pray that Stockdale comes out to this camp." And he was out there very, very quickly, inside of two days. I considered that another answer to a prayer.

Then there were a lot of little minor things like I'd been extremely intense in prayer at Alcatraz at night when there was utter silence, at two o'clock in the morning, and a bird would sing loud enough to almost wake everybody up. Just a lot of little things that make me know, not believe, that God answers prayers and that the prayers offered, as Catholic prayers, work. But you said something about my believing in Christianity. I do. I am a Christian. I'm a Catholic. I believe that Christianity is the true belief, but I don't believe that it's the exclusive means of getting to heaven.

I believe that the remarkable thing and the thing that we should concentrate on now in national and international affairs is the similarity in behavioral codes among the various religions: be they Catholic, Protestant, Christian, Jew, Islamic, Confucianist, or what have you. I just came back not too long ago from

Saudi Arabia and was amazed at what we share with them. I talked, of course, to many Hebrews and what God has given all men is a conscience. And when I talk here at the Armed Forces Staff College on this general subject of national principles and the impact on national strategy of the change in national principles, I don't talk Jesus Christ, I don't talk about Martin Luther, or even Almighty God. I quote The Republic, Plato's quotations from Socrates. He was a pagan. He believed in pagan gods. But the things he says are so beautifully in conformance with the behavioral concept of Christianity (we didn't have to wait for Aristotle) that I can use them, and I do.

I point out that Socrates was saying it pretty straight to a society that was on its way down. They poisoned him for his pains and then they went the rest of the way down the drain. There are a lot of people trying to tell them that now here and I hope somebody listens. I hope enough people listen.

Q: Yes, the ethical standards are pretty much the same in all the great world religions, which is more than a coincidence, I think.

Adm. D.: Yes, that's true, and if we'll just remain true to the unique national principles of this nation, you know, I develop that. They were truly almost exclusively religious in concept, not particularly political or economic, but the colonies, the settlements, over here were done in a fervor of religion; from Christopher Columbus on down through the Quakers, the Puritans, the Maryland

Catholics, and the Virginia Church of Englanders, and all that. And that which went into our governmental philosophy was a synthesis of their agonizing over the Judeo-Christian, particularly the Christian, concept of justice, the checks and balances; the "love thy neighbor" aspect of that, and the compassion for minorities is what has made us great. The source of all that is, in our case, Christianity principally, and now we're trying to tear it up and a lot of our youth and some of our old folks think that that's a new idea, and there's nothing new about it. It's only new to the United States of America. It's been tried in Greece and Rome and other places and it's always ended in such disaster that it's required centuries for the world to unlearn the lessons.

Well, the prosperity is here and the climate is here in which to forget those lessons again and we're forgetting them, in my opinion, in our own country to the erosion of our national security.

Index to

Interviews with

Rear Admiral Jeremiah A. Denton, Jr.

U.S. Navy

AFFLUENCE IN SOCIETY: p. 25-26; p. 33-5;

ALCATRAZ: p. 44; p. 64; p. 83; p. 102-104; divisions within the camp, 104-5; p. 145;

ALPHA STRIKES: p. 2-3;

ATTITUDE OF CAPTORS TOWARDS POWs: fluctuations due to changes in military status, p. 99 ff;

BRANDT, Ed: editor of Denton's book on POW experiences, p. 101;

BRIAR PATCH: p. 42;

CAPTOR's AIM WITH PRISONERS: p. 40-42;

CAT: Denton's comments on the Chief Gaoler, p. 43-6; p. 102-4; his confession and his continued attempt at favoritism with certain prisoners, p. 108; p. 110;

CHRISTIANITY - PRESENCE IN NORTH VIETNAM: p. 56-57;

COKER, Comdr. George: p. 131; his attempt at escape, p. 131-4;

COMMAND STRUCTURE - POW CAMP: p. 91 ff;

CZECHOSLOVAKIA: p. 56;

DAVIS, Comdr. Edward Anthony: fashions a cross for Denton, p. 138-4; Denton uses the story of this gift in speeches, p. 142;

DENTON, RADM Jeremiah A.: Details of his capture by the North Vietnamese, p. 2-3;

DESERT INN: p. 104; p. 106;

DIEM, Ngo-dinh: Chief of State, South Vietnam, p. 12-13;

DRAMESI, John (USAAF); p. 46;

FIFTH COMMANDMENT: "Render unto Ceasar" is of course a pronouncement of the Christ. It has relationship in theological terms to the Fifth Commandment - to honor father and mother, etc. - in fact "authority", p. 59-60.

FITNESS REPORTS: the captors in effect write the fitness reports, p. 64-65;

FLYNN, Col. John P.: p. 94;

FRATERNALISM IS A FAMILY AFFAIR: motto of National Fraternal Congress of America, p. 142-3; to be used in national campaign, p. 144;

FREE ENTERPRISE: p. 23-5;

FROEHIKE, The Hon. Robert F: Secretary of the Army, p. 84;

GAYLER, Admiral Noel M.: as CincPac greeted first contingent of POWs at Clark Field, p. 117;

GOD: man turns to God in moments of desperation, p. 19-21; p. 31; p. 59-60; p. 69-71; p. 73-4; p. 124; p. 126-7; p. 144-145;

GUARINO, Major Lawrence (Larry) N.: p. 94;

HANOI: p. 15 (and numerous other references throughout entire MS).

HANOI HILTON: p. 42;

HAPPY: a prison attendant and torturer, p. 127-8;

HEARTBREAK HOTEL: where Stockdale was incarcerated, p. 144;

HO CHI MINH: p. 43-5; p. 53; p. 101-2; p. 109-110; p. 120;

HOMOSEXUALITY: p. 58;

HOSTAGES: attempts of North Vietnamese to use POWs as hostages, p. 100-101;

JAPANESE REPORTER: the stage setting for Denton's interview, p. 49-50;

JEFFERSON, Thomas: p. 63;

JOHNSON, The Hon. Lyndon: p. 3; p. 100;

JOY, Admiral Chas. Turner: p. 5-6;

KISSINGER, The Hon. Henry: p. 16-17;

LAIRD, The Hon. Melvin: Secretary of Defense, p. 101;

McCAIN, Comdr. John S.III: p. 45; p. 102;

McKNIGHT, Capt. George G.: p. 136-7;

McNAMARA, The Hon. Robert S.: Denton's conversation with him in 1975, p. 8-10;

MILLER, Lt. Col. Edison W.: a POW who openly cooperated with the North Vietnamese, p. 104; p. 107; p. 113; qualified for first plane to Clark Field because of reported illness, p. 113; p. 120;

MORAL PRINCIPLES: a factor in a POW's ability to endure, p. 67 ff; their significance, p. 95-7; p. 146-7;

NATIONAL SECURITY: Denton's thoughts on the erosion of national principles, p. 84-5-6-7;

NATO: p. 17;

NAVY'S COMPASSION CONCERN - for POWs: p. 120-3;

NEW GUY VILLAGE: p. 138;

NEW YORK TIMES: Reporter accuses Denton of being briefed on his statement over TV at Clark Field, p. 120;

NIXON, The Hon. Richard: p. 14; his decision to bomb Hanoi, p. 15-16; p. 90; p. 100-1; p. 109; p. 110-111;

PATRIOTISM: Denton discusses patriotism as a necessary element in survival, p. 17 ff;

P. O. W.: title of book by John Hubbell (Reader's Digest Press - 1976) - Denton's evaluation of book, p. 123;

POW's: use of by North Vietnamese as bargaining chips in war, p. 13-14; p. 99-101;

POW WIVES - THEIR CAMPAIGN: p. 100-101;

PRAYER: used by POWs in preparation for torture sessions, p. 69-71; p. 73-4; Denton's description of his method, p. 74 ff; p. 124; a compelling example of answered prayer, p. 126-7; camp prayer that Stockdale be removed from Heartbreak Hotel - and he was, p. 144-145;

RETURNING HOME: the last months and days in prison, p. 110 ff; problem of dealing with Wilber and Miller (two who collaborated with the enemy) who returned also on the first plane to Clark Field, p. 113-4 ff;)

RISNER, Colonel Robinson (Robbie): p. 32; p. 47; p. 50; p. 73; p. 93-4; p. 100;

RUTLEDGE, Comdr. Howard (Howie) E.: p. 45; p. 103;

SHIELDS, Dr. Roger: senior U. S. Government official on plane bringing first POWs out of Hanoi, p. 113-116; p. 120;

SIEVERTS, Frank Arne: Special Assistant, U. S. State Department -helped in evacuation of first POWs from Vietnam, p. 113-116; p. 120;

SOFT SOAP FAIRY (SLICK): Camp Commander after Cat - withdrew punishment for communicating, p. 107-8;

SOLITARY CONFINEMENT - ISOLATION: use of this by North Vietnam with POWs, p. 69-70; p. 72-3;

SPOCK, Dr. Benjamin M.: p. 29-30;

STOCKDALE, RADM James Bond: p. 43; p. 49; p. 54; p. 64; p. 73; p. 94; p. 110-111; p. 113; p. 129; p. 131; p. 136; p. 137; p. 144-5;

TAYLOR, General Maxwell: p. 10-13;

THANH HOA: p. 2;

THE FAMILY - Marriage: p. 36-8;

THE LUMP: an arch tormentor and torturer of the P.O.W.s, p. 127-8;

TV COVERAGE - Vietnam conflict: p. 13-14;

VIETNAM CONFLICT - Opposition to: p. 4-5; discussion at the Naval War College, (1963-4), p. 6-8;

VIETNAMESE CHARACTER: Denton's comments on, p. 48; p. 52-5;

VIETNAMESE TORTURE - of North Vietnamese dissidents; p. 54-56;

WASHINGTON, George: his letter to a Jewish friend, p. 60-61; p. 64;

WATERGATE: p. 89-90;

"WHEN YOU RETURN HOME" -: session with captors on 'what you are going to say when you return home' (Feb. 1973), p. 108-9;

WILBER, Comdr. Walter Eugene: a POW who openly cooperated with North Vietnamese, p. 104; p. 107; p. 113; qualified for first plane to Clark Field because of reported illness, p. 113; p. 120;

ZOO: p. 42; p. 106-107;

Authorization

The U.S. Naval Institute is hereby authorized to make available to individuals, libraries, and other repositories of its choosing the transcripts of two oral history interviews concerning the life and career of the undersigned. The interviews were recorded on 6 March 1976 and 7 March 1976 in collaboration with Etta-Belle Kitchen for the U.S. Naval Institute.

The undersigned does hereby release and assign to the U.S. Naval Institute all right, title, restrictions, and interest in the interviews. The copyright in both the oral and transcribed versions shall be the sole property of the U.S. Naval Institute. The tape recordings of the interviews are and will remain the property of the U.S. Naval Institute.

Signed and sealed this 23rd day of December 1993.

Commander Everett Alvarez, Jr., USN (Ret.)

DECLARATION OF TRUST

The undersigned does hereby appoint and designate as his (her) Trustee herein, the Secretary-Treasurer and Publisher of the United States Naval Institute to perform and discharge the following duties, powers, and privileges in connection with the possession and use of a certain taped interview between the undersigned and the Oral History Department of the United States Naval Institute.

1. Classification of Transcript.

   ( )a. If classified OPEN, the transcript(s) may be read or the recording(s) audited by the qualified personnel upon presentation of proper credentials, as determined by the Secretary-Treasurer of the U.S. Naval Institute.

   (✓)b. If classified PERMISSION REQUIRED TO CITE OR QUOTE, the user will be required to obtain permission in writing from the interviewee prior to quoting or citing from either the transcript(s) or the recording(s).

   ( )c. If classified PERMISSION REQUIRED, permission must be obtained in writing from the interviewee before the transcribed interview(s) can be examined or the tape recording(s) audited.

   ( )d. If classified CLOSED, the transcribed interview(s) and the tape recording(s) will be sealed until a time specified by the interviewee. This may be until the death of the interviewee or for any specified number of years.

2. It is expressly understood that in giving this authorization, I am in no way precluded from placing such restrictions as I may desire upon use of the interview at any time during my lifetime, nor does this authorization in any way affect my rights to the copyright of my literary expressions that may be contained in the interview.

Witness my hand and seal this 6 day of September 1977

CDr. Everett Hoard Jr.

I hereby accept and consent to the foregoing Declaration of Trust and the powers therein conferred upon me as Trustee:

R. E. Bowker Jr.

Interview No. 1 with Commander Everett Alvarez, Jr., U.S. Navy

Place: Monterey, California - 17 Greenwood Way

Date: March 6, 1976

Subject: Prisoner of War

By: Etta Belle Kitchen

(Commander Alvarez is in Monterey attending the Navy PG school, from which he expects to graduate and receive his master's degree in September of this year.)

Q: The subject of our recording today, Commander, as you know, is going to be focused on your imprisonment by the North Vietnamese. I would like to have you begin the interview by describing what you were doing and why you were there and the circumstances of your being in a position to be captured. If you will give us some background on that, it will set up the framework for the interview.

Cdr. A.: To begin with, prior to 5 August 1964, the day I was shot down, I was an A-4 pilot on the U.S.S. Constellation. We were on station in the Tonkin Gulf, what later became known as Yankee Station, which is approximately 100 miles off Danang, due east. At that time we were there as part of our Navy's Western Pacific forces. At that period we had stationed one carrier off of

Indochina and then we had other carriers elsewhere in the Western Pacific.

Our particular assignments at the time - bear in mind that we're talking about a peacetime commission, peacetime as far as the Navy's concerned. You will probably recall that we had events leading up to that period in which we gradually increased our military assistance to the country of South Vietnam. We were also beginning to look into the situation that was developing in Laos, particularly northern Laos, and with respect to this we had some Air Force and Army units in South Vietnam, we had Air Force units in Thailand, but these were more or less reconnaissance types of operations.

Our ship off the Indochina coast was mostly concerned with reconnaissance operations also. We had reconnaissance aircraft that were starting to fly reconnaissance missions beginning about June, early June, of 1964 - or late May - over the Laotian areas, looking at what was then the beginning of the Ho Chi Minh Trail to lower Laos, Cambodia, and South Vietnam. We were beginning to take a more active role in that area by what began as weekly sorties but then turned into daily sorties. In early June we lost one of our aircraft to gunfire over the Plaine des Jarres, which is in northern Laos. We countered these measures by sending armed escorts with the reconnaissance aircraft so that, in the event that they would be fired at again, you could retaliate.

We were doing this under the auspices, I suppose, of the Laotian government or the faction we were friends with. It was pretty hard to determine really and I can't say who it was because we were supported by one part of the tripartate government that existed in Laos at the time. Of course, the other extreme of the tripartate was the Pathet Lao, which was opposed to us. But because of the situation that was developing we began flying these missions, and that's the reason we were off of Southeast Asia.

The particular incident that happened and led to my situation of being shot down occurred with the Tonkin Gulf incident, at which time two of our destroyers were intercepted on the high seas by North Vietnamese torpedo boats, beginning with the 2nd of August and again on the night of the 4th August, and then our retaliatory measure on the 5th of August in which we struck naval bases, torpedo-boat bases, and logistic supply bases on the coast of North Vietnam. Up until this time we had never ventured near North Vietnam.

Actually, what happened was that on the night of 4 August, the particular event that I'm talking about now occurred late at night, in which our two destroyers the Maddox and the Turner Joy were intercepted and came under attack by North Vietnamese torpedo boats. Aircraft from the USS Ticonderoga and from the USS Constellation went up to help the two destroyers. I was part of that, too. When that event culminated and we returned, the next morning we received word that we were to prepare for a mission to retaliate, and when the priority came from Washington we launched. We had aircraft from the Ticonderoga and from our ship.

On that particular afternoon I was in a strike group that had as its target the naval base at Hongay, which is at the northern extremity of the coast of North Vietnam, approximately 100 miles northeast of Haiphong. It was during our raid on the naval base, in which I understand we did considerable damage to the North Vietnamese Navy at Hongay, and as I was departing the area I was hit by gunfire and had to eject my aircraft.

I ejected, was not hurt seriously, I had minor injuries which took a few weeks to heal but they did heal. I landed in the water, just off the coast. If you should happen to look at a map and the topography of the area, you can note that it's a very rugged coast there. There are no beaches. It's mostly very-high-rising cliffs that come out of the water, and there are a lot of little inlets, a little bit like the inlets in Japan, where you have all these little lochs and little islets all over the place. I later found out that this particular area has the reputation of being one of the seven natural wonders of the world because of its beauty et cetera. I managed to land right in the seventh wonder of the world.

Q: Did you try to manage your parachute to see that you did go into the water? Did you just happen to land on the water or did you guide yourself?

Cdr. A.: Let me go into this. When my aircraft was hit by ground fire - I'm not really sure what it was, it might have been a missile, I could not tell - I was very low. I was just skimming the treetops as we were making our way out of the area by the bay there and I was heading right to the coastline. Almost immediately

I was hit my aircraft went out of control. I tried to maintain control but found I couldn't do it. I was also trying to gain altitude and I couldn't get much of that, so I had to eject fairly quickly. When I did I was very lucky. I managed to clear the cliffs. I fortunately had enough time for my parachute to open but it opened just as soon as I hit the water. So I really had no control of the situation from the time I was hit until the time I found myself in the water.

Q: What were your injuries?

Cdr. A.: My arms were wrenched and the joints of my legs were wrenched from the force because I was travelling as fast as my plane could go, about 600 miles an hour. The force of the parachute opening and just the windstream itself wrenched my shoulders and my joints. I had neck injuries just from strain, chest et cetera.

However, I was in shock and when I surfaced in the water I managed to get rid of my parachute and my hard hat, my equipment, and take stock of where I was. I was right in the middle of some fishing boats. At the moment, I thought perhaps I could avoid detection by swimming under water and perhaps manage to swim out to sea, where perhaps I would have a chance of getting myself picked up by friendly forces.

You have to realize that this was the first time that we had ever considered going into North Vietnam. We had no plans. There was no prior raid, no strategic planning of any sort or preparation, so we had no friendly forces in the area. We had no Navy out there in the immediate vicinity. The nearest ship was the carrier and that was about 400 miles away.

Q: How much briefing did you have about what you were going to do when you got there?

Cdr. A.: That was the point. We didn't know anything about this raid until the morning, when we woke up that morning. Our complete briefing was about two or three hours of here's where you're going to go, here's what you might see, and look for these kind of boats. But there was nothing about defenses or friendly help in case you should be shot. There was nothing of that. And, as I said, the nearest friendly ship was 400 miles away.

Somehow, intuitively, I think, realizing this, I decided that if I could manage to get away from those boats, I would need my raft, which was still in this pack and had not been inflated. So I started dragging it along under water. I would come up every now and then to breathe some air and then submerge again. I tried this for, well, it's hard to tell, perhaps about ten minutes. It's hard to tell time when you're doing something like this. It seemed like eternity.

At one point, I felt rather tired. My raft was like an anchor at that time, and I realized that the tide was taking me the wrong way. So I couldn't get away that way. Then I happened to find myself looking around and I didn't see any boats, so I inflated one of my life preservers and found that it did support me quite a bit, much more than I expected it to. It completely exposed me to anyone in the area, and they saw me and began shooting at me.

Q: They hadn't seen you before?

Cdr. A.: They had seen me when I came down and hit the water, but the fishing boats that were in the area ran as I hit the water. But then they came back with their militia.

I would say I was in the water between thirty and forty-five minutes, at the most, I would say.

Q: What was the temperature of the water? It was in August.

Cdr. A.: Warm, hot. It was a clear day where we were and it was very sultry. The type of balmy weather that you get in Miami.

Several fishing boats approached me and began shooting at me. I later realized that they were just warning shots. They weren't trying to purposely kill me, but when they first fired, one of them did clip me. I showed the scars later to the surgeons when I got home.

Q: Where were they?

Cdr. A.: Just on my elbow, just barely winged my elbow. It cut my flight suit. If it had cut the skin I'd -

Q: It didn't immobilize you?

Cdr. A.: No, it was just a scratch.

After a while, they came and I surrendered to them, knowing I couldn't get away. I was so tired I couldn't get away at the time, and I was fairly immobile. I couldn't really do anything else. They tied me up and picked me out of the water. They sailed around the area. I really sort of blacked out, I think. I came to and at times I would hear shouting. I was still in the bottom of the boat. They had me lie down in the bottom of the fishing boat.

One thing particular about this group that got me was that when they approached me, even though they saw that I was unarmed and everything, I think they were worse afraid than I was. They were shaking in their boots, and they were heavily armed. There were about five of them in this little boat. But they were more afraid than I was until after they'd pulled me aboard and securely bound me. They had taken my boots. Everything was relaxed then and they sat back and one fellow gave me a cigarette, stuck it in my mouth.

I received rope burns round my neck and arms when they tied me up, but they didn't do anything harmful after that.

I would say about an hour later a Vietnamese Navy torpedo boat came out, one of the boats I had been after, and they transferred me over to this boat and took me back to the Navy base where they took me ashore.

By the time we got back there it was getting dark and on the evening of 5 August 1964, I began my internment.

Q: How old were you at that time?

Cdr. A.: At that time, I was a lieutenant, junior grade. I had just over four years but almost four years of commissioned service in the Navy. Sixteen weeks going through aviation officer candi-

Alvarez #1 - 9

date school, from the time I graduated to the time I was commissioned. So, I had just over four years of active duty and was expecting my promotion to lieutenant any time. I was twenty-six at the time, and I was married. I had just been married for about eight months. Actually, it was eight months almost to the day.

Q: The name of the place where you were bombing was Hangay?

Cdr. A.: Hongay - H-o-n-g-a-y, or Hongai. The Vietnamese call it Hongai.

Q: Do you think the people in the fishing boats had seen your attack?

Cdr. A.: Yes, they had seen it. They were right near the area. Everybody in the area, I later found, of course, was aware of it because we went in, and the area is very populated. Then, just before I was hit, we were making our escape from the target area and I flew right over the town on Hongay.

Q: How large a city is it?

Cdr. A.: I really couldn't tell you. It's not as big as Haiphong, or as Dien. Haiphong and Hanoi are the biggest. It's an industrial area. It's a coal-mining region. They have soft bituminous coal in the area and in that port they also had docking facilities for freighters for the export of coal.

Q: Did you consider that you actually accomplished your mission before you were - ?

Cdr. A.: Yes. I got to see a little bit of the work when they took me off the boat and took me ashore. We had done good work!

Q: What kind of bombs were you using? Torpedoes? Or what was your ammunition?

Cdr. A.: We just had rockets.

Q: How many were in the group that went up there?

Cdr. A.: In our particular strike group there were ten A-4s like myself from our squadron, which was VA-144, and our sister squadron. So there were ten A-4s and then there were five what we refer to as Spads, A-1H aircraft, a propeller type that we no longer have now. At that time we did have the Skyraiders, the A-1Hs, and the A-4s, the Skyhawks. Incidentally, both of these are now out of the Navy's operational inventory.

Q: Were there any other losses on that strike?

Cdr. A.: We lost another man but he was not on our strike. He was in a group that was striking down at Dien, a fellow I knew. As a matter of fact, he lived next door to me on the ship, a jg from one of the Spad squadrons.

Q: And you and he were the two losses at that time?

Cdr. A.: The two losses. He was killed.

Q: So they took you on the train in to Hongay?

Cdr. A.: They took me on the boat and when the boat tied up at the dock they took me off and put me in a building, where I became a showpiece, more or less, a curiosity piece, and for the remainder of the night I was, of course, stripped of my clothing. It didn't take them very long, actually, to bring an English speaking interrogator in.

Really, the people I was facing at the time were unaware of what had caused this. They later found out, as everybody else did. But I think they were as much puzzled about what to do with me and who I was - it took them a while to discover who I was and what I was, an American Navy flyer and that it was the United States that had taken action and they really couldn't comprehend why. Of course, I realized this later, not at the time, because I was bewildered. As I say, I was in shock. Later on, it started to wear off and I started to feel very tired and I ached a lot.

About the middle of the night they put me in a jeep, took me through Hongay to a prison, a local prison, where they put me in a cell with two Vietnamese prisoners, and I fell asleep in that prison. They chained me and I fell asleep. Next morning I woke up and I was in this cell, my ankles were in shackles. I was in a small cell with two natives.

Q: Two North Vietnamese people?

Cdr. A.: Yes. Their jails are pretty full. They keep them pretty full.

Q: What did the interrogator attempt to find out from you?

Cdr. A.: Military information, of course. I was interrogated again that day several times. At night I slept in a cell. I found out that those two Vietnamese - one of them did speak very good English, I thought he might have been a plant. I'm not sure if he was or not. He told me about the raid. He had watched it from the window of the jail cell.

One thing that really surprised me at the time was when I asked him how long he had been in there and he told me he'd been in that cell for four years. And looking around that cell it wasn't any bigger than your bed here, the size of a double bed, and I could not believe that any person could live in such conditions for so long a period of time, and I asked him how could he do it.

Q: Did they indicate to you what the charge was? Why they were there?

Cdr. A.: Yes, I asked him why he was there and he indicated that he had been a jeep driver and had blown up the jeep or the jeep had blown up or something, and he indicated he was in jail for it. I never did get his story straight. These two fellows were my first non-military contacts. The fellow who spoke English, I asked him who he was and he told me his name. He gave me a Vietnamese name which I do not recall, but he said, "In English that means blue," he was Mr. Blue. He introduced the other fellow, told me his name and said his name meant sea. So my first two contacts were Mr. Blue and Mr. Sea!

Q: Did anyone threaten you? Did the interrogator use threats?

Alvarez #1 - 13

Cdr. A.: Not right away. They really didn't ask any military information the first day. They really wanted to know who I was. I gave them name, rank, service number, date of birth. They'd look at me and ask where I came from.

This was the second day now and they had not received word from headquarters in Hanoi yet, who had taken the action, what it was. They wanted to know where I was from, if I was married, about my family - those kind of questions. I told them under the new Articles of War I didn't have to answer questions and they said there is no war.

Q: Did they seem more curious than threatening?

Cdr. A.: Yes.

Q: Is that the implication you're saying?

Cdr. A.: Until the second afternoon when an interrogator arrived from Hanoi, an Army interrogator. Meanwhile, of course, all the pains had settled in and it was hard for me to get up and move. Every time they'd come in they'd take pictures. Every half-hour somebody wants to take a picture, these photographers. And to go along with this, Mr. Sea and Mr. Blue saw my cuts and bruises and put some kind of a lotion on them, they helped me wash the first day. They bathed me with wet rags and cold water in a bucket. I was sitting between them and Mr. Blue saw that I couldn't move very well so he gave me his pillow, which contained all of his earthly possessions. He had two bucks, a spectacle, a little bag of sewing needs. All he had was a T shirt, an undershirt and shorts, and he had this little sack which he used at night, he put his head down on it and made a pillow out of it. I complained about the hardness of the board and he said, "Oh, yes," we weren't used to such rudimentary types of comfort so he gave me his pillow so I should sleep on it. I said, "What are you going to use?" and he said, "That's okay, I'm used to it," and he let me use his pillow.

Q: What were the furnishings of the room besides a board bed?

Cdr. A.: A board bed, a straw mat, a mosquito net, and a little bowl to relieve yourself. These were his earthly possessions. He had a buck and some underwear.

Q: But you said the whole cell was no larger than a double bed?

Cdr. A.: Yes, about the size of a double bed.

Q: And there were three of you?

Cdr. A.: Yes. Of course, every chance I'd get I'd lie down and sleep I was so tired. Mr. Blue encouraged me to eat my food and I tried but I just really wasn't hungry.

Q: What kind of food did you have?

Cdr. A.: I don't know. I was not used to this prison food, some kind of pumpkin with grain mixed.

Anyway, about the middle of the second night, this was after the interrogator from Hanoi had arrived and had asked me questions and I told him I couldn't answer them, he called me in, in the middle of the night. He took me back into the other room. He told me that I had been used, I was a tool, that I didn't know what really had been going on. Apparently he had received word as to what the attack was about and he said that it was not safe for me there and he put me in a jeep. We drove for a considerable while. They put me in the back of the jeep where I was between two armed guards. We drove along the coast, as you would proceed from the Hongay area towards the Red River in North Vietnam, towards Haiphong. Then I'd say halfway along the way we turned off and went up into the hills, where we arrived at a farm house and I was put in a room in the farm house. A room with a table, a chair, and an old bed. The bed was a little board about three feet wide by seven feet long, which you could sleep on and put your mosquito net over. And that was it. I was locked in there and it was barred from the outside.

I stayed there for about three days. The interrogator stayed with me the whole time, or most of the time, and there I mostly slept. I told them that I was hurt. The interrogator would call me in twice a day, morning and afternoon, and they'd bring me food. Then in the evenings they would open the door so I could get some air - sit in my room and look out. I would look across a rice field, a little rice paddy, to a dike, an irrigation dike, and I could watch the local peasants working their rice paddy on their water buffalo. Over in the irrigation ditch, the buffaloes would go in there. It was almost completely dark, and the kids would play with the water buffalo. It was sort of peaceful and quiet.

Beyond that I could see a mass of fishing boats as they came in and out, so apparently it was a good-sized river so the fishing boats could go up.

I was there and I was interrogated. Basically, they were just keeping me there for safe keeping for a few days. They weren't really pressing me hard. They were asking questions that were more personal. What was your father's name, what's your wife's name, where do you live - you are just a tool of the U.S. imperialists, warmongers, et cetera, et cetera. I was just there for safe keeping.

I remember one night I had to relieve myself and they wouldn't let me go out to the corner of the rice paddy where there was an outhouse. They took me out, let me go under guard, and I looked around and the guard who was walking me out there shines his light on the area and I picked out at least three guards out there.

Q: But they had not been close to you at all?

Cdr. A.: No, I couldn't see them. I remember the following day under interrogation I happened to catch, as we walked by another room, I happened to look in and I saw these men sleeping. As I was sitting there listening to the interrogation, I wasn't answering questions, one of these individuals walked by and I asked the officer, "Who's that?" He said, "He's one of the men assigned to guard the place. He is a guerrilla. He's not military, he's a guerilla."

Q: Were they keeping you safe or keeping you from running away?

Cdr. A.: Of course, I was locked in, it was barred, and I was handcuffed. While I was there they did have an Army medical man come and look at me. He gave me some white pills. They brought eggs in the morning, which I couldn't believe. He'd indicate that this house belonged to a Chinese officer and the Chinese officer understood I was innocent, that I had been used, and he allowed me to stay in his house.

Q: How many people were in the house at the time?

Cdr. A.: I don't know. I was locked in there. There was a water girl who brought water and then they would let me bathe in the evening in my room. She would bring a tub and she'd bring the water. Then a guard or somebody else would carry the tub away. They didn't let me go out. And I got to shave there one time.

Q: We haven't talked about what you were wearing?

Cdr. A.: I was stripped of my flight gear, my flight suit, and I was given these pajamas, right away, these prisoners' pajamas, black pajamas.

Q: From the very first?

Cdr. A.: Yes. We always wore pajamas of some sort whenever we put anything on. Most of the time it was hot and we just wore shorts.

Alvarez #1 - 18

The day before I was taken from this place this same officer who had been with me all the time came in in the middle of the night and said, "Well, you have lied to me." What I had done, after a while, I had made up a story and he believed it. I made up a story that I was not involved, I had strayed from the area and was shot down. He came in that night and said:

"You did not tell the truth. We know that you were with the group," et cetera, et cetera, "we know that your father lives in Santa Clara, California, your wife's name is Angie. Now tell us the truth about your mission."

So, without even having thought of it, I made up another story. He seemed to be satisfied and he left. Then I got to thinking about this and, gee, I'm making up stories but I wonder how much he really knows or what's been disclosed.

Q: He would have heard it from U.S. news stories?

Cdr. A.: Obviously. I had no idea how much had been given, but here I am in a bind because under the code of conduct we give them nothing in the way of military information. But they're getting information from our sources.

Q: Was the information he told you accurate?

Cdr. A.: Yes. He told me where my father lived, where he worked, what his name was, what my wife's name was, where she was living.

Q: Did that come as a shock?

Cdr. A.: Well, in a way, I figured I knew what had happened. The press releases had told the story.

The next day another officer came in and they put me in a jeep early in the morning and took me to Hanoi, which was a good eight-hour trip on those roads in their truck. We arrived in the early afternoon in downtown Hanoi and we went to the prison that was later called the Hilton Hotel.

Q: Were you driven around the city before you went there?

Cdr. A.: No, by this time the jeep was - it was a covered jeep, obviously, with a canvas top and the windows were covered. There was a little window in the back and they had a blanket and sheet in front so I couldn't see out, and I was handcuffed. They had a guard back there with me all the way, but I did manage to peek out every now and then when he would sort of doze to see what we were doing. I knew where we were. When we crossed a long bridge I looked out and I saw a sign that said Hanoi.

I sort of anticipated as hope that our government said turn him back and they were going to release me, and that they were taking me down the coast to release me. All the while I thought I'm not going to stay, they're going to turn me over to the government. Why should they keep me? I wanted to go home. Then I saw that sign that said Hanoi, I said, well, they're going to take me to the coast and put me on a ship. Maybe they'll take me to a hotel. When we wound up at the prison I got off the truck.

It was a pretty good room, the best room I saw all the time I was there as far as the room goes. It was big. It was about 14 feet by 12 feet, had a tiled floor, a bed, the same kind of bed with a mosquito net, a mat, a table, and a stool.

Q: What about toilet facilities?

Cdr. A.: It had a little entranceway and a little bowl there. This was the front entrance, and it had a back entrance with a little courtyard and outside was a little Vietnamese outhouse in the corner that we wouldn't even consider. That prison was built about 1880 by the French and they had not done any maintenance as far as modernization. They had installed running water, a pipe, a little bath outside where I could wash my clothes, but you could not, of course, drink the water. I couldn't even bathe in there, it was so filthy.

I had access to the little courtyard about two hours a morning and two hours in the afternoon. They could come in and open the door and then at noon, for the siesta, they would shut the back door, lock me in, and come and open it in the afternoon, and after I'd finished my meal they would let me wash up my dishes outside, then they would lock it. So my access to the courtyard was limited.

The courtyard was very small. At the widest point, it was ten feet wide and then it narrowed down to a V. It was about twenty feet long, but it narrowed down to a V at the other corner because of the shape of the wall of the building, and that's where the little outhouse was, in that little V.

Q: You were by yourself?

Cdr. A.: I was by myself. I was in the room.

Q: Can you describe it more as to what was the wall. Was it concrete? You said the floor was tiled.

Cdr. A.: The building was brick and the walls were plaster, stucco, like a plaster of paris wall.

Q: Any windows?

Cdr. A.: No windows. The door opened at the top, the outside door that went to the courtyard.

I was in that cell, that room, from the 11th of August. I arrived there on the 11th of August and remained in that room until the end of March.

Q: Of 1965?

Cdr. A.: Right. I was interrogated all through that time. I was interrogated in a little cell next to it. I would just go out the door and go next door. I was left alone, completely alone, for the first six weeks and it took me six weeks to become used to the situation. Then I experienced a very interesting type food. I was not getting the normal food and I honestly believe that they were trying to feed me in a Western way so that I could sustain my health and everything. But these people, particularly those who were charged with this, - well, they didn't have any intelligence, the guards and so on - but they just didn't know. They tried to do something different, or perhaps they were purposely doing it, but the food I was getting was very weird. It made me sick all the time. I would get these strange foods. They would bring my meals - I was fed twice a day, once about eleven and once about five.

These people had been under the French for a hundred years and they knew how to cook. They definitely knew how to cook. They really had been trying to feed me Western cooking. I'd get dishes on my little tray that they'd bring this little stack on, dishes, bowls with a little handle.

Q: How many bowls would there be?

Cdr. A.: Two or three.

Q: Two bowls with a long handle?

Cdr. A.: Yes, but one would be a little more soup and perhaps a piece of bread. I'd open it up and I'd see this bird a good-sized bird, say, the size of a robin. I'd open it up and there it is. It had been gutted but that's all and boiled in grease. It was swimming in grease, all the feathers and the beak.

Q: The feathers were on it?

Cdr. A.: Yes, and sometimes the eyes would be open and sometimes the eyes would be closed, or the beak. Any time I ate that, I'd get sick, not because of the bird but because of the grease and the way it was cooked. Other times, they asked me if I liked pork, the interrogator did. The interrogator was another one who would come round twice a week, maybe once a week, to talk to me, he asked no questions but to see how I was. I told him I couldn't eat and he said, well, try, you must try. He asked me if I could eat pork and I said yes. So I'd get my pork, I'd get a snout and I'd get the hoof, you know, I'd get the hair and everything. One time I got shrimp, those great big shrimp, but they'd taken the shrimp and just thrown them in the pot, boiled them, and thrown them up in the air or a similar attitude, without cleaning them, without shelling them or anything, and they had put bread and made a thick soup out of them. Every time I ate this I got sick. They just never gave me a chance, and finally I kept it down with diarrhea and I experienced fever attacks. For the first six weeks I was just sick and I was beginning to get concerned because I was losing weight. I had dysentery -

Q: I meant to ask you how much you weighed when you were captured.

Cdr. A.: When I was captured I weighed about 160. I was concerned about this, so I kept asking them for a doctor. I found out that one time when I was sick I had dysentery. They got a doctor and he said, ah, dysentery.

Q: They did give you a doctor?

Cdr. A.: That's when I was passing blood down both ends for a couple of days and the medical doctor came and saw me. He gave me pills and told them to give me some rice soup with a little chicken... Well, it turns out that's hard to eat. I would eat rice soup and take the pills until I felt better. When I felt better they gave me the other food, and in two days I felt sick again. This went on and this went on and I was really getting depressed. I'm not hurting but I didn't know what was going on. The interrogator would come in and say, "What do you think your status is? Who in the world do you think you are?" And I said, "I'm a prisoner of war."

"How can you be a prisoner of war?" he'd say, "There is no war." And, you know, he was right. There wasn't any war.

This became a very traumatic period. Physically, they weren't punishing me but I was being punished by the conditions. And in another way I began to experience a lot of pressure, wondering what were they going to do with me. Initially, when they shot me down, I thought they'd kill me right away, but now that I saw that they weren't, I didn't know what was happening to me. It was the anxiety and the uncertainty that were beginning to pressure me, and then the conditions, too. My battles with the rats, huge rats in that prison, almost as big as cats. I remember the first night I discovered I was sleeping on a nest. I realize now, I soon realized, that one reason they gave you a mosquito net was not just for the mosquitoes. They told me to tuck it underneath my mat and lie on the mat, not just for the mosquitoes but for other reasons. As we later found out through the years, that's a good way to keep out rats and snakes and roaches and lizards and anything else I didn't want to get in bed with me.

The first night I was lying there I heard a noise. They would give me these little half-loaves of French bread - it's not French bread, except it's unseasoned - and I couldn't finish it one day, I was sick, and so I went to bed and left it, and I looked up and there was this huge rat carrying almost a whole loaf in his jaw.

Q: Where was he, in the rafters?

Cdr. A.: Oh, no. He ran out through the ratholes near the door. To show you how big the bread was, he couldn't get it out the rathole. He could get out but he couldn't get the bread out. So every night began my battle with the rats.

Q: Did this start right away?

Cdr. A.: Yes, it started right away, to protect my food. In other words, if they gave me bananas and what have you, I'd try to keep the bananas, and it was either me or the rats, plus this sickness and everything.

One day, I was coming down again and by this time I was really feeling low. My morale was very low. I'd been there six weeks. I had by this time decided that I was going to try and get a message, make a short tape to say I was okay. Yes, I did. I made a short tape that said I'm alive and well. I wanted to tell my wife this and my parents. And they did broadcast it over the radio, which was picked up and they heard it. Of course, I don't think they realized at the time whether I really was well or not, and so they let me write.

Mail at that time was very difficult because there were no diplomatic relations between the two countries and so it had to go by other means and this particular one took two months.

So, after that, and again I say I was about six weeks in this, I began to recognize the symptoms when I was going to be coming down with dysentery or diarrhea, and I thought I was coming down again, really coming down, so that morning when the turnkey came in - by this time I had learned Vietnamese, I kept asking my turnkey what does this mean, what does that mean and they let me have paper and pencil and I would write down the English equivalents and made myself a little dictionary. When the guard came in, I'd ask him, point, talk, point, and I learned how to pronounce the words. By this time I had learned enough to say "please give me some rice soup." He looked at me and said, "Dau, dau," which means sick. I said, "dau, dau." I said, "toy dau." He looked at me for a long time. He just kept watching and then he left. This was my regular turnkey, a fellow we later called Stoneface. He never cracked a smile. He looked like Alley Oop, and he probably came from the same period, too.

He left, then he came back. He indicated there wasn't any rice soup. "Today," he said something else." He pointed to his watch and said "eleven a.m. something, "five a.m." I said, "Well, okay, I can wait till five o'clock if I can't eat whatever it is at eleven o'clock." I just wanted my rice soup. That was on a Saturday. I'll tell you when it was, it was the 17th of September. He came in that day and gave me my food, my tray, so I took my tray, and I started to eat. I opened up the tray - he was watching me - and there on this tray is a real egg omelette, a real egg omelette. And I opened up and there were some French fries and a piece of bread. A plain egg omelette and French fries. I pointed at it and it smelled so good, and I looked at him and I said, "Tot, tot, tot," good. I tell you I started eating that and I started crying at the same time. It was never so good, to have something like this go down so fast.

Q: What did you eat with, fingers?

Cdr. A.: Oh, no. I had a fork and knife.

Q: They did give you a knife and fork.

Cdr. A.: I really bawled I think for the first time, being glad. I think it was the first time I actually emotionally broke down. I had not until that time. And that guard just watched me and left. That evening he brought me a piece of hamburger, fried. So they knew what I could eat and what I couldn't eat. The next day was Sunday, again good food. Monday morning, at six o'clock bright and early, he came in. He had given me a pair of trousers, khaki trousers, and a shirt. He told me to put those on and he took me next door to the interrogation and there I sat down on the stool and there were three interrogators, two high-ranking ones and one who was the boss and did not wear a uniform. The two assistants were majors in the Army. The other one I never did know his rank, but he spoke beautiful English. He asked me how I was. He said, "I understand you have been sick." I said yes, and he said, "Can you eat well now?" I said, "I like the food you gave me yesterday." He said good, "What we're here for is we've come to interrogate you. I make no bones about it. We're here to find out what you know. You're just a jg, you don't know anything much, any secrets, strategies, et cetera, et cetera, but you know other things."

He said, "If you decide you don't want to talk to us or tell us, there are many ways we have. You're in a very good room, you have nice clothes, and you have good food. So, think about it."

It was not physical pressure but it implied what would happen. This was the first day they came. He sent me back to my room to think about it. That day, actually, he talked just about nothing. He talked and I sat there and listened. Within a week, for the next few days, I did a lot of thinking about my situation and perhaps it may not have been according to the rule book, but I made the decision at that time that I had to throw away the rule book that I had because my rule book did not cover my situation. My rule book covered a military situation, a POW situation, in which a battleground or a POW camp et cetera, et cetera. I didn't know what my situation was but it wasn't this and hoping, or perhaps figuring, well, let's go along with this guy and talk to him and that would be a benefit more in the long run rather than to be a hardnose and say I'm not going to say anything. And then if they wanted to they could force something on me other ways over which I'd have no control. At least this way, I'd have control.

So it began again. I was interrogated every day, eight to ten hours a day, six days a week for the next six weeks, every single day except Sunday. I talked to them, but my strategy was I will answer or discuss anything that I thought I could get, anything that they thought I knew something about. I would deny or fabricate or somehow get out of discussing or covering anything that I thought they could believe or be made to believe I didn't know anything about. And that's how it went.

Q: Can you describe the room where you were? What did it look like?

Cdr. A.: Well, it was a room that was right next to my cell, my room I was living in in the prison, a bare room, a bare table. I was sitting on a stool. I'd go in there and sit on the stool and face them all day.

Q: Eight hours a day?

Cdr. A.: We'd take a break for lunch and a siesta, then come back in the afternoon. It went on all day.

He wanted to know, basically, every single thing I knew. A lot of things that he was asking about were common knowledge. I mean the average eight-year old or ten-year old who watches television, who used to watch the news media, who's ever seen an aircraft carrier from a distance, knew much more than he did, who'd ever seen "Wings of Gold" or planes riding on a carrier knew much more than this fellow.

These people did not have any concept of carrier aviation, but they wanted to learn. It took them weeks to comprehend when a carrier launches its airplanes and recovers its airplanes, it does not stand still in the water. They thought that perhaps the deck would extend because their pilots could not understand how they could land. Things like this. So I was being very helpful in showing them that when you take off an airplane you have ~~World War II, you have~~ a man up there who tells you to go and you fly the airplane off. They'd say, "don't you have radar?" No, we didn't have radar in our fighters, and they believed that. Things like this.

Q: Of course, at that point you were not telling them the truth?

Cdr. A.: Oh, no. I was denying knowledge for anything I could do, whether it was important or not. They went back and forth, back and forth. Sometimes they caught me in lies and I did a little bit of Hollywood acting. I'd come back and they'd say, "You go back and think about it," and they'd threaten me. But I could see that this was not their strategy.

I realized later on that their strategy was not to force me because of world public opinion, because I knew then that my name had been released, my family knew I was alive, and towards the end of the six weeks they gave me a letter from my wife. This letter had been written before she'd gotten my first letter, and it indicated that she didn't know whether I was really alive or not.

This fellow was playing me right along. It was a soft-sell program. If you show a good attitude, if you cooperate, of course, there's no reason for us to keep you, we'll let you go. Another reason was how can a little country like this stand up to the demands of the United States to bring my boy back, that type of thing. So, apparently, there were no demands, or, if there were, they weren't that strong. I wanted the U.S. government to know I was alive. There were a lot of other factors and basically it was back and forth. I got to know this head interrogator quite well.

Q: What was his name?

Cdr. A.: He never did tell me. I do know that he had highly polished boots every day and wore clean pressed shirts. It was mostly me asking questions and he lecturing on economics, the history of Vietnam, 4000 years, 2000 years under the Chinese dynasty, 100 years under the French, the history of the areas, the minority tribes, the fight for independence - he had fought against the French and been in prison - the economic growth, political, politics. This was his big thing. He wasn't an interrogator.

Q: Were there any other prisoners of war at this time in Hanoi, in that prison? You were the only one?

Cdr. A.: No. We'd only been up there one time.

Q: Oh, that's right, of course, so there would not have been any reason for others. Were you aware of the article about your capture that was in the U.S. News and World Report?

Alvarez #1 - 32

Cdr. A.: No.

Q: You've seen it since, of course?

Cdr. A.: Yes, but while he was interrogating me he said, "You know, you're not telling me" - after about three weeks - "anything I don't know." For example, you're telling me this and this. I know all that. Look," and he pulled out of his briefcase a copy of Time, a copy of Newsweek, flipped through the pages and showed me a picture of myself, flipped through again and showed me a picture of my wife - just flashed it. I said, "Let me see that." I had never seen that picture. I didn't know what was going on.

Q: Was that your picture?

Cdr. A.: Yes.

Q: Because it said in the article that it was supposed to be your picture, but it was in fact.

Cdr. A.: Well, no, he showed me the picture that they had in Time or Newsweek of myself in uniform. He flipped the page over and showed me a picture of my wife and a picture of my mother, but it was just a quick glimpse. I asked if I could see it and he said no. He said, "When you are finished and you go home you can sit in the library all day and look at it." He said, "Never give up hope." He was fairly honest because he believed me and that I was trying to help them, that I was sympathetic towards him, which was the impression I had not wanted to give but wound up giving, which might not be too bad after all. In the end, he said, "I think you ought to try to understand our situation. That's all we want you to do - just try to understand our situation so that when you are released you can go back and have a different idea of our situation. Don't look for miracles. You've only been here three or four months, but you know six months in prison are a long time."

This was a sort of a summary when he finished up. He said, "Six months is not a long time, a year is a long time, but don't worry, you won't be here a year."

We had closed off and actually after a while, after I was quite pleased with the way it came out and the fact that I gave them nothing. I've had several people say since I've been home that it was good, it was okay. I had one fellow remark to me - it was a visitor who went to Indochina right after and we had used it in our survival school - this fellow had talked to one of the delegates who asked about me, and he said:

"Oh, Alvarez, yes, he's okay."

"He talks and talks and talks but he doesn't say anything."

Q: Who was it who made this remark?

Cdr. A.: One of the North Vietnamese officials. The fellow had asked him if I talked. "Oh, yes, he talks. He talks a lot, but he doesn't say anything."

This was taught later on at the survival school as tactics or whatever.

After that they pretty much left me alone. The interrogator would come along when I was still living in that room. He would see me once in a while. One time close to Christmas there was a visitor who visited North Vietnam, a fellow who as it turned out later on had been kicked out of the United States and was living in Cuba. I think they were trying to release me into his custody, send me home. But before they wanted me to write a letter to Ho Chi Minh, apologizing for my action and telling about my good treatment et cetera. Up to that time, I had not written anything and I didn't do it. So I blew my first chance to come home.

After this first Christmas - by the way, it was a very lonely Christmas, they gave me a Christmas dinner, they brought some chicken, cut chicken, and a little bit of wine and some coffee, and that was not what I got every day. You don't get coffee or, of course, chicken. It was good, it was good food, but still I was very lonely. I used to wish many times that I had somebody to talk to instead of a wall or instead of that dumb guard who would come along and bring me my food.

It was a stale period, a dried-out, stale period which we now are getting into. At the end of 1964 and beginning of 1965, I remember when my birthday rolled around on the 23rd of December, I was celebrating. I smoked one of their cigarettes. I had saved up some cigarettes and smoked them all at once. That was my idea of celebrating.

By this time, I began to receive some mail from home. About every other week I'd get a letter. They were good about it. They let me receive letters and they let me write letters. So I was pretty much keeping my family informed with a diary account - I'd write a little bit every day about what I was doing, about how I was keeping my time occupied. Now the battle was not so much any more physical hell like it was the first six weeks. By this time, the food was not as good as it was during the interrogating period but it was substantial, the quantity was substantial the quality was still good. I would get buffalo meat and occasionally some potato with bread, perhaps a vegetable every now and then, and some fruit, bananas, tangerines, et cetera. But mostly it was how to keep my time occupied, keep myself occupied, and I started doing mental gymnastics, math games, I tried too. I still had a pencil and some paper and I would work out math problems or a design, homes or lay out a little farm on ten acres and what I was going to do with it. Just mental exercises to keep myself occupied. I found myself talking to myself a lot. I thought that was good therapy.

In the hours that I had access to the courtyard outside I would go out and physically exercise, do as much as I could, but not so much as to wear myself down. And other tasks such as trying to set traps for the rats, trying to stop the roaches from coming out, finding their trails, plotting escape plans which never did materialize. I began to picture myself as the great Mount Rushmore architect. On the walls, I started carving things with a nail on a rock that I would find out in the courtyard. Sharp objects weren't too hard to come by because the top of the wall - a 12-foot high wall - on the outside perimeter of the courtyard and it had broken glass on top and then barbed wire over that. It was going to be rather difficult getting over that wall. However, I could reach up, get up, and find broken pieces of glass. I started carving little sayings. I kept a diary of important dates like Halloween, Thanksgiving 1964, and Christmas day, my name day, and other dates that went by, Valentine's Day, Easter came. I judged Easter, I knew it was somewhere in that area but I didn't know the exact date. So I was carving my name. Of course, they spanked my hands for that. I wasn't supposed to do that, but it kept me occupied.

Q: Was there any actual punishment?

Cdr. A.: No, not yet.

On the night of February 11 or 10 there was a lot of activity in the camp and I found out that they were excited because we had another raid on North Vietnam, and I got excited, too. The interrogator came and told me the next day what happened. The guards were trying to tell me, but they were not able to make themselves understood. And at that time I figured, well, what do you know, it's about time, six months later.

But then a few weeks went by and nothing else happened. There were no raids in the Hanoi area; they were just down in the panhandle of South Vietnam at the time. However, I was getting their Vietnamese news bulletin, which was an English translation of what was on the presses. They were giving me copies of it.

Q: A mimeograph or a newspaper or what?

Cdr. A.: A mimeograph, and it was filtered so that they would give me just what they wanted me to read. I read about the attack, the raid, and I read about the body of an American pilot that had been found, his ID card. This fellow I knew. His name was Ed Dixon. He was at La Moore, I knew him back in the States. Then I read about the next pilot being captured. They showed his picture in the <u>Vietnam Courier</u>. I was getting a copy of that. This fellow's name was Bob Schumaker, who's here at Monterey also.

A few weeks after the raids started they came in and wanted me to help them again. This time I wouldn't answer their questions, wouldn't even talk to them.

Q: The same man questioned you?

Cdr. A.: No, it was not the same man. It was one of his assistants who came by this time.

They came and they tried. I would not talk to them because now I knew that the war was starting, at least I hoped it was starting. Now we're going to go by the war rules. Now it's clear cut and I wouldn't even say boo. They tried again, they tried again. They still didn't force me. After that they took me back to my cell. A few minutes later they came in, told me to wrap up my mosquito net, map, and my little belongings that I'd accumulated from the guards, an empty jar for water, my pencil, my clothing, and moved me to another smaller cell, where I remained for about a month.

Then they moved me out of there and took me to a tiny 7-foot-x-7-foot cell with no windows, where I remained for the rest of the time that I was in that camp. I was in one of those cells, out of contact. I knew then that we were starting to get American prisoners in that camp, but I was never able to achieve any communication with them.

The food deteriorated little by little, I stopped getting any mail from home, of course, right away, I received no cigarettes, no goodies and, by the summer of 1965, it was really bare minimum, very, very bare. No outside time. Locked up in the cells.

Q: No ventilation?

Cdr. A.: No, no ventilation. They sort of stuck me back out of the way and forgot about me till September when I did manage to make contact with a prisoner who was in another part of the same area in that prison camp. I managed to scratch my name on the bottom of a plate on which they brought food because I knew they were bringing several trays in. So I did make contact and I found out that a man was near me. I told the guard and pointed over there, because I wanted to talk to someone. The camp officials found out that I knew so within a few days after that they took both of us out to a prison in the country, which we later called the Briar Patch.

Q: Why did they do that?

Cdr. A.: I think that they were just trying to keep me separate the whole time and when they found out that I was in contact with the others or communicating with the others in some way, they decided to put me with the others. And the others were not kept isolated very long because it turns out I was completely isolated for thirteen months and continued to live alone, in solitary, but I was able to communicate with others.

The conditions? As I say, the food was bad, not enough to eat.

Q: How was your health, as a result?

Cdr. A.: As a result, I was tired. I was just sleepy all the time I was in that cell to myself, and I think I had actually mentally gone downhill. As far as sanity goes, I think I may have lost. I can remember doing things that are not rational. It was not a good place to be.

Q: Can you remember what you did?

Cdr. A.: Well, if you want to go into detail here. In this particular cell at that time, I can remember that they used to have like a foundry right outside my walls, continual banging on metal, steel grating, all day, all day. The women's section was nearby and they used to torture the women prisoners. I could hear screaming.

Q: These were Vietnamese prisoners?

Cdr. A.: Yes. They were all Vietnamese prisoners around me in that section. I had made contact with another Vietnamese prisoner in my cell block. I had a little pinhole I used to be able to look out and see him. He knew I was there. He'd been there for quite a while. And standing in front of his door or sneaking a glimpse at him now and then I was able to make contact. It turns out he was a military man. He indicated by his actions that he had been in the military. I have a feeling he was on the wrong side or something because they had him in prison for blowing up something. I was slipping him part of my food because he wasn't getting much, either.

It was interesting. I remember that I had to escape from that, not physically, but mentally, get away from that. So one day I just lay down and went to sleep. I slept all day. I would sleep all day. I'd close my eyes and dream. All that noise around me was going on. I just mentally did something else to keep myself away. I dreamed or I daydreamed or I planned, just to get away from it. That went on for a couple of months. After that, one day the banging stopped and that's when I made contact with the others. I really don't have much explanation of what I could do or what I did. But by this time, I think I was down to about 110 pounds.

Q: This is when you were in the Briar Patch, was it?

Cdr. A.: No, no, no, this was before I was put together with the others. This was the summer of 1965, and I was down to 110 pounds, with hardly anything to eat.

Q: This is when they had separated you at the Hanoi prison?

Cdr. A.: Well, they kept me separate. I was never with anybody. They just completely separated me from the area where the others lived.

Q: But you knew others were there at that time?

Cdr. A.: Yes, and I eventually made contact with them.

Q: In 1965?

Cdr. A.: 1965.

Q: How did you make the contact?

Cdr. A.: Well, the first time was when I found a name on the bottom of the plate and I scratched my name. I used to also hear the jeeps coming in and a lot of excitement. This was before they put me in the real small cell and I could look out the door through a pinhole and I could see Americans walk by. I couldn't make anything out. It was just dark but I could see their uniforms and that they were being brought in. I was not there very long. They put me in this other cell, where I remained for the rest of the summer.

Q: How many months would that have been?

Cdr. A.: I really don't know, but about May, June, July, August, September.

Q: That's about five months.

Cdr. A.: Yes.

Q: Is that what you described as being in solitary confinement?

Cdr. A.: I would describe that as complete isolation, because after they took me out of there and put me in another camp I remained in a cell to myself. Now that's solitary confinement, but I wasn't isolated. I could talk to others and I began to talk to other people. Gradually, I began talking and began to come out of whatever shell I had gone into. I could associate myself with them and talk to them, and that did a lot, just getting to other people.

Q: Although you were in solitary confinement, you still could make contact?

Cdr. A.: Yes. We did it covertly.

Q: I'm going to ask you whenever it's appropriate to describe how you did develop your communications.

Cdr. A.: I learned the tap code and we tapped on the wall and just whispered whenever we could out the window when they were in the area. It all had to be done covertly.

After September of 1965 we were out in the country at the Briar Patch. The first fifteen Americans that were shot down were out there. We got to talk from one cell to the other in a little building which was in the center of a little area which was walled off from another building. We could talk over the wall, if conditions permitted, to the other fellows in the other buildings and so forth.

So we knew who was there. I was brought up to date on what had happened, how the war was going, the war was starting, and we thought we'd be home by Christmas of '65. Our optimism was good. This is one thing I have to really say. The guys really kept their optimism up and it kept them going. This is not going to last very long, we'll be home, because we're just now starting to get geared up. This is how it went.

I was just out there for a couple of weeks, then they brought us back to Hanoi, to a new camp that later became known as The Zoo. We were the first ones in there, twelve of us. It was not a prison camp at the time. It was just some deserted buildings and they boarded up the windows and doors and put us in different rooms. And gradually they brought the workers in and started to turn it into a prison camp. So, as they were working on one building, constructing cells and making bars on the windows and all this stuff and putting beds on floors, I was living in a bare room. The cooking was done outside by the Vietnamese guards, who'd give you rice and fish and stuff. But as they'd finish one room they'd move us into one area and then go to work on the others. Then they'd move us out and come back and do something else on these, so we were just being shuttled around under guard and living under these conditions.

On the night of the 17th-18th of November 1965, that evening I got my first roommate, an Air Force first lieutenant. He was new, fresh, somebody alive who could speak English.

Q: He was the first person you had had as a roommate since you got there?

Cdr. A.: Yes. Tom Barrett was his name. I can remember the guy was wide-eyed and young. He thoroughly believed we'd be out of there and home by Christmas and he had me convinced.

From here on, from late '65, all the way through, conditions were very changed. The Vietnamese would be very hard at times, ease off at times, but generally speaking from the fall of 1965 until late '69, after Ho Chi Minh died, our conditions, generally speaking, remained the same. In that period, late '65 until the following Christmas, 1966, they did a lot of really physical things, strictly for propaganda. That's all it was for because we'd been there quite a while.

Q: What did you know about military at that time?

Cdr. A.: They didn't want us for military. They wanted us for propaganda purposes. You know, how well we were being treated, protest against the war, write to Senator Church, Senator Morse, Fulbright, support these people in their activities. And they were actually outright brutal. Statements of surrender, all these things that they wanted.

Q: Were you brutalized?

Cdr. A.: Oh, yes. Everybody was. Things would get hard physically. The food, whenever they would give us food, they would increase the quantity, but basically it was rice and green weeds in the winter or pumpkin soup in the summer when pumpkin was in season, kohlrabi in the winter.

Q: What was that word?

Cdr. A.: Kohlrabi. It's like a cabbage, like a radish, like a turnip. We didn't get salt in our food in the early part of '67. We didn't get any sugar. We kept begging them for sugar through the interrogating officers, something sweet. Finally in the summer of '67 they started giving us sugar. Then we'd go out and pick up our meal outside. We'd come out of our cells and there would be sugar with the meal.

We were living two, three men - a few men were still in solitary - but mostly two or three men per room. We generally lived in terror at times, because we never knew when we'd be taken out of the room for interrogation or other purposes and never come back. This type of thing.

In the spring of '66, Tom Barrett and I were still living together and we were taken from the Zoo back out to the Briar Patch, and it was out there that we began, along with the other prisoners, to undergo this treatment, you know. First force you to give your biographies, different ways, different tactics. In July we were both brought to Hanoi with others from out there and marched down the streets of Hanoi. After that they got really hard on us. We were being punished for our bad attitudes. We were tied up all day, released from our shackles at night to sleep. That was the normal condition. Those who were being punished were shackled twenty-four hours a day and this kind of thing.

They'd take you away for a week or two and you wouldn't come back and do things, deprive you of sleep for all that time to outright physical punishment. I don't know how many guys didn't make it. When they'd get something they'd work on you for a while, ten days, two weeks, until you gave in and you gave it to them. You'd come back to your cell, to your roommate and tell him what happened. A few weeks would go by, then they'd take you out for something else. This got to be a way of life.

Q: Now we're talking about 1966?

Cdr. A.: We're talking about the summer and fall of 1966, right. By the summer of 1966 they had pretty much achieved their purpose as far as subduing us, subduing us as a group. In other words, they feared our military unity, the type of unity in which if you unite as a group you could organize and be an effective group. And they start to isolate you, to deprive you of any ability to organize, to resist. Not only that, but to defeat and completely eliminate any incentive to do so. Just completely do it and we weren't that able to do a lot of things, like fear. This is a communist tactic. By fear, by living in fear, conditions of prohibiting you to communicate with the next room, but still giving you the good, the humane and lenient treatment. You had a roommate, you had food, all this stuff. By being completely subservient to the people, to the guards, everybody, you had to bow and you go along with it after a while. They forced you to bow. You had to bow, you had to be polite. After a while, you became like a trained puppy. Show respect, follow the camp regulations, don't have a bad attitude. Have a good attitude.

This is basically what they do to their own people. People in their own society are fearful. They go along because not only from the government and the policy system but from their own cadre, informers, the spy system. In other words, you'll be punished in the society if you don't conform. Anybody in that society, once he gets in it, can't break away. You can't do it. It's too hard. This is how their regime has power over the people. Nobody can protest, nobody can change it, nobody can rise up to a position of strength unless they're in the party. Ideologically and politically, you're motivated from the very beginning to follow the Marxist-Leninist line and Mao's thinking and so on.

Q: I wanted to ask you, did they give you propaganda?

Cdr. A.: Oh, yes.

Q: Can you describe that?

Cdr. A.: They gave us propaganda literature, translations about the war. We heard a lot about the anti-war activities here in the States. We heard every time there was an anti-war speech by somebody, especially in the government. We got it, and, of course, a lot of things that were questionable, whether anti-war or not, that part was cut out.

The whole thing was to keep us subdued. That way they could control us, and they did it fairly effectively, yet they never really achieved their objectives because their main objective was to have this political indoctrination and lectures. That began to arouse people. You'd listen to their lectures. That never did them any good, I'd say, because in 99 per cent of the cases, they'd have to force somebody to go on.

There was always the search for who's keeping the prisoners from following along or being good students of the camp authorities. In other words, willing to learn the truth. Who's keeping them down. So our senior officers were hit. Whenever a troublemaker was found out or spotted, he was separated and he was punished and then they'd work on the rest of us. And then they wouldn't understand why we didn't go along with the thinking. Every time something new would come up, a new method would come up, guess who got chosen, was one of the first chosen to try it out?

Q: Explain that a little bit more.

Cdr. A.: Well, in other words, when they started to have the radio broadcasts of taped doctrine, we were one of the first to get it. In '67, when they went to a new program, you'd have to sit there on your bed fully dressed and listen quietly. We were the first to do that for several hours a day, twice a day.

Q: Listening to the radio?

Cdr. A.: Yes, and the guards would come round and look and if you weren't paying attention to something you'd be punished. Later on, they said, well, let's have personal across-the-board talks. They were having all these English-speaking students come along and lecture, and we'd sit there all day. I called them English-speaking, but they couldn't speak English very well. They were trying to explain the doctrine to us, the whole thing.

Q: They were military men?

Cdr. A.: Yes. And you'd sit there and you knew it was all baloney, you'd know this was not true. They didn't understand why this didn't get across. So, finally, by threats. We'll teach you and those who refuse to learn will be sent to the blackest of camps, Alcatraz. And others would be tried again, and again, up to 1969 when they realized that they weren't having any success with their programs. They would single out people, take them away, work on the rest, but it still didn't work. This is why I call it indoctrination. You can't say it's brainwashing. I don't really know what brainwashing is. Nobody I have found could give me a quick definition, this is brainwashing. I could see where they could go through what I would consider brainwashing, methods of torture where a man is insane, he's pretty much wiped out. But we weren't. Most of us just sat there and closed our ears to what they said.

With me, every time a radio speaker came on, gosh, they're talking, and I instantly just shut them off like that. I wasn't listening to what he was saying. You couldn't argue with them, you couldn't discuss it with them, especially the ones who were younger.

So, as a result, we were punished.

Q: When you say "punished," what are you talking about?

Cdr. A.: I'm talking about punishment. I'm talking about methods of forcing you like this. You're being forced, you're being punished for your action, or for weeks you sit there like this, with your hands cuffed, and you can't move. You can't go to the bowl, you can't do this, or they let you out an hour a day, or like that. (References to the pictures in Prisoner of War by John M. McGrath.) In a small cubicle until you win. That's how it went.

Q: Do you want to go back to 1966 and go into a little more detail?

Cdr. A.: In 1966, it was hard. In 1966 they wanted propaganda statements. They came. They finally got three in six months from me, but it was a continual show. Then somewhere down the pike I guess the word came down from higher-level government that all these tapes were being used, shown, had gotten out or what have you and our government got upset about it because they stopped coming after us directly. They started using other means. So it was off. There was a breather. It was a restful period.

Of course, a lot of the guys would get sick out there. I think what they said we had was beri-beri. Resistance was low, conditions were very bad, sanitary conditions. They closed that camp up and brought us back to The Zoo.

They would alternate roommates, move us around, two and sometimes three. This was when they began indoctrination.

Q: Descriptions I've read of The Zoo make it sound unbearable.

Cdr. A.: The Zoo was much better than some of the others, much better than Alcatraz and better than Heartbreak Hotel. Heartbreak, that's in the Hilton, a section.

Yes, they sealed off all the ventilation ducts, except the two little holes way at the top, no light, we never got out.

Q: Day and night you were in the dark?

Cdr. A.: Yes. Oh, no, no. They had the light on. But you didn't get out. The summers were very hot. The summer of '67 was very hot. You were always in fear, you know. When you heard a door at night, you knew somebody was going out to be tortured, or when you heard a key jangle you knew there was a turnkey in the area and you'd have the fear he was coming to your door. My God, if that key got into your keyhole, you'd say, "Oh, God," and your heart would drop, because you didn't know what was going to happen after a while. You can put up with silly things for a while, but after a while it gets to you and you start to fear. Yet, you say, well, that's the way it goes, this is my life, this is how I live.

Q: Would they not generally take them out at night?

Cdr. A.: No.

Q: Any time?

Cdr. A.: Any time, day and night, but if it should happen at night because normally there'd be no other reason for a turnkey to come to your door at night. In the daytime he'd have regularly scheduled hours, but if he came outside of the scheduled hours you'd say, "I wonder what's going on. Who's going now."

Then they'd have a break and you'd get roommates. Roommates were great because you'd talk and you'd learn from them, you'd pick his mind clean. You knew all about him, his experiences, his childhood, where he lived, his biography, you knew his family, his kids by name. You picked his mind clean. You talked. It's hard to live with a period in confined conditions, very, very hard.

Q: How large were your cells at that point?

Cdr. A.: Twelve by sixteen or fifteen by twelve, something like that with two or three men in it. You set yourself a routine. You exercised every day. You exercised as soon as you'd get up. You'd do several hours of calisthenics, you'd sleep, you'd talk, if you knew any chemistry or math or psychology or he knew about the stock market - you know, anything. You'd talk about it and learn. Basically, this is how life went from 1969.

Alvarez #1 - 53

Q: Did you stay in the Hanoi Hilton, as they called it, for the rest of that time?

Cdr. A.: No. I was in The Zoo. After we got back from the Briar Patch, I went back to The Zoo. I was in The Zoo until 1970 when they took us all to the Hanoi Hilton. That was after the Son Tay raid.

Q: I wanted to ask you about that, but tell me those years again, the movements that you made from prison to prison. You were at The Zoo when?

Cdr. A.: I was in The Zoo when they first opened it up in late September of 1965 till May of '66. In May of 1966 they took us out to the Briar Patch till about the 27th of January when the guys were all sick and they decided to close it down because of the unsanitary conditions. We had one well out there. We used to go down there and draw our water and everything. Then in those cold winters up there it wasn't too healthy. They moved us back to The Zoo and I was in The Zoo from January 27 of 1967 until the 26th of September 1970.

Q: How did you keep track of the days?

Cdr. A.: We knew the days. A moving day was a big event. We did all kinds of things. Mentally, we kept count. Of course, after Ho Chi Minh died, after the letter-writing campaign to your home, there was a lot of pressure throughout the world, a lot of notoriety, a lot of publicity was given to the POWs, and that's when conditions began to improve. That's when they started letting us out. That's when they started knocking the walls down between rooms, and we'd have bigger rooms with six, eight guys in a room. That's when we started going out. They let us get some sun. Some of us got to play games so they took movies. We played basketball or volleyball, but they took that away.

That's when they just started easing up. One day they came in in the summer of 1970, opened the door and right away we bowed from the waist down. That was a big day. There was a new camp commander and he came in and said, "You no longer have to do that." Then they got mad if you did it. We were so automatically trained and a door opening like that we'd bow, then they'd slap you down and hit you for breaking the camp regulations. It didn't take us very long, though, to learn that we didn't have to bow. It was sort of a decontaminating process, gradual. We were able to go outside, get fresh air a few hours a day. Little by little, we got more. They started opening up windows. We started seeing others, talked to them more, in bigger groups, started getting panicky to get home. So I got mail, pictures.

They cut off my mail in 1965 and my next letter was a letter with pictures and it came in a package at Christmas of 1969. I'm just going to be very general. I cannot get too specific. I'd be here all week!

Q: Can you tell me about how they did organize the POWs?

Cdr. A.: You mean our own organization?

Alvarez #1 - 55

Q: Yes.

Cdr. A.: Well, we're military. We are trained to remain as a military unit and through our survival school in a normal POW environment you will maintain yourself as a military unit, so this is the way it is for us. And if you're the senior officer you will take commands, just as in the Code of Conduct. Well, anytime we got a group together, whether we were physically together or were just in a building and we could communicate within walls, okay, I'm the senior officer or he's the senior officer and here's what we're going to do. We're going to follow these policies or we're going to follow the regulations as laid out by the camp senior officer if we happened to have contact with him, or just do the best you can. This kind of thing.

Q: Who was the senior officer? Do you remember who they were at various times?

Cdr. A.: When?

Q: That's my point. When you were at the Hilton.

Cdr. A.: Yes, I could name every single senior officer but it changed about every other move. The senior officers of the camps were changed. At the time we were there Robbie Risner was the senior officer until Admiral Stockdale was shot down. He was a commander at the time. He remained the senior officer of all the prisoners. He wasn't with us all the time. General Flynn of the Air Force came in in 1968 and we had other people who happened to be the senior officer in the camp. They would change sometimes almost daily, depending on the situation, depending on how active the Vietnamese were, this type of thing. But we found out.

Q: Can you describe more about how the communications took place? You spoke of writing on the bottom of a tin plate.

Cdr. A.: That was early stages. That was before we developed the tap code. Once we lived in a building and we were in separate rooms, we could tap from one room to the other. We could keep our line of communications open that way. At other times, we learned to communicate from building to building. We developed the hand alphabet code. You could see someone's hand or else tap the code so it could be heard by someone or other means, covert means, message drops and things like this.

Q: Tell me what you mean. I'm interested in this.

Cdr. A.: Some things I can't tell you.

Q: Oh, because of some security?

Cdr. A.: Yes, but, you know, message traffic. We'd leave a note in a message drop or a hand code, hand alphabet, the tap code, or just plain talking, if we could do it. Some way to send signals. If you could get hold of a piece of glass and make a mirror out of it, you could use that.

Q: Building to building?

Cdr. A.: Right.

Q: What leadership training and disciplinary training in relation to the Code of Conduct had you had before?

Cdr. A.: Just survival school. That's general, there wasn't anything specific. We had to make up and improvise our own method of communication, and we had to improvise our own policies as far as the way to go in this situation. Here's our situation and here's what we're going to do.

Q: But you did have training, of course, in the Code of Conduct before you went over there?

Cdr. A.: Yes, but the Code of Conduct is a very general directive. It's to give you a guideline. When you're in a specific situation, you have to adapt yourself, you have to adopt a policy or course of action that's within the guidelines or to the best of your ability. You have to decide, now, is this worth dying for? By God, I don't think that this is worth dying for, but I'll resist as much as I can do it.

Q: Did you ever come in a situation where you had to make that decision? Many times?

Cdr. A.: Yes, several times. When I had to give these propaganda tapes, I said, is this worth dying for? Who in the United States is going to believe this?

Q: And you thought negative?

Cdr. A.: I thought that nobody in the United States would believe that garbage when they listened to that, but nobody in the United States that I know of hears this, except perhaps some anti-war groups. Actually, what it comes down to is it's not the people in this country, it's for their own people as much as for other people in other parts of the world.

Q: Did the training and the awareness of the Code of Conduct play any part in your interrogations?

Cdr. A.: Oh, yes, continually. It was always the guideline. This is what you live by or you try to.

Q: Do you think any changes ought to be made in it other than what I guess you perhaps have already said of adjusting to situations as they arise?

Cdr. A.: I think the code as it exists now does give you the leeway to do that. It does enable you to look at a specific situation and say this is what I think I will do. The code has given me the guidelines and now I can apply myself to this particular problem. The code is under a lot of fire, but I don't think it's justifiably so. I think the code did a lot for us. People say the code didn't do us any good. It did. It did us a lot of good. In other words, we weren't able to live up to the code itself, but the code is just a guideline. We were able to live up to an objective that we set. You know, everybody's different. What it did for us was to enable us to come back and not be ashamed of anything. I don't have anything I'm sorry for or anything I'm ashamed of. In other words, I'm not going to hide my face from anybody because I did something I shouldn't have done, because when I did do something I held out as long as I could, and I think that's all anybody could ask of me and that's all the code asks of you.

Q: I'm curious to know whether you feel that when they did torture people or threaten them with things of that nature, did that harden their resistance, do you think? Did it actually accomplish anything for them?

Cdr. A.: Well, everyone's different, but as for myself I wouldn't say it hardened my resistance, but it hardened me to the point where when I gave in it angered me because they'd made me give in, to the point that when they came again I'd say no again and I'd keep saying no as long as I could. But then others, I think it scared them to the point where they were afraid to say no and it bothered them to say no because they didn't want to do anything. Others did. It angered them and hardened them. Every person has his own limits and every person has his own reactions.

Psychologically speaking, it was a big psychological game.

Q: The people who came over there, Ramsay Clark, Jane Fonda and their visits and their activities, the release of the Pentagon papers, things of that sort, do you think that had any effect on the length of the war?

Cdr. A.: Oh, yes, I do.

Q: Do you think you'd have been brought home sooner?

Cdr. A.: I think that these people who went over there, all these things that happened here, did a lot to keep the Vietnamese going. They had told me before it even started that they were ready to fight a long protracted war, and when they say that they're talking about a war similar to the war they fought against the French, in which they just kept hammering and hammering, but hoping that eventually the French - and in this case we - would become disgusted, discouraged, and turn away, hoping that it would lead to dissension like it did with the French. They told me this before the war even started out there. They started their war with the French in 1945. When it got to the fifties the people of France were tired of this drain and it even caused a change in their government. This is what they had experienced before, so when we got involved this is what they were shooting for.

If we had gone in there militarily and fought a military war, they couldn't have been able to stand up to it. They'd have come to a concession, knowing that militarily they could not compete and would have conceded and would have released the prisoners or they would have negotiated, if we had put the handle on like we did eventually. But being that there was a war of escalation, there was a political war, it wasn't a military war, and knowing that they were getting more and more towards their objectives, it was building, and things weren't going smoothly, this was all they wanted.

If we had not had people sympathetic towards them and visiting them, I think it would have taken a lot away from their enthusiasm.

Q: Were you aware of their being there? Did you know when those people came?

Cdr. A.: Oh, yes, we heard their tapes.

Q: Did the Vietnamese try to get you to appear for them?

Cdr. A.: No, they didn't try to get us to appear. They took others who were more cooperative. Some of those fellows they tried to bring court-martial charges against them, but I didn't. They had those people picked out. There were a few who would go along with them.

Q: Did they have to threaten them and mistreat them and torture them in order to have them appear before these delegations? Do you know?

Cdr. A.: I don't know. You see, they had already forced us to do so many things before, see delegations and what have you, but these were French people, or Europeans, or Russians. By the time the Americans started going over there, they couldn't trust us to do what they wanted.

Q: How do you attribute your ability to resist? What do you think made it possible for you to resist or gave you the courage to survive?

Cdr. A.: Courage, I don't think so. I'm not any more courageous than anybody else. Everybody, I think has a lot of courage. It's just the point that you think about it and you say what alternatives do I have? Do I really want to do what they say? Well, first of all, I don't believe these people, I don't believe what they say. I'm not sympathetic. I can see where a lot of innocent people are getting hurt in a war. This happens in all wars. But their rationale, their reasoning, their blame, I say no, I don't agree with that. And this is what the whole battle is about. This war is a product of the battle. It's an ideological battle, political. Yet, I say to myself, well, first of all, these people, I think, are evil. What they're doing to me, what they want is wrong. And even though you have wars why another human being would do what these fellows are doing to me for the purpose he wants is completely wrong. It's evil, the way I see it. So I'm going to fight it every way I can. I have no alternative and I'll fight them as hard as I can and I'll resist as long as I can. If he wins out, well, he wins out because he's got the upper hand in the beginning. In my situation I've got nothing going for me, except to show them that I don't agree with them and I'm going to resist them, and that's it.

I cannot go against my convictions and my beliefs and nobody else can. Nobody else can be so hypocritical or something. I could see where they did and a situation would happen which is what actually did happen when they'd give in.

Q: Did religion play any role in your ability to resist or live or to go through the days and months and years?

Cdr. A.: Yes, in my case, it did because I was raised as a Catholic.

However, I think that the books that have come out overplay this. Religion was a big part but it wasn't everything. There were a lot of fellows there who were not Christians, who are atheists, didn't believe in God and yet were just as strong as anybody else, maybe stronger, because they have their own god. They have themselves and they have their own principles and they have their own strength. Maybe it was money, dollars, but it was a strength that kept them going. Some guys used to count how much they had in the bank accumulated every day, every week. The longer I'm here, I'm getting so much a month and at a certain per cent interest rate. I hope my wife, I hope my mother is putting this in this plan or something, and this is what kept them going, and you know, I wouldn't mind being here another year. Well, you could take that guy and that's his strength. It keeps him going, enables him to get up in the morning and face the day.

Not me. For me, I relied a lot on prayer, but I think it's been overplayed. Every book I've read had too much faith in God, prayer. I'm not saying that this wasn't a big part, but nobody spent twenty-fours hours saying prayers like in a monastery. No, he was living with his people. We had church services and I'd say my prayers at night, and the rest of the day I just survived, living with the other guys and doing something, communicating. It would take us hours to communicate.

Q: How would you spend a day? Can you describe getting up in the morning and going through a day?

Cdr. A.: Okay, to answer your question about a daily routine or what a day was like, let's first take into consideration that through the eight and a half years we're talking about various phases that we've gone through. Each phase might be as long as six months or it might be several years. But from 1964 to February 1973, we went through several phases of which each one had its own routine because of the situation or the pressures on the government, on the Vietnamese, at the time. We experienced different conditions. We were living in different time periods and each time period had its own routine, had its own similarities, and what have you. So, if you consider 1964, a normal day when I was there by myself, it was much different than 1965 or 1966 when we were going through the various punishment phases, to 1968 when we were not being punished but were just existing. Okay, in 1968 the bombing stopped in North Vietnam. From 1968 till 1970 there was nothing going on. In 1970 conditions began to improve so much that they were completely different. And in 1972 after we started bombing again, it was completely different altogether.

What was a day like? Well, a day in 1964, I could describe. A day in 1967 when I was living with, say, Tom Barrett or Red Berg, I could describe that. It's also much different when you have two men and three men, like when there were four of us in one of these rooms in 1969. That was much different. We had to adjust ourselves to a different routine. You've got four people, you know, and you could schedule things, you've got to organize yourself to be able to do the daily tasks.

You might laugh when I say the "daily tasks," but it was a daily chore. I used to think about it at times when I'd say, my

God, here I am and from the moment I wake up in the morning till the time I go to bed I'm so busy I don't get everything done that I want to do. How the heck am I ever going to survive when I get home and I've got a normal life to lead. I'll never exist. I'll never make it. Because about 1970 or 1969 we had two sets of pajamas, one was being washed and put away while you had the other one on. You had two blankets each. They were really good to us now because things were much improved, we had two blankets and sometimes in a cold winter we had three, and we had much more food to eat, much more rice, our bodies had more fat, maybe, and we could stand the cold better. It seemed like the winters got warmer as they went along. But then you realized, too, that the reason they were giving us more blankets in the winter and more food was because now we were important people.

In other words, they could not militarily win the war. It would have to be a political negotiated war, which is what happened when the Paris talks started in 1968, and it didn't take long to realize that that was what they were going to have to do, and, lo and behold, what was one of their biggest assets? We were, because the American people began to care about us, especially in 1970. So they had to take care of us. Now we were a prime asset, now we were something that was worth value. In 1972 they were giving us more food than they themselves were eating. They were fattening us up for market. Even then, when I came home I weighed 140 or 145 pounds, after being fattened up for two years.

Q: You'd gone from 160 down to - ?

Cdr. A.: 110, then about '69 I was down to 110, and after that when they started feeding us in 1970, they started increasing the food little by little as the months went by, I started to regain. We started going out and exercising and getting fresh air, your appetite builds up and you start to gradually gain. In the last six months they were feeding us so many beans and potatoes and canned fish from Russia and canned meat, it seemed like all the food that was coming into Hanoi was coming to us because their people were getting bombed and their people were hungry. We were getting the good because they wanted us to look good when we got home.

So you're talking about a completely different pattern as you go along.

Q: What was the worst part of it?

Cdr. A.: When I was by myself in the summer of '65, the way I described before.

Q: When did you come to the realization that it wasn't going to be a short experience and that you weren't going to be home by Christmas?

Cdr. A.: After I wasn't home for the Christmas of '66, say, the start of 1965. It was in 1966 when we began to really realize that this could be a very long, long war. We were getting input, you know, from guys who got shot down. We were starting to build bases in Thailand; we were building more bases in South Vietnam, ports, our objectives were long range. You don't want to admit it but you're thinking this could be a long time, whereas before we were hoping it would be short. Now you're getting the whole strategic picture and you say, my God, it's going to be a long time.

A typical day in 1966 when we were arriving at the Briar Patch. The Briar Patch had no electricity, had no running water. I had a roommate, Captain Berg, Red Berg, and we'd get up in the morning. The room was about 8 by 8, maybe 8 by 10 something like that. We'd be in our cells all day. Let's say today is a good day. Today nobody was taken out and interrogated. At that time, we weren't doing a lot of exercising in the morning. We were weak, we weren't getting enough to eat, to really do a lot of exercising, and it was cold out there. They'd make us go out at 5:30 in the morning. The guard would say, "you've got to get out of here," so we'd get up.

We'd fold up our blanket, fold up our mosquito net, put our mosquito net under our blanket at the head of the bed and then sit there. I've got pajamas on, I've got my shorts underneath, you know, the little blue shorts that the Vietnamese wear, and a T shirt. If we were lucky they'd give us a pair of socks, others didn't and we'd just be barefoot.

Q: And the temperature was what?

Cdr. A.: Oh, it got down to freezing.

Q: No heat?

Cdr. A.: No, no heat. If it was a cold windy day, well, you'd close the shutter and it would be dark in there, but at least it would keep the wind from coming through because it was a biting wind. You know, a Siberian cold front comes down through that area in the winter. You'd sit there and if it was real cold you'd huddle in your blanket. You start talking to your roommate and you start with, "Well, what are we going to talk about today?" Red Berg was from a town near Seattle and he's a big hunter, did a lot of flying in light aircraft, and I learned all about Seattle and his boyhood experiences. A whole morning would pass and he'd tell me about, say, an experience or somebody's family. I'd tell him about mine.

Then about ten o'clock the guard would come around and let you out and you could dump your bowl. Say, today was Red's turn, so we'd take our bowl, walk down to a dump. There were two of us in that cell, so we had two bowls, and, as it was cold, one bowl was for fluid and the other was for whatever solids you could pass. When you had diarrhea, you were using the other bowl most of the time. Diarrhea was common. Everybody had it. It was a normal day to have diarrhea. If you don't have diarrhea, either you're real sick or something's wrong, you're well. So diarrhea is normal.

As you walked down to the bowl dump you passed other buildings and their shutters are shut so you can't communicate. They can't see out and you can't see in. You get to the bowl dump and all this time you're taking in what's new because this is one of the few times you're out of your cell and you look around and you catch the signs as you go from your courtyard to another courtyard and past other buildings. You go to the bowl dump and you dump your bowl. You come back. As soon as you come back and the guard left, this is what I saw. I went by what's his name's door, I saw that they had a plate out there which means he ate late. He must have been taken out for interrogation late last night. Or, hey, there's only one plate out in front of Room - we had each building named, Building C, Building D, and then each door to each building - hey there's only one dish in front of 2C. That means somebody's gone. Maybe somebody moved, see if you can find out. Yes, I saw that.

There are some new guards in the camp. Looks like they're beefing up. Or you look around the area, say, I saw some new defense things, they're digging ditches up on the hill out there. It looks like they've got some new batteries moving in or something's going on. Things like this.

Whenever you left, it was what intelligence you could pick up, what you could see. The guard who walked with you, they never left your side, was always batting you on the back of the head to keep your eyes straight down, look down, don't be looking around, don't be trying to see what's going on.

This is what we did every time we left the building.

Q: Did you walk with shackles or were you unshackled?

Cdr. A.: No, you were not shackled when you were carrying bowls down to dump them.

But most of the time you're sitting there and you're talking. If it was during that time period we're talking about there were periodic air raids. The gongs would go up the hill when you'd hear an air raid coming. In this small room underneath your bed you had foxholes about four feet deep. Everybody in the foxhole. So you'd jump in your foxhole while the guns are going off all round you, planes come by, and we knew they'd got a raid somewhere in the vicinity.

After it's gone, it's clear, the gongs went, and you could come out of your foxhole. Immediately, of course, you had to shut the shutters if we had an air raid. The guards would shut the shutters, lock them from the outside. Most of the time in the winter you kept the shutters closed anyway because it was too cold, and you sat and you talked. Of course, you had to talk in hushed whispers because you could not be heard outside the room. If a guard came by and stood outside your shutters, about as far away as two feet, and he heard your voice, you would be accused of trying to communicate with the people in the next room. So everything was a whisper. When I say we talked, we whispered. After getting beat around so much for trying to communicate or punished severely, if a guard outside heard your voice, then, you know, it's better to just go ahead and whisper.

For years we were whispering. I didn't even know what a normal voice sounded like.

Q: I was wondering. Your voice is low. Was it always this low?

Cdr. A.: No, this is because I'm getting tired.

Q: I wondered whether you had picked up a different manner of speaking.

Cdr. A.: No.

Q: Has your voice always been soft?

Cdr. A.: Yes.

About eleven o'clock in the morning, the food-carrier, whoever it was - sometimes they had food girls, sometimes food boys - would bring the food in. You could hear them dishing out the chow. They'd come around to your building. Outside our door we'd have a little vat with water and you stacked your dishes right next to that. They would take your dishes, serve you your food, leave it out there. The guard would come by and let you out there to take it in.

Q: Everytime with a guard. You didn't ever go out alone?

Cdr. A.: Oh, no, you could never go out. They had to unlock the doors. What you had to be careful of was a lot of times they would let the cows or the buffalo in the yard where the grass was growing and they would graze. You had to watch that because those cows would come and drink your water, and a lot of times we'd go out and find dead rats in our vat, stuff like this. That's what I mean, it was not sanitary.

Then after you ate, in about a half-hour, the guards would

come around, unlock your door, you could go out and you had a couple of minutes to wash out your dishes. You had a little bar of soap like Fels Naptha, rough soap. You were issued a bar every forty-five days, sometimes every sixty days. That was our ration. That was to bathe ourselves, to wash ourselves, and to wash our dishes.

So we washed our dishes with the water we had in the vat, and it stood there. We'd go back inside and he'd lock us in. Then it was nap time. We'd take a nap, a siesta.

Q: You were required to?

Cdr. A.: Required to. If you couldn't sleep, you just lay there or what have you. But normally you grew accustomed. You looked forward to the siesta. After the siesta, they'd ring the gong, get up, get up. We hardly ever put our nets up for the siesta, but sometimes if it was too cold, it would be added warmth and we'd put our net up and get underneath it with our blanket. Then it would be a little warmer.

And we'd spend the afternoon the same way. We'd talk and what have you until dinner. At five o'clock they'd bring the food along, feed you. By this time, it was getting dark. At dinner time during the winter you had to eat fast and be careful, as soon as you got your food. If you set your plate down the roaches would get to it.

Q: Inside your cell?

Cdr. A.: Oh, yes, the roaches would come out of the wall. Also, every time you got your food, you'd fill up your little teapot - we each had a little teapot for water supply. They'd fill it twice a day. And you had a little metal cup and a little metal spoon, and that was it.

Incidentally, I brought my cup back with me. I brought my things with me. They're in the museum back in Washington, D.C.

You'd wash your dishes after dinner, they'd lock you back up, and then it was too dark to put your net up, so you got underneath your net and talked, whispered, until you fell asleep.

That was a good day because nobody was taken out. Sometimes you'd have an exciting day when the guards would come along, take you out, and punish you just for no reason at all. You know harassment.

Q: What kind of punishment, like in the book?

Cdr. A.: Just, just plain beating you around, hitting you with sticks and things like this.

A day would be when you'd be eating your meal and the air-raid alarm would go off, you've got to get in the foxhole. So Red and I would get in our foxhole and stand in there and eat our meal. This was something a little different. You had to keep your sense of humor up, that was one thing. You really had to keep your sense of humor up. If you let it get to you, it wasn't good. You had to keep optimistic and you had to keep your sense of humor.

Q: I think that's a miracle.

Cdr. A.: You have no choice, you really don't. In 1969 I was living in a room with four men. We'd get up - by this time we were getting more rice. No ventilation. Say it's a hot summer day. You wake up and you're sweating like crazy, but they were by now giving us baths every day and we knew how to build up. Each day you'd do more push-ups, you'd do more set-ups, you'd run a little longer in place. So now we'd get up and we'd exercise for two hours, 200 push-ups, 500 sit-ups, run for 10 minutes, so many miles. You'd pretend. As I'm sitting there in place, I'm jogging through the hills of Monterey or something like that.

At seven o'clock or eight o'clock they'd come, they'd open your door, and you could take your bowls out. We'd go out, we'd dump our bowls, and we'd bathe. It was all brick-enclosed out there at The Zoo. If it was the winter and it was cold, it was a quick bath, but at least by now, 1969, 1970, they were giving us baths. Christmas of 1969 they let us have playing cards, whereas before if we made our own playing cards and they found them we were punished, contraband. So we had four and we played bridge every day, every night, or if we were lucky and we had a guy who could tell movies we had a movie. He'd tell a movie he'd seen, television movies or -

Q: He would just tell it?

Cdr. A.: Yes. One of the guys had got shot down in '67, my gosh, that's two or three more years of movies, and he was a young fellow so he would tell a movie. Real good.

Q: Did you have to whisper then?

Cdr. A.: No more. Well, we were whispering but we didn't have to worry about it then because the buildings were heavily constructed and it was hard to talk from one room to the other, anyway. We couldn't do it. They had not opened up our windows yet, anyway, they were sealed up. So you'd sit there and you'd have the air-conditioner, a little fan, and we fanned ourselves in the summer. We didn't do any talking. Continually drenched, but we'd tell movies or we'd be telling experiences, relating something amusing.

Q: I should think nothing would be so bad as to be alone in the dark?

Cdr. A.: You're right.

Q: I was going to ask you about the very worst part, but I think you've already said it?

Cdr. A.: Yes, the worst part I've said.

Now in '71 they let us all live in big groups, twenty men to a group or what have you. It was fantastic. It was like going to UCLA because now you had twenty guys, we had the senior officer, the executive officer, he would designate you as, perhaps, educational officer, in charge of educational programming, and he would designate the clean-up crew for the week. In other words, they would do the dishes for the week, we'd have so many bars of soap for the group for the month. Now we were starting to live like a normal POW camp under those normal conditions.

We'd organize our classes. I taught Spanish, another friend of mind taught French, another friend taught calculus. We'd get up at five o'clock with the gong, exercise for an hour, clean up details, and then we'd have classes until lunchtime. We'd knock off the classes. We'd have French three days a week, we'd have Spanish three days a week. Everybody wanted to take French if they were in the group; everybody wanted to take Spanish. We'd have Spanish days. Everybody would be speaking Spanish. I would not let my students speak anything but Spanish on Saturdays. If you talk to me and you're not speaking Spanish, I'm not going to listen to you. So they learned. A French day, we all spoke French. On German day, we all spoke German. Of course, German is harder to learn so we weren't quite so stringent. I never did take German very long because I couldn't stick with it.

Then they started giving us paper, pencils, we started making our own dictionaries, we wrote our own grammar books, we made our notebooks, we started writing all this stuff down.

We'd have lunch, everybody would eat lunch, the same amount of food and what have you. The dishwashers would clean it up and other guys would clean out the bath area or the bowl area and then we'd take a nap or the guys who didn't want to take naps would play cards. After that, we'd have classes again. If you're taking French and it's a French day, you have a morning class and you have an afternoon class.

Then we'd have dinner. Oh, don't forget, all the time now

we have communications at certain times, like during the siesta. That's why we never did sleep because we were always communicating during siesta. That's when the guards would relax and we'd start communicating with other rooms, things like this. At night we'd communicate for a short period of time and then have movies.

Q: You make it sound as though it were almost liveable, but I'm sure it wasn't as good as you make it sound?

Cdr. A.: It was much, much more liveable. It was 100 per cent more liveable.

The rec officer would say, "Tonight's movie is told by John." So he'd get in there and he'd tell a movie or a book review. We had a couple of fellows who were fantastic book reviewers. They'd take two or three days to tell a book. If they couldn't remember it, they'd make it up, certain portions. Some guys would even write their own books, they wrote novels, mystery stories. Pretty good, much better than the actual books we had read.

At nine o'clock gongs go off and everybody into the nets.

Q: Was there still the filth, the animals?

Cdr. A.: No, because at this time we were starting - they were letting us take care of our own cells, we took care of ourselves, we kept the camp area cleaner, policed the area. We made our own outside areas. We took care of ourselves much better than they took care of us.

Towards the end things got better. We started to play volleyball, basketball. We put up a basketball net. This was when they just opened the doors. The last six months there anything you wanted - we ran it ourselves. They let us cook our own food, we had a detail go down there and clean our own food and cook our own food in the kitchen. The whole camp opened up.

Q: That would be the fall of '72?

Cdr. A.: In the fall of '72 we were doing our own cooking, a community shower out in the middle of the courtyard, we fixed up a shower stall, had running water in the showers. You could go out there and get a shower anytime you wanted to, except they'd lock you up during siesta in your room and they lock you up at night. Open up the door in the morning, lock it during siesta, open it after siesta, and lock you up in the evening about six o'clock. And then they left you alone. They had the guards in the towers around and that was right at the end.

Q: You had optimism at that point, too, to keep you going?

Cdr. A.: Well, we were bombing them again and we had new people coming in and we were talking to the people who were just coming in, especially in December. In December of 1972 they were coming in so fast and so furious that they didn't even try to keep them separate. We happened to be in Hanoi. There was another camp elsewhere. There were other camps, but they were bringing them into this camp and we were getting all the hot news, the latest news, right up to date on what was going on at home, you're getting pictures, you're getting magazines. It was like a regular camp that you see in the movies at that time.

Q: Before we go on any further, I wanted to refer back to the raid at Son Tay. How did you learn about that and what were the effects of it?

Cdr. A.: At the particular time when the Son Tay raid occurred, I was at The Zoo. They never told us about the raid, of course. We didn't get it directly, but we had indications. For example, the day after the raid there were a lot of Vietnamese officials coming round with the camp commander, walking around, inspecting the area, pointing up to the top of the walls, and they would be talking at length about things. And we always had speculations whenever we saw some strangers, Vietnamese strangers who appeared to have a little authority or what have you. We always suspected that something was up.

Anyway, these people came around and they were looking at the walls, the guard towers, et cetera, looking over the walls and discussing at length amongst themselves what lay beyond the walls, and a lot of pointing and jabbering. Then they started to beef up their guard towers. They reinforced, doubled, the guards and did a little patchwork on some of the perimeter of the camp. So we thought something might have happened somewhere, perhaps there was an escape attempt at one of the other camps.

This happened in September or October of 1970. I think

that's the right date, but I might be off. Anyway, they were pretty cautious but they still kept us in the camp and went through all the propaganda plans that they had at that time in our camp, but they had started to let us play volleyball and basketball and we built a little dirt basketball court, leveled it off, put up some backboards, and put up a volleyball net. They were letting us out to play quite a bit and they were feeding us pretty good. Then, just prior to Christmas, one day out of the background there appeared about two dozen photographers taking pictures as we were playing. We thought, of course, that this was the situation all throughout. We had no idea that our particular group had been primed for this.

Q: They were letting you do it just for propaganda purposes, are you saying?

Cdr. A.: No. You see, we were in contact with other areas of that camp, of The Zoo, and we knew that they were playing ball, too. They had their volleyball nets and they were getting out and doing a lot of exercise, so we figured this was in accordance with changes in the treatment, every prisoner must be experiencing this. Also, at the same time we were receiving packages and we were getting more mail from home, they were knocking down the walls between buildings, knocking out the bricks that they had blocked the windows up with, the windows were opened, we had fresh air in the rooms. This was a complete change, so we figured something was in the wind and they were going to let us go home.

Well, as it turned out, just prior to Christmas - this is what I refer to as the great Potemkin episode - we were playing as we normally did and around the building come about two dozen Japanese and foreign photographers. They weren't allowed to talk to us. We're asking what they're doing, what's going on, and no, just keep playing, they're just taking films. We didn't like this and so we told them we didn't want to be photographed and yet not knowing if this was the case or not, if this was the camp policy throughout all the camps. So we hesitated about doing anything and they finally took enough pictures - they had taken a few pictures of us - they left.

As soon as they left, down came the volleyball net and we didn't see the basketballs any more, and we knew we'd been had. That happened right before Christmas, and the day after Christmas, after they gave us a good Christmas, a big dinner, the upper portions of the camp - we decided after they had taken away our volleyball that this was another big frame-up, you might say. But we did see them taking movies of the Christmas dinners. Other photographers came in on Christmas Day. They came to our building and we said no, we don't want them to take pictures and we don't care what you do, so they left us. But they did go elsewhere and they did take pictures, I think, of other people getting gifts and stuff.

Then the day after that, they rounded us up and we packed up our belongings, and they moved us back to the Hanoi Hilton, where everybody else had been since the Son Tay raid. So we knew then that they had kept us in our camp for these purposes only.

Q: Was that The Zoo?

Cdr. A.: At The Zoo, and then they moved everybody back to the Hanoi Hilton. At that time, there must have been about 350 or 360 prisoners, all together, from me all the way up to the Christmas of 1970. I mean, that's up until '68, when the bombing stopped. Nobody came in after the '68 cessation of bombing. There weren't any more new prisoners shot down.

There were about 360 of us there and they just packed us in there like sardines, but we were able to keep our programs going like I described earlier, yet conditions were extremely crowded. They tried to keep us separate in different rooms, but we managed to maintain communication. Actually, it was like knowing everybody there.

Q: It was like what?

Cdr. A.: It was like having everybody in one big camp. We were able to communicate with each other.

Q: You were not in a room by yourself then?

Cdr. A.: Oh, no, we were in large groups, 40 or 50 men per room. Our room had 20, we had a small room.

Q: You have mentioned that several people like Red Berg and Barrett –

Cdr. A.: Tom Barrett.

Alvarez #1 - 83

Q: Tom Barrett. Can you remember names of other roommates you had, other POWs that you came to know, even though you perhaps didn't see them?

Cdr. A.: Oh, yes. We had the names memorized of everybody who was there, definitely.

You know, in 1969, they were starting to release about three prisoners a year for their propaganda reasons, also. Most of the guys had most of the names memorized of the guys who were actually there. So our services, our people back here, knew who was there. There were a lot of questionables, those who never did show up. We weren't really sure and they weren't sure. But everybody who was there was correctly - we knew who was there, we knew who was not there.

Q: What was your feeling about the reasons for the early releases, why they chose those people to release?

Cdr. A.: They were picked from the beginning. In other words, the people they released, the first group, did not have the punishment. They were shot down at the end, prior to the cease-fire in '68. They were shot down in early '68, perhaps late '67. The Vietnamese were waiting, they knew that they were going to do this long before, so they got them and never did anything to them. They never tortured them, never treated them badly, they had a separate camp where these new people were going. They worked on them but it was another soft-sell type thing. When they did release them, the fellows had been kept separate, they could never say that they had been mistreated, that's what they were trying to -

Q: That's what they wanted them to say?

Cdr. A.: Yes.

Q: Let me go on, then, a little bit further. Can you place what period it was, what was happening when you learned that there was going to be a release, and how did you learn of it?

Cdr. A.: Well, to backtrack a little bit from that point, let's backtrack about a year, to the beginning of 1972. Actually it was in late December '70 when we heard about bombing again in the southern portion, different portions, but we did not have any raids up in what we called Route Pac 6, which is the area of North Vietnam that included Haiphong, Hanoi, the major industrial and metropolitan area. At that time we thought, well, the bombing had stopped but is it really serious, are we really in earnest. Our treatment remained the same.

By this time, they had started to reopen camps and moved our particular group back to The Zoo, back to the same building.

Q: Did you stay with the same group?

Cdr. A.: We'd been our same group since the fall of 1970 when they put us twenty fellows in a group and we went through that picture-taking episode, and we all went into the same small room, twenty of us. When I say "small room," I mean a room as big as this room including that space where you have your tape recorder.

Q: Twenty by twelve?

Cdr. A.: I'd say it's about thirty by fifteen, at least.

Q: And it contained twenty men?

Cdr. A.: Yes. We could fit in there. We were packed but it was habitable and we made it comfortable. We made it as comfortable as we could. We were sleeping almost one on top of the other but you get used to that, also.

Q: Were your bunks actually racked up above?

Cdr. A.: We didn't have any bunks. We were sleeping on wooden slabs, palettes.

Q: On the floor?

Cdr. A.: On the floor. And sometimes no one palette, we'd just throw our mat on the concrete floor.

When we went back to the Hilton, and that's what I'm talking about - don't forget that's an old French prison built in the 1880s by the French, and the floor was heavy concrete, just a big slab, and we would just throw our mats down and sleep. And then when we wanted to make room, we'd roll up our mats and go back and forth during the day and conduct our classes and do our business, whatever we were doing. We exercised, let's do this exercise because I'm doing this exercise and we don't have room to do both kinds of thing.

Q: I would imagine there'd have been a lot of conflict, possibly, unless you were extremely careful and were aware that it could happen?

Cdr. A.: Yes, but nothing did. We'd been under worse conditions for a lot longer period of time and by this time everybody had learned to live with someone else. That's one thing. By this time, everybody had been there an average of four or five years. I'm talking about 1970, so they'd been there an average of four years, anyway. You have learned to give and take. You learned control and you learned patience.

After about a year there, in that camp, they took us back to The Zoo. They reopened it. This was just prior to Christmas of '71 and spent Christmas of '71 in The Zoo. We then again started to fix up the basketball courts and play volleyball. And this time we said, okay, we're going to play but if there's any hanky-panky, no, sir. They did try coming around; they'd bring photographers around, and we'd just throw the stuff we had away, books - they'd given us books and they'd give us a guitar to play - we would just drop everything and walk back to our rooms. Go ahead and lock us up if you want, but we're not going to pose for you. So they finally gave up on that.

We didn't think that they would try to force us again like they used to do in years previous. We weren't going to give it to them. It's presenting a lie, that's what it is. Yes, we were playing but we're not there for -

Q: To be exploited?

Cdr. A.: Yes, and that's what they will do. They'll exploit you as long as they can and for as much as they got out of you.

Then, in May of '72, on a Sunday afternoon, we heard the alarm and we heard the jets coming in, and this time it was big bombing and every one of us was jumping up and cheering in our rooms because we had figured, by gosh, we were following their reporting of the happenings in the Paris peace talks. I'll never forget that this was four years of peace talks and it was a big farce. We knew, also, that we had started to pull out and we had figured when we started to pull out of South Vietnam. Well, they didn't, and we figured if they're going to gradually withdraw they should gradually get some of us out of there. But it didn't happen and this was disappointing. By '72 a lot of the Americans, the GIs, had left South Vietnam. They were supposed to be down to some force that was - compared to what we had there before, it was nothing, and yet nothing was happening to us.

Q: You logically felt that if they were taking the troops back they were going to release some of the POWs?

Cdr. A.: Sure. Then we started hearing the latest reports, the Vietnamese reports. Now their demands were that they were not going to be satisfied until we gave up the whole thing, and then we realized that we were okay. President Nixon and the government said we're going to pull everything out, we're leaving South Vietnam entirely, hands off. Is that still going to mean all of us. Some of us might go home, but not everybody, because they had the upper hand then. They could come around and say we'll let those go who have a good attitude.

I mean they'd gone this far, why not take Cambodia, Laos, everything, and give their friends back here everything they want for our return, if we are that important. And we were so many, why don't we just come in here and level the whole place, wipe it out. This really got to us after a while.

Q: Did you ever give up hope?

Cdr. A.: No. We'd get discouraged, sure, but we never gave up hope because you figured, well, something's going to happen. And we were getting indications by our treatment, which indicated that they were still taking care of us and there's a reason. Maybe there was nothing they could do, hooked, you know, but our treatment is still good. By God, we're better off than we were before, we can survive longer now, if these conditions continued, and there's something up their sleeves. Maybe they do want to trade us for everything, for the world! That's an extreme thought, but tending along these lines, gearing the camp for us -

Q: How did you get the news of what was going on? Did they broadcast in your rooms?

Cdr. A.: Yes, they broadcast the news in the rooms. We would get the Voice of Vietnam or an edited version of the Voice of Vietnam, which was an English language broadcast to the soldiers of Vietnam. Hanoi Hannah would get on there and speak. Then they would be very nice and they'd play American music on their radio for the GIs. But the news we heard was filtered news.

Q: The news they wanted you to get?

Cdr. A.: Yes, but we could glean out of that. You know, they would say - for example, back in the '68 Tet they'd killed hundreds of thousands, wiped out hundreds of tanks, shot down 500 airplanes. Well, we don't have that many airplanes and tanks, but we could sense there was a battle. They would say from some period to some period there was a battle. It must have been a big battle because it lasted a week.

Q: And it fit into what you knew about Tet offensives, didn't it?

Cdr. A.: Yes. Well, we heard about the Tet offensive, of course. That was their big victory. They had won the war. The war was over now.

Q: They almost did.

Cdr. A.: I'm sure it was nothing compared to what we heard. Anyway, we were able to glean information. Then that May, it might have been the 5th of May - these dates stick in my mind, but I'm not that sure - the middle of May when we first hit up there, everybody in our room was extremely happy. A few of the pessimists, the guys we called the pessimists because they'd say this is not good because we can't beat them, but these were guys they had thrown into our building, they were newer. The guys would be separated quite a way from us after this happening because they did not think that we could force these people into anything. We're just hopeless.

Now, we had really done it. In other words, we hadn't a hope now as far as they were concerned. There were a couple who felt this way, and these individuals were separated from us and taken to another group. Everybody I know, except for these individuals, was very happy because we knew now that we had been away so long, we had negotiated for so long, we had not done anything for so long, we were pulling out of South Vietnam, and there's no reason they'd come back to North Vietnam except to come in hard. And we did.

We heard about the blockade. They were condemning the blockade of Haiphong Harbor. Hooray, it's about time. And they were condemning the raids on these power plants that had never been hit before. It's about time, because they'd all been flying missions and we'd say why don't we bomb their power plants. Then in the summer they'd condemn the raid on these airfields. By God, it's about time. These were always off limits.

Then after a few months they took us all back to the Hanoi Hilton, in the summer of '72. When we got back a lot of the people had gone, but as we found out later on, they had opened up another camp, way to the north, near China. There were quite a few of the fellows up there. Half of them were up there and half of the prisoners were in this camp. They did, through the years, manage to pick out a few people, a total of about ten altogether, most of these were new guys who were being shot down then, young, they didn't know, but four or five old-timers. When I say "old-timers," I mean '67, '68. They kept them in a different camp strictly to see the visitors, to see Jane Fonda, Ramsay Clark - these are the people who were pessimistic.

Q: Did you know who they were at the time?

Cdr. A.: We knew the ones that we had had contact with. We found out and heard their names through the broadcast, that these people had interviewed Jane Fonda, Ramsay Clark, and these others, and they were the ones who were later - there was talk about court-martialing them and all, but these charges were all dropped. Charges were brought against them but then they were dropped.

Meanwhile, back at the Hilton, every day we had continual air raids in high-density downtown Hanoi in August, September. We're still getting, as I said, better conditions, feeding us, but they're mad, they're really mad. The guards and the officers would love to punish us again because before '68 whenever there was an air raid near our camp it would infuriate the guards and they were so mad they had no one to take it out on but us. Then they would just raise havoc with us. Now they would love to do that, but it was hands off.

There was some heavy bombing going on there, especially in

October and again in December - all night there'd be 52s coming in, and when 52s started coming in we knew it was a matter of time. We'd hear the raids at night. We had gathered some planks - this was a big cell, it could hold fifty people but in ours we had about forty - in the corner and made a little bomb shelter. The Vietnamese had pretty much let us dig foxholes. I know when the bombing started and the ground would shake, I'd jump under those planks. The only injury I received during that period was when I fell and hit my head on the concrete. We'd get in there for hours. They were pretty close but they knew where we were. They knew the prison was there. There was only one near miss, a corner of the prison was damaged but that was an afternoon raid and what happened was a plane was hit and he lost a portion of his load and one of his bombs fell near the camp. Nobody was hurt.

We weren't concerned about bombs. We felt that in wartime our forces had things pretty much under control. We were concerned mostly, and that's when I would duck under cover, because the Vietnamese have no concept of safety. They throw everything they have up in the air. They're shooting off missiles like crazy and everything they have is fired up, and what goes up has to come down. I was afraid that some of their missiles would probably come right back down, so my big concern was to get in there. I was a little concerned at times but after a while you get used to that, too. They really did a good job when they built this prison - double-thick walls, heavily reinforced with steel, but even then the plaster was coming down and it was rocking all night.

I would hate to be a target of a B-52, I tell you that. But it was exciting and we knew that it couldn't last. They were letting us at this time, as I said, do our own cooking, but they were hurting, they were mad. After a while the guards were so dejected, they wanted it to stop. They really did. You could tell -

Q: This was in December of 1972?

Cdr. A.: In December of 1972 and the guards would look at us when there was a raid, they wanted to say, "Enough, enough." The people had had it and they were hungry. They weren't getting the supplies, the city was hungry. We were getting what they could give us and we'd say, "Can we have something to eat or some other thing." And they would say, "Look, you're getting everything. The people aren't getting anything. We have nothing else." So they'd had it.

This is what it took and this was the only way, I'm convinced, because I lived through it, I lived with these people, I know what they're like - I'm convinced that you could never have negotiated. As it turns out, they haven't lived up to the agreement, anyway. The only way to get us out was the way we got in. That was the only way we could have done it. If we had said, okay, we'll take out all of our troops, then they would have wanted all our military assistants and advisers, everybody out, everybody who was State Department, because they would say these are military advisers under the guise of the State Department or mission or something. And not all of the guys would have come home.

Q: How long did that bombing take before they actually agreed?

Interview No. 2 with Commander Everett Alvarez, Jr., U.S. Navy

Place: 17 Greenwood Way, Monterey, California

Date: March 7, 1976

Subject: Prisoners of War

By: Etta Belle Kitchen

Q: I think we're going to pick up on this tape, Commander, with around Christmas 1972?

Cdr. A.: Right. I'm still answering your question about finding out that we were going to come home. Now I'm ready to lead up to answering your question.

Around Christmas, especially just before Christmas and December 27, 1972, we'd been hitting them so hard and, as I said, we knew that the Vietnamese had had it. People can just take so much. The whole country, I don't care how geared up they are, they can just take so much pounding, and we were pounding them in the right place - the railroad depots, the stock depots, et cetera - day and night. In the daytime it was our tactical air force coming in, at nighttime it was the B-52s and other heavy bombers, and they were firing everything they had, missiles - it was amazing how many missiles I could see at one time in the sky going up. They no longer had the capability to track our planes. They were just throwing them up in the air, and they were hitting quite a few of ours, not that many but for the amount of missiles they threw. I remember one afternoon within an hour they must have shot 100. We were counting them right and left, and at night you could see their trails.

After Christmas they weren't shooting them any more. We figured and as it turns out they didn't have any more. So it stopped on the 28th of December and it was quiet. No air raids that morning. We knew this was it. Something's happened. He's not going to stop for very long if it's not real because he had stopped in October, he had stopped again in November for a few days, started again and kept coming. Every time he came back it was heavier and heavier. Stopped just before Chirstmas for a day. They didn't bomb Christmas Eve but they bombed Christmas night. Then on the 28th it stopped. It was heavy on the 26th and the 27th. So the 28th we got up and there was nothing. It was quiet.

There weren't any guards around or anything. The jailer came and let us out, but the guards weren't visible. We figured, well, we'll know in a couple of days. Maybe something's happened. A couple of days went by and nothing, quiet. Okay, something's going on now.

In the meantime, we're busy with our routines, busy talking to the new shoot-downs. They were bringing them in so fast there that they were bringing guys in in the morning in our camp, we could see them bringing them in on stretchers, or walking in, injured people, with their flight suits still on. They had just been shot down a few hours previous. This is how fresh they were. And they would just put them right into the buildings. They had a couple of rooms in which they had new guys. We were talking to them. Some of them had broken bones which they had just bandaged and set and that was it. Now, with the bombing stopped, we were talking to them daily.

Q: Any restrictions on your movements?

Cdr. A.: No. We were not allowed to go in their rooms. We could mingle with them out in the courtyard. What they did at first was paint some lines and you cannot cross that line, you have to stay on your side of the line. We congregated around that line and talked and talked. We soon erased that line. They finally just gave up on that.

Then they came through with a bunch of pocket books, soft-covered books.

Q: Paperbacks?

Cdr. A.: Paperbacks, and packages after Christmas. They started coming across with stuff that they had had for years, packages. You'd get a package from home and, "Another one? I just got one last week." The stuff is moldy and the clothing had a greenish mold. I said, "Where in the heck have you had this?" "Oh, this just came."

Then they started moving us around within our camp, rearranging the rooms, and the new people moved out. They took them somewhere else. This was after the first of the year. Pretty soon we found that all the old-timers were being put in one of two rooms right next to each other and the rest were across the courtyard. There was myself and Bob Shumaker, No. 2, and Haydn Lockhart, No. 3, Bill Butler, No. 5 - No. 4, he didn't make it.

Q: Why are you using the numbers? Is that the length of time you'd been there?

Cdr. A.: No, these are the order of shoot-downs. I was No. 1, Bob Shumaker was the second.

Q: Shumaker?

Cdr. A.: Bob Shumaker, 11 February '65. Haydn Lockhart was No. 3, 7 March '65. And then Smitty Harris on 3 April, another fellow on the 4th of April, Lay Bowden. Another guy Ross Storz, on the 20th April. Ross Storz didn't make it.

Q: What do you mean "didn't make it"?

Cdr. A.: He died.

Q: Died in prison camp?

Cdr. A.: Yes.

Another thing happened. All this while now they have had the senior ranking officer, the real high-ranking senior officers, who were colonels, lieutenant colonels, Navy commanders separate, but we had contact with them. We had communication but yet we did not mix with them and they still did not let them mix with us. And all of a sudden here they come in our room. Robbie Risner, Jim Stockdale, these people. They were commanders, colonels, lieutenant colonels when they were shot down in '66, '67, so they were our ranking officers. Now here they come, mixing in with us. Pretty soon in these two rooms were the first sixty men shot down. Then we looked around and, yes, it fits, there's the next group in that room, the next in seniority. Then we knew something was going on. What could it be? They're ranking us, they're going to let us go home. We said there was only one reason why they would do this. And then we saw the figure, there were so many in our camp, and these were the first guys shot down, the ones that were in our camp.

We rationalized then that the only purpose for this could be that they were going to release us in groups, not all at once, and we would be going out. This was a contingent. They're going on the contingency that they may release us in groups, the first group being the first guys shot down first. Or, the first guys shot down last! We never knew. By this time, you have developed a sense of pessimism in that, oh, well, let's go on the basis that they're going to release us last. That way, we'll be surprised and we'll be happy. We sort of developed this attitude through the years, after having been disappointed for so long, because for so many years we'd had so many ups and so many let downs. We'd build ourselves up for something really good and then in '68 when the bombing stopped, boy, this is it, it won't be but a month or so, a few weeks, they're going to get us out, and then the letdown.

The good treatment started in '70 and then the let down. We're still there. So you naturally build up this defense.

I think I mentioned it in one article. I don't know if you read it?

Q: Yes.

Cdr. A.: In other words, this build-up and this let down gives you a skeptical outlook. Optimistic yet skeptical. So we had this. We said it looks like they're going to do something but let's go on the basis that they're going to release the new guys first because they're fresh and healthy-looking. That's logical. And yet, we said, maybe our government won't go for it. Well, maybe they can't do anything about it, maybe they'll take it. Then we think, gosh, what if it falls through and only part of them get out. Oh, well, buckle your belt and say I'm going to have to stay here, we'll do whatever we can type of an attitude.

Sure enough, they were shuffling people back and forth. All of a sudden one guy would be in a room, then they'd move him to another room, or else he'd be in this room and they'd change their mind and take this group and move part of them over here. So we pretty much had it defined to the day from what day to what date time period this group consisted of.

We then were called out one morning, our two rooms, adjoining rooms, and the camp commander's out there with all his officers and one of the other high-ranking people is here just to watch. Big smiles. So we shuffle out there - by the way our prison garb is what you see in there, the pajamas, the sandals - and it was in January, about the 15th of January, and he says:

"We have an important announcement," and he read off the agreements which stipulated how we were going to go home. Within thirty days the first group would go home, followed by etc., etc. Those who would go home first would be those who had been the longest there et cetera. He read out the whole agreement.

We were all standing there just listening and I looked around - not one smile. Nobody was smiling, just plain stone-faced, everybody's sort of reminiscing or perhaps contemplating, but no outbreaks, no laughter, no hooray, because we knew what it was. And I think the Vietnamese were disappointed because they saw no emotional display - they had photographers somewhere. I didn't feel any real big emotion and I looked around at the cells where the other guys were, they were all looking at what's going on, and we said, "He's reading us the agreements." Oh, okay.

Q: You did not feel any enormous emotion?

Cdr. A.: No. What I felt, and talking to the others they felt the same, was that it was over and the Vietnamese had a sort of "why aren't you happy" expressions, why aren't you celebrating, why aren't you jumping. They just sort of looked at each other. And we just felt, well, congratulations, we made it, now let's go back in the rooms and finish our card game or whatever we were doing.

Q: Why didn't you feel anything?

Cdr. A.: Because it was long overdue. I felt, well, here it is, it's about time.

Q: Had you worn out all of your emotional reactions, perhaps?

Cdr. A.: Yes, it was anticlimactic. I had expressed more emotion and jumped for joy when they read the announcements on the Hanoi radio in late September or early October about the United States has proposed that and we've proposed this and the government of North Vietnam has agreed to the proposal as set forth by the United States et cetera, et cetera, and she read off this agreement, and we yelled, "There it is." We were in our rooms. This was in September. However, the bellicose U.S. government has changed its demands and are now demanding something of the North Vietnamese people, we will never succumb.

In those few minutes when she was going on reading the agreements - and I don't know what this was all about but apparently they had agreed to something which was not what we wanted - we felt emotion. It was a limited amount, but it was emotion. It was "Hooray," and were shaking each other's hands, a couple of guys were crying a bit because it was over, we were on our way home. She came through with this later and you just look at that speech there and "how can you do this to me?" Then the bombing started getting heavier.

So now we were drained, emotionally we were drained. It was anticlimatic. It was too long overdue and, who knows, maybe you are leaving and it's the truth, maybe you're not. We'll see. I'll believe it.

Q: A wait-and-see attitude?

Cdr. A.: Yes. It sounds good and it stands to reason because there's no more bombing, and I don't think we would have agreed to this paper - I don't think we would have stopped the bombing unless we had agreed to the proposal. But, we'll see. Something else may come up and spoil it all. This was the feeling that we had. We'll believe it when we see it, but it sounds good.

A few days later we looked out and here come guys drawing these little carts - Vietnamese peasants are pulling these little carts into the courtyard, and we said, "Okay, looks like we've got little suitcases, satchels, coming in." In the middle of the night more cartloads would come in with clothing. "What are those?" They'd point and they'd show the shirts. Well, it looks like they're getting ready to send somebody home. They're bringing in a bunch of shirts, trousers, belts, shoes - a boxful of shoes. Where in hell did they get the shoes? We probably can't wear shoes any more. It's been so long.

We knew that according to the agreements they had read, from the date they had signed them, that they were going to release the first group within thirty days, and here thirty days was approaching. Well, maybe they're not going to release us, maybe they're going to release the new guys who aren't in this camp.

Then, one evening, just about two days before the deadline, they took ten of us, Bob Shumaker, myself, and right down the line, the first ten guys shot down, and marched us over to see the interrogator, one of the officers, in what used to be the interrogation room and he said:

"Henry Kissinger is coming in to Hanoi tomorrow. He will be here and a mission is going to come into the camp, and tomorrow morning you will be taken on a bus and you will go to Gia Lam Airport, and you will go home. Tonight we'll give you your clothes and a suitcase."

They gave us our trousers and our shirts and an undershirt and shorts - new clothing - in a little suitcase. What they gave us the suitcase for, it's hard to say. I just put the things I wanted to keep in it, artifacts, you know. The only thing I brought back with me that I had all the time was a Navy watch cap, one of these woolen pull-downs. I had stuck that in my survival equipment a couple of years before I was shot down and forgotten about it, and when the Vietnamese captured me they took everything off me. They were going through this survival vest I wore at the time and they pulled this cap out. I saw that and I thought, gee, I'd forgotten I had that in there. Later on they returned my socks and my underwear, and the first winter it got cold and I asked them if I could have this cap back. I told them it was very dear to me, that my father had given it to me when I was a child and it meant a lot to me. At that time - this was back in '64 - they were responsive to this and they brought it to me. This really helped me every winter. When I'd go to bed at night I'd pull this thing down over my ears, over my eyes. I could snore to the world, you know, and it really kept my head warm.

Other guys would make rags from a pant leg from their pajamas, an old trouser or an old pajama bottom. They'd make some kind of headgear. It looked like a circus. We really looked funny, but this thing really helped me and I still had it with me. I had had it taken away several times, but I'd always managed to get it back. It always showed up somewhere. When they used to take away a lot of your own personal things, you were not allowed to have those. They would take it away but then they would give it back later on during the good times. One time in the spring they took it away and at Christmas they gave it back to me as a goodwill gesture for Christmas.

So the last few years I had it and I still have it. I brought that home and I brought my cup with me, my water cup. My last birthday in December '72, one of my roommates made me a little ditty bag. He sewed it out of an old rag, embroidered my name, and it had a little design. I brought that back and Vietnamese cigarettes. All these things are now in the Navy Museum in Washington.

Anyway, they gave us our clothing and shoes and everything and we carted all this back to our room, and there was a lot of

"Hey, look at this, how does this fit, how do I look? Does this look good?" "Don't you think you need a little bigger size", or "My God, look at this belt, look how loose it is. I can't believe it."

It was a little difficult getting to sleep that night, but they didn't give us our clothing till nine o'clock. They're continually, at this time, giving us coffee, more packages from home - I don't know where they had these things stored. We can't drink enough coffee and they're giving us oranges, bananas, and I'm just bloated, just eating myself silly.

Q: How about your shoes? Did they give you a pair of shoes that fit?

Cdr. A.: Yes, I got a pair of shoes. Whether they fit or not didn't bother me. I wasn't going to keep them that long, anyway.

All this activity's going on because after the first group of ten they took the next group of ten out, and the next. I think there were something like 65 in that first group. So there's a lot of activity late into the night.

About midnight - he told us they were going to wake us up early, before the gong goes off at four, so we could get dressed because they wanted us on the bus at 5:30 so we could go out to the airport - so I thought I might have trouble falling asleep tonight, but we'll wait and see what happens tomorrow. Maybe tomorrow they'll say something's happened.

We went to bed and I managed to fall asleep and, sure enough, at four o'clock they woke us up. They really didn't have to wake us up. Some of the guys were awake. We got up and we dressed and we left a lot of things there for the other guys, things that we couldn't eat, coffee. We said, "Give it to the other guys. They can have our coffee and our fruit and read our magazines." I just brought these little artifacts I had. Also in these packages we were getting from home we were getting underwear and stuff like this, thermal underwear and T shirts, so I packed a few of those things and I left some for the other guys. There were some, perhaps, who didn't have any. Everybody had extra underwear and extra blankets. It was a land of plenty.

Then they took us out, lined us up in groups of ten, first group, next group, and we decided we were going to look military so we formed ourselves up in rank and file in the courtyard, and everybody else is there, waving, "See you in a few weeks," "See you in a few months," "Hope you get to call my wife." Everybody the day before had been saying, "When you go, give my wife a call."

We marched out of the courtyard to an adjoining courtyard, a small one, which leads up to the outside entrance. They lined us up there, and we stood there, and we stood there. Finally, they came along and said, "You can go ahead and sit down. There's been a delay." "How long?"

"We don't know yet."

So we sat down. After about an hour we're still there. Then we turn around and go back in that big courtyard.

"Here we are, back again, guys!"

We sat there and everybody's saying, "Well, I wonder how long it will be before they turn us around and we go back to our cells." There's been a breakdown in the negotiations or something.

Apparently there had been a breakdown so they held us up there. I recall this so well because I was waiting out there and I told the guard I had to go to the bathroom. Okay, go ahead. They're using one off what used to be called New Guys Village. So I go back in there. I had been drinking so much coffee, I guess, or what have you that I had a little diarrhea and there's no toilet paper. What am I going to do?

Q: Here in your new uniform!

Cdr. A.: All of a sudden these other guys start saying, "Hey, Al, we're going, we're going."

Oh, God, of all times to get stuck. So I scrambled out to the yard and got some old newspaper, and hurried, and came running out and,

"Come on, we're waiting for you."

Q: You're the No. 1 man and you're holed up in the john!

Cdr. A.: Yes!

So we marched out and loaded up into the buses. The buses were outside.

Q: Were you No. 1 on the bus or did you go by grade?

Cdr. A.: No, we went by rank, but the first ten guys shot down were in this group and what they did was they stuck another group in front of us. They had brought them out from a different area and it wasn't until we were out there ready to load on the bus that we saw these guys come on. And these guys were wounded. There were only thirteen or fourteen of them. They were wounded people who had been shot down within the last few days, kept separate, and most of the group that were seeing the visitors, the delegations, they put them on first.

Q: Did you recognize them?

Cdr. A.: Oh, yes. We did not talk to them. We wouldn't talk to those guys.

Q: Do you want to mention names?

Cdr. A.: No, everybody knows who they are. We wouldn't talk to them.

Q: They were the wounded and the --

Cdr. A.: Some of the wounded were being released because they were wounded.

Q: And the rest were the ones who had cooperated?

Cdr. A.: There were a couple of stretcher cases, but the wounded guys were going. Some of them were new, they were young kids, they were hurt, and all of a sudden they're being put out there and they don't know why. But those guys, I feel no animosity towards them. I don't have any animosity toward any of them. I feel pity for some of those fellows. But the others you say, look at that, right out there.

So they got on first then we went out. Bob and I were side by side.

Q: Bob?

Cdr. A.: Shumaker. We got on the bus and they took us through a back route, through town, across the Red River, a circuitous route to Gia Lam. We came in the back way. They stopped, they let us out, they put us in a building, which is on the back perimeter, away from the field. We sat there and we asked:

"What are we waiting for?"

"We're waiting till we get the go-ahead from here to take you to the airport."

Then we're waiting and waiting and they gave us beer. "Do you want beer?"

"No."

"Do you want sandwiches?"

"No."

I wasn't going to eat any more. I was going to save myself for a steak sandwich. After a couple of hours of sitting there, I said,

"Maybe I'd better have a sandwich and a beer. We might wind up going back to the camp," because there had been a breakdown in the negotiations. This is the word that they told us.

"Okay, give me a beer and a sandwich."

I still couldn't eat. I was getting real excited. I said:

"What do you think? Do you think we'll make it?"

"Well, we'll see what happens." This type of an attitude.

You're trying to doze and it's hard to sleep. About one o'clock, Hanoi time - it may have been about eleven o'clock, Hanoi time, now that I think about it - it was quite a wait, at least two to three hours, and we're saying:

"Well, here we are, another exercise, another drill."

They came and they said:

"Okay, get on the bus."

We didn't know if we were going back to the camp or where. Sure enough, they pulled up to a hangar. We were in the first bus - I don't know what happened to the one with the wounded in it and the other guys. Oh, yes, I do. It was behind us. They were lined up behind us. We were the first bus and in our position we could see around the corner of the hangar and the hangar was sort of bombed out - but we could see around the corner of it and we could see two C-130s sitting out there on the ramp, and there was a bunch of people under an awning. There were some tables out there in a canvas tent.

Then they got the go-ahead and they pulled up - oh, no, before they pulled up, as we were sitting there, we looked up and here comes this C-141 MATS with a red cross. It comes in and pulls up. We watch it and we're thinking, "Don't stall,"

"Don't crash," "Go ahead and put her on." It taxied by and we all yell and cheer because that was our ride home we realized. Then we pulled up and there was the negotiating team and our people.

They let us out of the bus, you must obey the guard, and all this. By that time we were just oblivious to what they were telling us. I was looking across and the American Air Force officers one guy came over and he said:

"Just take it easy. A few more minutes and we'll have you."

Then they told him to get away and he had to go back on the other side of the line.

As they marched us up to the gate, photographers were taking a lot of movies and all that. First they said:

"Make room for the stretcher cases." They brought the wounded through, then they said:

"Make room for these others."

The stretcher cases came through and the injured came through, but if they had brought these other fellows walking through I was going to clobber them. We just didn't want that to happen, and it didn't. They came out last, but still they were in the first group, and that left a - well, there was nothing we could do about it. That's why I pity these individuals. I don't have any respect for them. I don't have any hatred for them. I pity them because we were coming home now and all this while we had resisted and we had done our best because we knew that we were going to have to face up to ourselves when we came home. We were going to have to live with ourselves, and I don't see how those guys can and

I don't believe they can. I think it's very hard for them.

Anyway, we got through and as soon as you crossed they called your name and you passed through. I had two fellows take my arm, they escorted me to the airplane. Boy, I think those fellows were more excited than we were, "How do you feel? Do you feel okay?", and they were huffing and puffing.

"Yes, we're fine. I'm okay."

Q: It must have been terrible excitement for everybody?

Cdr. A.: Yes, it was exciting for everybody but still, you know, there's this long overdue type of feeling.

When I got to the back of the airplane, I looked up and here's this very beautiful blonde Air Force nurse. My God, I said, "Bob, look at that." They got us all aboard and we sat down. I was sitting next to Bob again and I said,

"Well, what do you think? Are we going to make it off?"

"I don't know."

They got everybody aboard and they closed up and pretty soon the engines started up. There was a big cheer when the engines started up, and it was taxiing along. We could tell when we got to the runway, and they revved the engines up. We go rolling down the runway, you're counting and counting, and pretty soon you feel it lift free. Everybody cheered, except Bob and I. We didn't. We shook hands: "We're in the air, Bob." And that was it. I just didn't feel like yelling and cheering.

I was happy and I was excited. I was excited now but I wasn't

Alvarez #2 - 114

- I couldn't get myself to be over-emotional, break up. I just couldn't do it. Just like you said before, I guess I was drained.

Q: But you were on your way home!

Cdr. A.: We were on our way home.

I think the only time I really experienced emotion, there was emotion when we got to Clark and we saw the people there, and we got on the bus. It was emotional to get in a hot shower and stand there for hours. It was emotional to get your first meal. They tried to put me on a bland diet because I had parasites and I looked up at these other guys going through the line and they had steaks and eggs and all that and I said to heck with this, I'm going to have steak and eggs and milkshakes. To heck with the bland diet. I ate the bland diet and I ate the steak and eggs, too.

They couldn't believe it right away, you know. You can't do that. You're going to hurt yourself. Well, if I go, this is the way to go! After a while, they said okay, go ahead, eat whatever you want. They couldn't believe it.

The only time, I think, I really felt emotional and wanted to break down and cry was when we left Clark and were on our way to the States and we had to make a stop at Travis. When we got to Travis, no, not Travis, Hickham, in Honolulu. When we got to Hickham, we got off the airplanes for a couple of hours and I was in the terminal where they had little refreshments and what have you - it was in the middle of the night, about four in the morning,

Honolulu time - there were a lot of people out there to see us as we came through. It was really gratifying to see that, but as I got in there they asked me if I knew Captain John Nicholson. I said, "Nick." He said yes, a captain.

Well, this fellow was my operations officer when I was shot down. I was flying with him and when I was hit he was the last guy I talked to on the radio. You know, as I described before, as I lost control of my airplane. I didn't go into that much detail because of the time element, but I was talking on the radio and doing other things at the time. I was trying to go through my emergency procedure, I was trying to keep the airplane under control, and I was talking on the radio when I could. It was intermittent, but I did manage to tell him I was hit, and the last thing that came through was that Nick and he said, "Okay, Al, you know what to do." I said:

"Okay, I'm going to get out. I'll see you guys later."

I always wondered if they heard that because my equipment was failing rapidly and I don't know if that transmission got through.

They said, "Well, would you like to see him. He and his wife are in the next room." They were real good friends from before. So I walked in there and that's the first time, I think, I really did start bawling and so did they!

Q: Had he heard your transmission?

Cdr. A.: The first thing he said was, "You know, Al, I never forgot what you said and I always knew that I'd see you because you said, "I'll see you guys later.'" And they all did, they all heard it.

That was a very emotional experience, seeing him. I don't know why because when I got home to Travis a few hours later and they took me to Oakland Naval Hospital I saw my folks, but I didn't break down and cry. It was emotional but it wasn't -

Q: Well, he had been part of the thing there with you, hadn't he?

Cdr. A.: Yes. It was funny because I saw him and we all stood there and hugged each other, bawling like babies. His wife was just bawling like a baby. That's what made me bawl, I think, but I said:

"Where did you guys go? Why did you go off and leave me like that?"

He had been there the whole war. He went back to Vietnam and was out there the whole time. Any time he could, he'd ask for orders. So it was sort of we guys stay in.

Q: That's a very touching recital.

Cdr. A.: One of the other guys who was a JO or a JG also did the same thing. He had gone through the war and came back and gone through as a pilot flying missions. When I saw him in San Diego the following summer, his wife said - when we were released and I came home in February he was out there in the Tonkin Gulf on the <u>Enterprise</u> - and he had told his wife when they left on that cruise that this time they were going to get me out. That was emotional, it was really emotional.

Q: To me, just listening to it, it's just as unbelievable and incredible that you were gotten out at the end of eight and a half years. I just never understood how you lived through it.

Cdr. A.: Well, as I said before, we had no choice. You can't just lie down and give up.

Q: Some people did, didn't they?

Cdr. A.: Yes, but I think what helped us - you mentioned earlier that religion was a big factor. Yes, it was to a lot of us but that isn't everything, you know. I said before that everybody has his own source of strength, whether it's a dollar or whether it's his own physique or whether it's booze or what have you.

Q: Have you ever found out what yours was?

Cdr. A.: Not really. I thought perhaps religion. It is a great source of strength for me, I know it is, but I didn't rely on that completely. And we all did rely on our own source of strength because we learned and it didn't take long to learn that we all relied on each other. We really did, and we really did a lot for each other.

Q: I would assume that's why being in solitary would have been the worst?

Cdr. A.: Yes. When a guy was in solitary, we did everything we could to communicate with him, to get to him and communicate, to keep him going. We'd spend hours each day to talk to a guy in solitary, just pass the time.

Q: So he'd know you were thinking about him?

Cdr. A.: So he knew we were there.

Q: But when you were in solitary in the first months there was no one else there to try to help you?

Cdr. A.: No, but I had my religion, my strength, but I also felt that I had my family, and I was lucky to get some letters eventually. I knew I had my friends and I had my family, that was my strength.

Q: The worst time for you was when you were by yourself and the foundry was making a noise outside, if I interpret correctly?

Cdr. A.: At that time, I pretty much lay down and gave up in the sense that I put myself out of reality into a dream world. Physically I suffered and I think mentally I was out of it because I didn't pray. I don't remember praying or thinking of anything. I was off somewhere else.

Q: How many months did that last?

Cdr. A.: I would say it started around June and lasted till August.

Q: Of '65?

Cdr. A.: Yes, or September. I can remember lying there and screaming, trying to drown out the noise.

Q: Was that day and night?

Cdr. A.: No, it was all day.

Q: I mean the noise.

Cdr. A.: Yes.

Q: It was all day long. It did stop at night?

Cdr. A.: It stopped at night, sure, because those people went home.

Q: Would you know whether they put you there because of the noise? This being an extra -

Cdr. A.: No, because there were Vietnamese prisoners in the next cells.

Q: Oh, I see. It wasn't punishment or being brutal, it just happened that you were put in that location?

Cdr. A.: Yes. That was my worst period. That was a hard period mentally and physically. I came out of that. One day I was out washing myself - they used to let me out for ten minutes a day to wash and empty my bowl - and I looked up and the sky was beautiful. It was a clear day. I could see a little bit of sky between the walls and the roof and, to show you what state of mind I was in, I was out there singing as loud as I could "Oh, what a beautiful morning." It doesn't even occur to me that it's against the regulations and I could get punished. I wasn't supposed to make noise. I was out there just singing away. Maybe I thought I was Mario Lanza. And the next thing I heard was this voice over the other side of the wall saying, "Oh, my God" in English.

I yelled, "Who's over there?"

And he yelled back some name. To me it sounded like Geronimo.

"Did you say Geronimo?"

I couldn't make contact with the fellow. This was August or early September of '65. I didn't hear from him any more but I knew he was over there in my little area. That's when I told the guard to give a T shirt or a towel or something - they had given me a couple of extra towels - to him, and I pointed over there, "Give it to him." That's when they knew that I knew there were other Americans there.

So, on the night of 17 September 1965 when they took me out and put me in a jeep to take me to the other camp, I got in the jeep and I sat next to somebody and he said:

"Who are you?"

I said, "Who are you?"

We were blindfolded, handcuffed, and so forth. He said his name was Guarino, and I said:

"Oh, you're Geronimo!"

He said, "No, no, Guarino." Larry Guarino, he was a major shot down just a few weeks prior to this and he had been put in there for punishment and was suffering hallucinations and everything. He was really badly off.

He asked me who I was and I told him.

Oh, when I hollered across, "Who are you?" and he said, "Geronimo", he said, "Who are you?". I then realized I shouldn't be shouting my name over the wall, right out, because I didn't know who else might be hearing this, so I said "Al." He said, "Al?" Then we lost contact, but I figured he could deduce who Al was. But he had no idea I was there, so when I got in the jeep next to him that night he said, "Who are you?"

I said, "Al." I figured he knew who it was. He said, "Al, who?"

I said, "Alvarez."

He said, "Oh!" Oh, my God. Holy smoke," like holy smoke, you're still alive.

This is how we got together and this is how I first made contact.

Q: Was that the first time you knew there were other Americans there?

Cdr. A.: No, I had known. I had found out there were other Americans there by other ways - notes and messages on the bottom of the plates.

Q: But to me noise, that constant noise, would be almost as bad as physical torture and I wondered if it just happened to be -

Cdr. A.: I think it just happened to be there.

Q: And they weren't doing that as punishment?

Cdr. A.: No. That was a hard period. In '66 and '67 when they were using these methods for propaganda, that was a hard period physically and mentally.

Q: They were trying by threats and torture to make you - ?

Cdr. A.: Well, you know, you developed a fear. You lived with fear and that's what was hard. The physical pain didn't last very long but that was hard. The fear was worse or as hard for me.

Q: You have a phrase in one of your poems some place about the fear of fear is almost as bad as the punishment.

Cdr. A.: Yes. Then in '71, six months prior to my learning about my wife, was very hard emotionally, then when I finally did know about it, the first six months of 1972, I was shocked. I was no good. I was just drained emotionally. I mean I was just hurt. That's when my friends really came to the rescue.

Q: Did you learn it in a letter from her?

Cdr. A.: No. I stopped receiving mail. They started giving us mail in '69. I got a letter from her in '69 and got a letter at Christmas of '70, but it was a year old. Then no more mail. I'd get packages and letters from my mother. The first two packages came from my wife. After that I didn't know what was going on. I didn't know if she was sick. I didn't know if she'd been in an accident. I didn't know what had happened, and this not knowing was hardest because all these years now, six years, everything I've got going for me to keep me going. My strength was her and our future. It's part of you, you know, this is what kept you going, this is why I wanted to live. If I hadn't had her to come back to and start again, I think I would have just said oh, the heck with it.

Now things were better physically for us, yet now I didn't know what had happened to her. Had she found someone else? But she couldn't because she's not that type of girl, she's not like that. So I had to know. I was writing to her and my mother was answering. So I wrote my mother and I told her I wanted to know what was going on. I wrote her in the summer of '71 and at Christmas of '71 I got her letter in response. All this time, I'm biting my nails and saying, "What could have happened, what could have happened?"

Christmas of '71 I got a letter. It was short. We were getting these six-line letters. That's all we were allowed to write. She did a very good job of telling me what had happened and I wanted to know. In the following letter, several months later, I got a little follow-up more, but it was a real blow and it took me about six months before I began to say, "Well, you know, I'm still alive and I'm going to come home. I've got a life to lead." I started coming out of it towards the summer, the end of the summer, of '72. I started realizing that there was still something I could do.

Q: It's horrible to think of but better you knew to give you the chance to adjust so that you were adjusted by the time you got home to start a new life. Is that true?

Cdr. A.: Yes, because a lot of the other guys found out when they got home. That way, it was another blow. It was bad enough to find out many things had happened, personal things had happened. At least I had gotten that out of the way.

Q: You have a beautiful life now?

Cdr. A.: Oh, yes, we're very happy.

Q: There are a few topics I wanted to discuss with you. For example, your physical and mental condition, your height and your weight when you were released.

Cdr. A.: I think I mentioned it before, but you recall that I was 160 when I was shot down - 155 to 160 - and I'm 5 feet 10. I lost an inch somewhere along the way. I'm a little over 5'9" now, and I think part of it was probably due to the ejection, I'm not sure. I was surprised when I measured my height. I went down to about 110 during the years and then gradually they started feeding us and I went back up. I weighed 140 when I got to Clark, and I weigh 160 to 165 now, depending on what I've had to eat the day before.

My health is good. There is a program in which the Navy returnees are examined thoroughly every year. We go back to the Navy Aerospace Center in Pensacola and the captain in charge of the program back there is very, very interested in us. He takes a personal interest. We do get a thorough going-over each year.

Yes, we did have some lingering effects of parasites. Eventually I got rid of mine, and everything's fine. Most of us do maintain a good physical fitness program. I don't have the time to do what I want to do, but I still keep pretty active. Physically, we're pretty good. I feel real good.

Q: You said that by the time you were released you almost had a skill, at least you had a workable skill, with the North Vietnamese language. Is that true?

Cdr. A.: I had a better skill at it when I was first there by myself. I was really eager to learn and I built myself a little dictionary and I studied the vocabulary. Part of my mental exercise was to go over my vocabulary and add to it and use it talking to the guards, et cetera. Then when the bombing started the guards became a little nasty and they started demanding that I be polite and say it correctly. Like a trained dog, they wouldn't give me water unless I asked for it politely. So I said, the heck with it, I'm not a trained puppy, so I stopped using it.

Then after I started living with other fellows, Americans, we asked for things when we had to, but I lost a lot of the words and eventually the Vietnamese would know when we said we want water, "hungry," "wash" - they knew the words.

Let me put it this way, I was at my peak after I'd been there six months, then it dropped off for those reasons.

Q: At the time you were captured you were a JG and you had automatic promotions so what was your grade when you returned?

Cdr. A.: I was a JG but I was expecting my promotion any day and my promotion did come through, I understand, the following month and I was promoted automatically. It had already come through and then I was a lieutenant, then I was promoted automatically to lieutenant commander 1 July 1969. Others at that time were making it much sooner, but I went along on the automatic promotion cycle. However, when I did return I was a lieutenant commander and I was picked up two years early for commander. That was sort of a bonus, I think.

Q: And not any more than you deserved, to put it mildly.

Let me ask you about any revenge that you felt about bad treatment you received from the guards or from the camp commander or from the interrogators?

Cdr. A.: No. As I said before, I don't really bear any hatred or revenge. I don't like some individuals because a few of the officers and some of the guards were very brutal, barbaric. I don't like them for that, but when I look at the guards or think of the Vietnamese in general, no, I don't have a lingering hatred for them, gooks, commies, or Vietnamese, because they're human beings. They're illiterate. It's an underdeveloped country, but these people are under control and it is what is controlling them that I have a hatred for. It's a hoax. They did what they have to. The policies come down from higher up. In other words, when we were punished or tortured, they didn't decide to do it, they followed the orders. The manner in which some of them responded to the orders, some of those people I don't like. They didn't have to do what they did.

But it's the system, their system, that evil force in there that would direct these orders down to get these things they wanted for the purpose they wanted them. In my mind, it's evil. It's wrong. And I'm not talking about an ideological concept of communism or socialism or pure communism or capitalism, because you can have those and yet not be evil. But it is the method in which it is applied, their methods of terror, their methods of brutality that I detest. It is the concept of evil that goes along with it - the party, the cadres, the ones who direct it, the ones who come out with these methods. They have the control and it's the controller that I don't like.

Q: Did you have any feelings of hatred for certain individuals at the time?

Cdr. A.: Oh, I developed a hatred for some of those individuals who were unnecessarily brutal, for what they were doing to my friends and myself. There was no need for that.

Q: How did you feel at the time about having a war crimes trial?

Cdr. A.: Let them call them war crimes. In my own mind and in our own minds, they could call it whatever they want to.

Q: I meant for us to have tried some of those brutal people for their war crimes against you? As we did in Germany.

Cdr. A.: Well, the thing is - the factor here is that there was no winner, no outright winner. If there had been a winner like we had in World War II, yes, we would have had war crimes. If they had won, they could have had war crimes. If we had won completely and captured them, destroyed their government, we could have had war crimes.

A lot of people here have told me about what happened in South Vietnam and how we treated theirs. I don't know. We did have our own trial. We tried our own people, some of those like the Calley trial and things like this. There was a lot of publicity given to the tiger cages on that island down there. When I saw pictures of that and saw movies, I would love to have lived in one of those cages. You've got to realize that the ventilation they had, the conditions they had were much, much better than we had. I would have loved to have a tiger cage where I could have ventilation, where I could have the ability to roam around like they did - I really would. They were much better off than we were. We had no ventilation. We couldn't roam around, we were chained to our beds, things like this.

So when you talk about the harsh, brutal conditions, I can't see it. Besides that, those were their prisons maintained by their own army for their prisoners. We didn't build those prisons but that's how those people lived. I wish we had had conditions as good as they had them on that island down there. It's really something.

Q: Some psychiatrists have expressed the opinion that our POWs came home in such good shape because of the fact that they were a special group. You've read of that, of course?

Cdr. A.: Yes.

Q: What was your reaction to that?

Cdr. A.: I agree with it 100 per cent. All these fellows had a lot going for them. They were all college graduates, they were all professional men, they were all above average, and they were all aviators. When you look at the fellows who were captured in South Vietnam - of course, their conditions were different - but you got a different cut of person. This is another thing, too, the Vietnamese realized this. That's why they worked so hard to keep us separate, to keep us under control. They also, I think, respected it. They respected us because we could still organize ourselves, we could still hold our values and hold our principles.

Q: In some of the material I read frequently you're described as being an inspiration to the other men.

Cdr. A.: In that sense it's just because I happened to be the lucky guy to be first, because I was there first.

Q: Lucky guy!

Cdr. A.: Yes! I'd been there a year when these other guys were just sitting there, and at that time they thought this war's not going to last but six months or a year and, if he can make it this far, I can make it, too. Then later on, he's been here two years, I can make it - or he's been here four years, I've been here three, I can make it one more or two more. It was this kind of thing.

So it's implied. It's not a "rah, rah, let's get going" kind of thing. I'm not that type.

Q: Did you ever attempt to exert any inspirational leadership that you were conscious of?

Cdr. A.: No.

Q: Just the fact that you had lived through it perhaps made you a living inspiration?

Cdr. A.: After I'd been there four or five years the newer fellows would, if I happened to be in a position - normally it was the senior officer who set the policy, but when I happened to be available, they'd say, "What do I do?" and I would try to listen and suggest "I would try to look at it this way." But that's not the time when you get up in the pulpit and give your Sunday sermon or the time to get up there at halftime and give them the cheer to get up there and put some fight into it. It's just that I'm not cut that way, or I didn't feel that I was one who should go out

Alvarez #2 - 131

there because I'm as weak as anyone. I gave in. So I'm not model.

There were others who resisted much better than I did, physically, others whom I admired because they went all the way. They didn't come back. It's a question of the image, of whether you would want -

Q: Do you think you came back with a different set of values, or were you able to just simply maintain the values for your own personal life that you went in with?

Cdr. A.: I did not come back with a different set. I thought about this a lot, specially when I was there. I do not feel I have a different set of values. I feel I am more convinced and more firm in my own values. Others I have defined, whereas I never considered them before. I was only twenty-six years old when I was shot down. I was a young pilot, a gay blade, you know, I'd fly and go to the bar and drink, chase pretty girls, and drive nice cars, and I didn't have a penny. It's not that having money is important, but here I was in different countries and I never took advantage of the opportunities I had.

I have different values now towards family. I never considered it before, how I would feel towards the family. I was ready to go to sea and fly any time and the family stayed home. I didn't give it that much thought. Now I don't want to go to sea. I've got different values. I've got the same values. I consider a family important. I always did. I always placed my family, my parents and my sisters, very highly, but now I look at it differently. Now I have more feeling towards them, more responsible. I was fairly responsible, but now I have more of a responsible feeling.

Everything's interrelated. I look at politics, I look at our government, and I look at our school system, and I can see a deterioration that hurts. I can see things that are being taught to our young children and it bothers me that they no longer say the pledge of allegiance in our schools. It bothers me when I go to a basketball game in our nation's capital, a big arena, and when they play the national anthem, half the people are turning around with their hands in their pockets talking and looking elsewhere, not even caring if they sit down. It bothers me. This shouldn't be.

Q: It seems to me you might have had somewhat of an inspirational influence on people because I'm going to quote in just a moment, but I did want to ask you did you have any feeling that the time you spent in whatever it was that we had in Vietnam, call it war or whatever you will, was worthwhile?

Cdr. A.: Yes, but we went about it all wrong. First of all, it was a political war, it was not a military war. That was the first mistake. The military was not calling the shots. Somebody else was calling the shots. Yet we had to try because, as I say, it's this controller that we're fighting. Look what happened in Cambodia. That's a perfect example. The Vietnamese are too subtle, too smart, to do something like that in South Vietnam, yet they don't have to worry. We're not going to go back in there. They've got all the time in the world to take over, mold it in their own way, and get them the way they want them, to get the people as they have them in North Vietnam. There's no big rush. There's no purge. There's no need for it. But it's going to hurt us here under our system because they consider us their biggest threat. They consider us an evil force that they eventually have to get rid of because capitalism is a threat to socialism.

I thought we had to try and I think we're going to have to try it again somewhere else. We've given up a couple of chances here and we may give up a few more chances, but eventually we're going to wake up and say we've got to do something, if we want to preserve our system as we have it now. But there are many people in our country who don't believe that, who would like to see a change. If the majority of the people want to see a change, okay, as long as the change is an ideological change, a political change eventually, where they're going to be happy with it, but not where you have this control group that dominates and instills fear, where you and I are afraid to talk out against what's his name up there, he shouldn't be doing this, this is wrong, where we have a chance to express our opinion. If it comes to that some day I hope we see that.

Q: You hope what?

Cdr. A.: I hope we see a peaceful change.

Q: If there has to be a change, you mean?

Cdr. A.: Yes. But I cannot see it today. You see it in segments. You see people like these outlaws, these SLA people, that's exactly what these people are over there. Exactly.

Q: Do you feel there are items that we may have omitted that you'd like to include in the interview?

Cdr. A.: No, I can't think of anything right now.

Q: Let me close, then, with a quote that's attributed to you. It was in Time magazine on March 5, 1973, and I believe some of the media had been saying these men come home and they all say the same thing and it looks to me like maybe they've been told what to say. Do you remember that?

Cdr. A.: Yes.

Q: And you said, "For years and years we dreamed of this day and we kept the faith, faith in God, in our president, and in our country." That seems to express your feelings.

Cdr. A.: Yes.

Q: Well, I think you have been an inspiration. Thank you.

Cdr. A.: Thank you.

INDEX

to

Interviews with

Commander Everett Alvarez, Jr.

U. S. Navy

ALCATRAZ: The worst of the prisons, p. 49;

ALVAREZ, Commander Everett, USN: details of the incident over North Vietnam that made him a POW, p. 1-12; interrogation by his captors, p. 12-18; p. 28 ff; Hanoi Prison, p. 19 ff; he participates in the Hanoi March, p. 46; his wife leaves him - the emotional shock, p. 122-3; p. 129-30;

AMERICAN SYMPATHIZERS OF NORTH VIETNAM: value of their visits to Hanoi, p. 59-60; p. 91;

BARRETT, Lt. Thomas J. USAF: becomes roommate of Alvarez, p. 44-45; p. 64;

BERG, Captain Kile Dag, USAF: (Red) a roommate of Alvarez, p. 64; p. 67-8;

BRIAR PATCH: Alvarez moved there in Sept. 1965 when others began to come into prison, p. 38-9; his long period of mental inaction, p. 40; p. 43; p. 45; p. 67;

CAPTORS: attempt to subdue entire group of prisoners, p. 46-7;

CODE OF CONDUCT: p. 57-8;

COMMUNICATIONS WITHIN PRISON: p. 42; p. 56; p. 118;

USS CONSTELLATION: p. 1, p. 3;

EARLY RELEASES: p. 83-4;

EXIT - FROM HANOI: p. 104 ff;

GIA LAM AIRPORT: p. 110.

GUARINO, Major Lawrence (Larry) N. USAF: p. 120-1;

HANOI - BOMBING OF: Final days in prison, p. 91-6; p. 98-100; agreements between U. S. and N. Vietnam are read to prisoners, p. 101-2;

HANOI HILTON: p. 19-20; p. 81; p. 85; p. 90;

HO CHI MINH: p. 34; p. 44; p. 53;

HONGAY: U. S. raid on naval base, p. 4 p. 9.

LAOS: reconnaissance missions over, p. 2-3;

LETTERS FROM HOME: p. 25; p. 34-5; p. 38.

NIXON, President Richard M.: p. 87;

PEACE TALKS: p. 87-8;

POTEMKIN EPISODE: p. 81;

POW - ABILITY TO RESIST: discussion of factors involved, p. 61-3; p. 117-119; p. 129;

POW - DAILY ROUTINE IN CELLS: p. 63-4; a day in the Briar Patch, p. 67-73; routine at the Zoo, p. 74-5; conditions change by 1971; p. 75-8;

PROPAGANDA: p. 47-8; p. 50;

REHABILITATION - NAVY PROGRAM: p. 125;

RISNER, Colonel Robinson (Robbie): p. 55; p. 99;

SHUMAKER, Lt. Comdr. Robert H.: second man to become POW in Hanoi, p. 37; p. 98; p. 104; p. 110; p. 113;

SON TAY: p. 79; repercussions at the Zoo as result of raid, p. 79-80;

STOCKDALE, Rear Admiral James B.: p. 99;

TET OFFENSIVE: p. 89;

THE ZOO: Alvarez moved there in fall of 1965, p. 43; Tom Barrett becomes his first room-mate, p. 44; p. 51; p. 53; p. 74-5; p. 86;

USS TICONDEROGA: p. 3.

TONKIN GULF INCIDENT: p. 3.

VIETNAMESE COMMUNISM: p. 126-7;

Appendix

UNITED STATES MILITARY ACADEMY

West Point, New York

The Second Sol Feinstone Lecture

THE MEANING OF FREEDOM

by

Rear Admiral Jeremiah A. Denton, Jr., USN

2 April 1975

The Meaning of Freedom

In my lifetime, I have learned enough about West Point - its principles, its purposes, and its graduates - to recognize that there is no more appropriate place than here to address the subject: The Meaning of Freedom.

My treatment of the subject will be based on an assumption. I have assumed that it would cause extreme disinterest if I were to engage in the exercise of reciting too many of the previously expressed meanings of freedom - beautiful though so many of those definitions are. We must begin with the knowledge that freedom, like love, is a many splendored thing and that no lecture can do it justice.

This talk is the second of a series on this topic. I believe the subject is so big and the series aspect of its treatment so important that each subsequent lecture should try to build on the previous talks. Thus, let us commence our initial approach on the subject tonight by examining a superb definition of freedom by the man who makes this lecture series possible - Mr. Sol Feinstone. It reads:

> *In the beginning there was the void of sameness; the spark of life made everything, and made everything different.*
>
> *The stamp of sameness is the stamp of death.*
>
> *Freedom to me means a social order based on individual freedom to live differently and to dream differently.*
>
> *I dream of a brotherhood of free nations of free men.*

Analyzing that definition, we find two main elements of freedom emphasized.

First, the right to be different, specifically to live and to dream differently. We note that the word "dream" includes, but poetically transcends, the verb to think.

Nowhere than in America has there been more variety in the kinds of life styles, the kinds of dreaming, working, playing, and dressing. The freedom for exercising that variety has been the key which has unlocked the innovativeness of this nation - producing historically notable innovations in politics, economics and the technical sciences, as well as in the arts - especailly in music. In Mr. Feinstone's definition, these freedoms are appropriately analogized with life, and their absence with death, and indeed freedom has given us our national vitality and underlaid the growth of our spiritual and material power.

The right to live and dream differently has an invaluable and sacred application to the abundance of religious beliefs which have flourished in the United States.

Not only is freedom of religion important, but the most fundamental principle of American Freedom itself, as conceived and built into our Constitution by our Founding Fathers, was the factor of religiosity. The United States was indeed founded as one nation under God, and the distinction between the precious and positive quality of the man of liberty on the one hand, and the empty and destructive nature of the libertine man on the other, is the distinction which verily defines freedom in the original American sense - indeed, in any favorable societal sense.

This distinction is made nicely in another splendid definition of freedom by a great soldier and great American, your former Army Chief of Staff, General Harold K. Johnson, who gave the first lecture in this series, and whose name and deeds are familiar here and so importantly associated with the subject. I quote his concept as he gave it on that occasion:

Freedom means the maintenance of order or a climate of stability within which a person may pursue or advance his individual dignity unobstructed, unimpeded and unfettered - except - except that he not interfere with the ability or right of any other individual to do the same thing.

His emphasis is essential to an understanding of the only kind of somewhat constrained individual freedom that can work successfully for long in our own free national social order, or in any free societal environment - national, tribal or familial.

Indeed, it is that idea which is the most important single ingredient of the progress of civilization.

It is that idea which is implied in the second of the two main points of Mr. Feinstone's definition. I refer to the last sentence of his definition which says, "I believe in the brotherhood of man."

For brotherhood means being cooperative, helpful, considerate and, most of all, loving - tolerance and understanding of other human beings though they think and act differently from us.

Such thought as this was in the forefront of the minds of our Founding Fathers.

George Washington, conscious of the potential danger of intolerance resulting from mutually perceived differences of the many strongly-held religious beliefs among our early citizens, mostly Christian, closed a letter to a Jewish friend with the following beautiful statement:

May the children of the stock of Abraham, who dwell in this land, continue to merit and enjoy the good will of the other inhabitants; while everyone shall sit in safety under his own vine and fig tree, and there shall be none to make him afraid. May the Father of all mercies scatter light and not darkness in our paths, and make us in all our several vocations useful here, and in His own due time and way everlastingly happy.

We who are Christians must remember that Judaism is the Father of Christianity. And we who enjoy the heritage of Judaeo-Christianity would do well to note that Islam shares Judaen history down through the prophet Abraham.

All mankind, believing or not in Jesus Christ as God, admires His teachings which can best be summarized briefly as "Love God, love thy neighbor as thyself."

It would be good if all mankind would agree with Him when He defined the word "Neighbor" in "love thy neighbor as thyself", by His parable of the Good Samaritan. In that parable the loving and helpful neighbor was shown to be a foreigner, a person of different religious beliefs, and of a different color.

The main thing to respect in a man is not his degree of conformance to perfection as judged by our beliefs; instead, we should respect his earnestness of effort to try to be good, his effort to perceive God and His will, his effort to try to avoid abusing his access to freedom by over-indulgence of his desires at the direct or indirect expense of others and at the cost of his own self-degradation. In that sense we must love and respect Moslems, Buddhists, Confucianists and those of other faiths for their earnestness of effort in that respect. We must love those of our own respective faiths whose behavioral imperfections are disproportionately and distortedly publicized.

I do not think it necessary to try to gloss over the fact that I am a Roman Catholic. Needless to say, I believe in my religion, but I am aware that my religion is a faith, not a knowledge.

What I now regard as knowledge, as a result of many rather remarkable experiences in Hanoi, is that there is a God, and that my God answered my prayers. Further, what I believe to be the same God answered the prayers of Jews, Protestants, other Catholics, as well as Confucianists and Buddhists who happen to conceive of God in a different but similar way.

Why do I dwell so much on religion in this talk on freedom?

I dwell on it because before, during, and after my captivity, I have had the conviction, tempered like steel in captivity and rendered urgent by what I have found since my return, that too many Americans are forgetting what made this nation great, and are suffering from misconceptions of the meaning of freedom. They are losing their orientation - the orientation of the human species with respect to God, of the citizen with respect to country, of child to parent, of parent to child, of the places in society of law and order, sacrifice, and cooperation, and ultimately the relationship between international peace with the collective personal integrity of each citizen in each respective country.

In particular, I am shocked to find that too many of us are forgetting, in a repetition of an ancient and historical cycle, that people must make a special effort not to lose their spirituality in an environment characterizable as one of material surfeit. Surfeit tends to bring on a materialistic mentality which, ironically and justly, in many cases has caused the forfeiture of the wealth and, more importantly, the freedom of the people of that nation.

As most or all of you know, it is truly ordinary to ask and then to receive help from God under painful physical pressure. However, it is much rarer and nobler to rise to the occasion, to pray, and to behave conscientiously by virtue of our own intellectually self-generated pressures in a comfortable and affluent environment. I believe that such an effort is the only hope of this surfeited nation - the only alternative to rising from the ashes, if rising is possible, after a great fall toward which the nation appears to be headed. When I call this nation surfeited, I hasten to recognize that there are pockets of real poverty in America. But having seen men in North Vietnam fight over empty tin cans, and having myself eaten human waste (boiled) in the hope of gaining some protein, I believe that there is much here that is falsely perceived as poverty and related to the desire to have what others have - things which are luxuries, not real necessities.

Now, let me try to develop a definition of human dignity which is, I believe, at the heart of the meaning of freedom. Webster gives a number of meanings for the respective words: human and dignity. Some definitions differ sharply and even contrast with one another. Of extreme importance is that, since 1970, the dictionary definitions given for the word "human" appear to have changed in a vitally important way.

For now, allow me to discuss a few pre-1971 dictionary definitions for our purposes today.

First, the word "human" which comes from the latin humanus, akin to homo, a man. "Of, belonging to, or typical of mankind (the human race)". Further "having or showing qualities, as rationality or fallibility, viewed as distinctive of such individuals." Here the key aspect of man emerges.

This definition declares that among all known species of life only man has the power to do wrong. Plants and animals cannot do wrong. Plants have the capabilities of sustenance, growth and reproduction. Animals have these, plus sensitivity and instinct. But man alone also has rationality, with consequent fallibility. This combination implies conscience and intellect, and the history and feats of mankind, though full of examples of fallibility, also prove the almost incredible power of his reason and conscientious effort to avoid fallibility.

A code of conduct is also implied when one speaks of fallibility.

Until recently, to Americans that code was the Ten Commandments. But as the song says "Times, they are a-changing."

Next word, "dignity" from latin dignus: One dictionary definition given, which we shall reject, is, "a high position, rank or title." Let us use this one: "worthiness, proper pride and self-respect."

Let us disqualify all other definitions regardless of their popularity. This disqualification includes denial of the idea that dignity is something that can be given to a person. Dignity, defined as worthiness, proper pride, or self-respect, has to be earned.

So, certain voguish nostrums about "imparting" human dignity, or all people being "entitled" to human dignity, just do not make sense. What does make sense is a strong effort to impart to all human kind the opportunity to earn a sense of worthiness, proper pride or self-respect. In this regard, equality of opportunity for education is a legitimate, and as yet unfulfilled, goal even in this land of freedom. Further progress is still required in other areas such as achieving equal pay for equal work, irrespective of color or sex.

The questions of what a citizen is entitled to from the State, and what the State is entitled to from the citizen, are also directly linked to how we define human dignity.

In my personal opinion, the right answers are to be found only from arguments predicted on the proper orientation of man as a species subordinate to God, of citizens subordinate to State, of State responsibility to the citizen.

When Christ was asked by his enemies what he thought of the people of Israel having to pay taxes to the Romans, his answer was clear, "Render unto Caesar what is Caesar's and unto God what is God's." The United States Army in Vietnam and the Charge of the Light Brigade, if not directly comparable, may both be sad, but glorious, examples of conformance with that dictum - and such readiness by armies to conform thus is the sine qua non of nation states. Peace is an ideal, but it takes "two to tango." No nation has done more to prove its interest in preserving peace. But we are forgetting that peace has a price in the face of raw aggression. We are forgetting that strength - not weakness - preserves peace. We are forgetting the sacrifice of those from whom we inherited not only peace, but the power and responsibility to try to preserve it. Not just peace in the sense of preventing fighting, but peace by promoting the betterment of life for people all over the world, including those in Communist countries.

Citizens, especially American citizens, owe much to their country. At this moment in our history's shifting tides I believe we, the citizenry, are relatively overconscious of what the States owes to us. Unity behind our leader, whether Democrat or Republican, is certainly more needed now than destructive criticism. Familiarity with affluence has inverted the Mavlovian hierarchy of values among too many Americans, with security and sustenance assumed as rights to be afforded by the government while the citizen dabbles only with self-gratification.

We are tending now to ask too much recompense for too little output, which is the simple cause of inflation.

The Bible, in both Old and New Testaments, holds numerous statements about the need for all men to work for their living and for the well-being of their families. Helplessness, but not laziness, should receive hand-outs.

On the international scene there is much helplessness which cries out for us to do what we can to get the ignorant and hungry on their feet and self-sustaining as soon as possible. Such an effort, charitably conceived, would usually result in achieving material as well as spiritual gain for ourselves in the longer range of a decade or two.

But on the national scene we need now to remind ourselves that the performance of manual labor is a major source of human dignity, and that no nation can long survive without her citizens' willingness to do an honest day's work for fair wages. David Ben-Gurion once said:

We don't consider manual work as a curse, or a bitter necessity, not even as a means by making a living. We consider it as a high human function, as a basis of human life, the most dignified thing in the life of the human being, and which ought to be free, creative. Men ought to be proud of it.

Our school system, parental guidance, and the tremendous power of television must help communicate to our young what is unique and precious about the American way of life which places such high value on human dignity. How sad that the opposite trend seems to be the case.

It is self-evident, but not widely enough appreciated, that the American way of life has proved itself to be the best in the history of the world. Measured in terms of economic prosperity there has never been another nation with so much accumulated power and goods, nor a nation with its power and goods so equitably (not equally) distributed among the masses of its populations. This pinnacle of material prosperity has been reached in spite of our not having the largest population, nor the most natural resources per capita, nor the greatest size of the world's nations. In addition to economic prosperity, the United States of America has been generally regarded, even secretly among its enemies, in spite of its imperfections, as a spiritual beacon that has gleamed with unique brightness throughout the world.

I have learned that, if asked to define the American way of life, individual Americans are likely to give markedly different answers. Many of the answers would contain such terms as "freedoms" of one kind or another, or "government by the people"; and, increasingly as the years go by, more and more of the definitions offered tend to include the term "human dignity".

In closing, let me try to grope even closer to the definition of the peculiarly American connotation of the word "freedom" by developing a rough definition of the American way of life.

Let us define the American way of life, or the United States form of freedom, in specific terms:

A democratic, pluralistic political order consciously exploiting individual motivation for material gain as the reliable prime mover of its economic system, which is free enterprise in principle and regulated by the political system only when and as necessary to guarantee application of the principle of love thy neighbor as thyself. The legal and judicial systems are based on the Ten Commandants.

More briefly, we can state it as an equation: America equals free enterprise, plus love of God and neighbor.

Consider this definition as generally analogous to a sort of chemical equation in which the interaction between free enterprise and love is a perpetually on-going process, with the product (the American way of life) undergoing constant change.

For example, the eradication of slavery was a terribly needed change, one of the many products of the on-going confrontation between that which free economics can lead someone or some group to want and that which majority conscience will permit by virtue of the love factor in the equation. Free enterprise is driven by the reliable desire for self-improvement, but includes freedom to raise flowers for beauty not profit. The love factor instills compassion for the helpless, the disadvantaged, and the needy; it includes regard for fair play even among power-equals; and it ensures consideration for minorities on the part of the mandate-empowered majority. In sum, the love factor, basic in the principles of our Judaeo-Christian and Revolutionary heritage, tends to keep free enterprise hones and empathetic in both the national and the international sense.

Going back to our definition and discussion of human dignity, which is the same concept our Founding Fathers embraced, we can see why this nation originally chose free enterprise as our basic economic system. They knew that more people would benefit from this system over the long term. Further, their consciousness of the true meaning of human dignity is why we chose to regulate that enterprise with the milk of human love as it was derived from the principles of Judaeo-Christianity. Thus, the accelerating corruption of the national concept of human dignity directly threatens the manner of exercising both the free enterprise and love factors, each of which is essential to our way of life.

We must reverse a swelling tide which is tending to cause national abandonment of the bedrock of principles upon which we base our version of the meaning of the terms human dignity and freedom.

How ironic that the very prosperity we earned through conformance to spiritual values is the root cause of our ever-expanding sense of materialsm. Coping with prosperity has been a fatally difficult problem for a number of empires, nations and peoples; and, the end has always come by drowning in a sea of materialism and selfishness. Thus, the root cause of our problem is as old as Adam and Eve and is indeed identical to theirs. But the degree of our prosperity is so advanced that the degree of our national temptation to abandon that which made us great is also relatively severe. Beyond this severe degree of temptation, there is a new unprecedented operational aspect to our present day problem. There are now fantastically prolific means by which these temptations are spread among our people and are conditioning us all to social acceptance of yeilding to the temptations.

I refer to the television medium in particular and to certain other media which now exercise unanticipated, uncalculated and increasingly harmful power over our citizenry through redundant access to their minds, Especially the minds of our children. There are many exemplary men and women employed in the industry; but, unfortunately, this power has more of profit-motivation than sense of national or moral responsibility in the manner in which it is so freely wielded. Sex is being sold as the invention of the devil, not of God; and it is not subject to God's rules. Violence vies with illicit sex in salability. I believe this new aspect of our "coping-with-prosperity" problem is now resulting in a downward step-by-step process, with each step being deeper and broader. The family, as an institution, is in the process of destruction and with it - so is the nation. This tide must be reversed as a matter of priority, and

I am among those who shall try to reverse it.

While in Hanoi I planned to buy a piece of land on a pretty bay called Perdido Bay. I have bought the land and plan some day to build a little place on it with a rose trellis at the entrance to the walk. In Hanoi I thought up the name that would be inscribed on that trellis as the title of my villa. The name will be, "Perdido Y Encontrado". Lost and Found. It would go without saying that what was lost and found is freedom.

Yes, having lost it, I have grown to appreciate it more fully than before. I have seen the converse of freedom, not only from the perspective of one of many Americans who was treated badly by the Communist system, but from the perspective of one who sympathetically observed North Vietnamese suffering grossly and unjustly at the hands of their own government. I learned from personal contact what that system is, what it is based on, how and why it began, as well as the direct and indirect methods it uses to crush freedoms inside and outside its borders. What I have been talking about is what basically differentiates their system from ours.

Hopefully the entire country will learn enough of how horrible that other system is perceived to be by the millions who do understand its horrors and who have been fleeing to avoid coming under that system at any cost. Hopefully we will experience a conscience-stricken re-awakening if, and when, we look back on the unprecedented betrayal of our own principles. This betrayal is spelled out by our too general willingness to put the unambiguous, naked aggression in Southeast Asia in the "too hard file", and by our rationalizing that South Vietnam enslaved is preferable to allowing them to fight with the promised means to defend themselves, which they were doing so well until they knew that the help was being cut off.

We should also be shocked now by the clear story spelled out in our own over-crowded jails, our jammed psychiatric wards, our rising crime and divorce rates, our depreciating educational systems, the increasing number of illegitimate, abandoned, mistreated, bewildered children, and the tens of thousands of draft-dodgers. Hopefully from all of this we will be shocked into a new appreciation for the meaning, the source, the pricelessness, and the threatened transiency of America's freedom. Otherwise we may bitterly learn the truth of the warning of William Penn: "If men will not submit to being governed by God, they shall be doomed to be governed by tyrants."

We are members of this nation's most admired profession, the military. I think that to deserve this admiration, we now have not only the duty to defend this best of all Fatherlands, but the duty to speak out within our lawful limits and to give the kind of example that will preserve the honor which makes this country worth defending.

So, again, West Pointers, it is Duty, Honor, Country, but with new and urgently pressing connotations. God bless you and help you in your dedicated efforts.

The Adaptation of, and Dependence on

SOUND

As Experienced by

American Prisoners of War in North Vietnam

A research paper submitted in partial
fulfillment of the course requirements in
Behavioral Science
MN 2106

by

Everett Alvarez

7 November 1974

TABLE OF CONTENTS

	Page
Forward	ii
Introduction	1
I. The Nothingness of Four Walls	2
II. Adapting to Our New World	4
III. The Effects Began to Show	8
IV. Sound -- Our New Weapon	11
V. Conclusion	13
Bibliography	16

FORWARD

The purpose of this paper is to explore the effects of sensory deprivation as was experienced by the American Prisoners of War in North Vietnam, and the methods that were adopted by the POW's in order to counter these effects.

Many stories have recently come out in the open as to the treatment and conditions under which the POW's existed. I have referred to a couple of books written by some of my good friends, as sources for some material I used here. However, the bulk of meterial used in this paper stems from my own experiences, having lived eight and one-half years as America's longest held prisoner in North Vietnam.

Not all the prisoners experienced exactly the same living conditions. However, from 5 August 1964 until February, 1973, I had the opportunity to personally experience just about every type of living condition and situation that was faced.

Human Sense and Perception

. . . and men should know that from nothing else but from the brain come joys, delights, laughter and jests, and sorrows, griefs, despondency and lamentations, and by this, in an especial manner, we acquire wisdom and knowledge, and <u>see</u> and <u>hear</u> and know what are foul and what are fair, what sweet and what unsavoury . . . and by the same organ we become mad and delirious and fears and terrors assail us, some by night and some by day, and dreams and untimely wanderings, and cares that are not suitable and ignorance of present circumstances, deseutude and unskillfulness . . .

Hippocrates, On the Sacred Disease

INTRODUCTION.

To most of us, this world is a maze of things that continually fill our senses. During the course of a normal day's routine, our senses of vision, of hearing, and of touch are constantly taking in countless objects and events. Regardless of where we may be, be it the downtown district of a large metropolitan city during the evening traffic rush, or involved in the busy academic schedule at NPS, or even in the quiet solitude of a few relaxing minutes in the privacy of our own homes, our senses are the receptors of an uncountable number of items.

Furthermore, to a great degree, this reception or ability to receive, is as much a conscious part of our basic every day existence as is eating, drinking, or breathing. Subconsciously, we accept these inputs as a matter of fact. The ability to have and use our senses is part of our natural being.

But, have you ever asked yourself? What would happen if you were thrust into a situation where you were deprived of the ability to employ your senses? True, many people, whether by accident or by chance of nature, have lost their sight or their hearing or have lost a limb or even more. It is obvious this person must undergo a great adjustment process if he desires to continue a useful existence in one form or another.

Such an adjustment was imposed on the Prisoners of War who were detained in the prison camps in North Vietnam. This adjustment was different in the sense that the prisoners did not physically lose their senses; but the adjustment was there due to the conditions imposed in which we were deprived of the normal function of our senses.

I. <u>THE NOTHINGNESS OF FOUR WALLS</u>

Almost immediately after capture, the aviators that had been shot down and apprehended by the North Vietnamese were confined in almost unimaginable conditions.

> Bodies built for movement were confined to closet-like boxes, active minds were forced to be idle within the numbing nothingness of four walls in a dingy little cell . . .
> (Risner, Introduction)

Many lived in cells 7 feet by 7 feet. All through the day there was no light—save whatever daylight could filter through small ventilation ducts near the ceiling about 18 feet above the floor. The concrete walls were barren. The concrete floors were almost always moist. Most cells had two concrete slab beds on either side—each just over two feet wide and running the length of the cell. This left a narrow aisle about two and a half feet wide and seven feet long in which the POW's walked. And at one end of the aisle was the entrance to the cell which was blocked by a heavy steel reinforced door. If a person was fortunate, sometimes this door would have a crack or a termite eaten pinhole in it through which he might be able to peek out, or through which a small ray of daylight might find its way to penetrate into the cell.

Most of the prisoners had a straw mat, a mosquito net, a water jug, a metal cup, one blanket, a set of prison striped pajamas, and two pairs of shorts. These were all our earthly possessions. Each cell was also furnished with a "Bo." (A small wooden bucket which served a combined purpose as our commode, our sink, and our stool—whenever the need for one arose.)

For the first few years that the North Vietnamese had American prisoners, the Viets would allow the prisoners out of their cells for just five to ten minutes a day to wash, rinse our clothing, and dump the "Bo's." (If a prisoner was being punished or under maximum security for some reason, he would not be allowed these "privileges.") Except for the times that the prisoners were taken to interrogation, one never ventured more than a few feet from his cell, and then for the reason stated above.

Nothing, absolutely nothing, was provided for the prisoners to occupy their time, or amuse or entertain themselves. Furthermore, if the Vietnamese discovered that a prisoner <u>had</u> smuggled something into his cell in order to occupy his time, he would then be beaten or punished in some other form for violating the camp regulations.

These conditions persisted for a long, long time. I personally know of individuals who lived in solitary conditions such as this for as long as one, two, three, and for a couple, as long as four years.

It was not that we were treated radically different than other POW's in history, "for the Korean POW's experienced

similar treatment under the North Koreans and Chinese whenever the opportunity presented itself to the captors..."
(Eastman)

> There were thousands of POW's in the Korean conflict, whereas in North Vietnam, the average number of American POW's for the greater part of the eight and one half years that we had prisoners there numbered less than 350 Americans.
> (CNO Roster)

Thus it can be easily seen that the North Vietnamese had both the time and facilities to handle the prisoners in the manner best suited for their purposes. At least this was true for the first two or three years. Most prisoners spent the early years in solitary. Then in 1966 the North Vietnamese gradually started moving men into groups of two and sometimes three when the influx of new prisoners became greater. These men then lived in similar types of cells—cramped for space, barren, with little ventilation or daylight and almost no outside time.

> The North Vietnamese went to great extremes to construct cells for one to three men. They made every effort to prevent communication between PW's... PW's caught communicating with each other outside their cells were immediately punished... cellmates had to speak in a whisper so PW's in adjacent cells could not hear... Complete control through isolation was sought by the captors.
> (Gaither, page 86)

II. ADAPTING TO OUR NEW WORLD

For almost all of our waking moments, there was nothing to see. One could just as well have closed his eyes, and kept them closed. (Some, for the most part, did just that.) There was very little to touch or feel. And most of us who spent a very long period of time in solitary confinement may just as well have lost the ability to talk. We had no one with whom to speak.

As a consequence, and out of necessity, we had to adapt ourselves to a new manner of living. We depended primarily on sound. Our hearing was now our primary sensory in our new existence. We came to know our new immediate world through its sounds. As time passed and as the weeks rolled by--turning into months, then years--the sounds we lived with and learned to know so well were our only real world.

From the time the gongs would ring in the early morning, until they rang again at night marking the end of another day, familiar noises filled the long hours signifying the passing events of the daily routines.

We learned to tell by the particular way the turnkey (guard) rattled his keyring who the turnkey was for that day. We could tell by the manner in which he handled his keys and the rate at which he opened the cell doors if he was being hurried or if he was in no particular hurry. We could sense anything unusual that was happening or if the turnkey was just in the area conducting his routine chores, and if he was in a pleasant or "sour" mood.

We could tell by the particular creaking noises the doors made as they were being swung open whose cell it was. The shuffling noises as the rubber sandals scraped along the concrete floors gave us the clue as to who was out of his cell washing himself or dumping his "Bo."

We learned to recognize each prisoner's peculiar cough, or the manner in which he cleared his throat, or wheezed, or sniffed his nose. We also learned to recognize each of the guards by their gutteral commands, their individual vocal characteristics, the peculiar tones of their voices.

We also learned to keep an open ear for danger signs—especially when we were engaged in some covert activity, such as communicating. The swishing of a guard's ammo belt against his trousers, or the pat of his gun butt against his leg were warning sounds of a guard approaching. As we quietly pressed our ear against a crack in the door or lay on the floor with our ear against a rat-hole at the bottom of the door, these same noises indicated if the guard was equipped with an AK-45 semi-automatic rifle, or an old World War II model carbine.

Our sense of hearing in a fashion became so sophisticated that after some training we knew whenever a guard was in our area making his rounds, if he was daydreaming or lollygagging, if he was unusually alert or wary. His pace indicated his intentions, if he had seen something or discovered something out of the ordinary. We could even tell by the combinations of many noises that he generated where he was looking and at what he was looking. What was more amazing to me was that all this time, unbeknownst to the guards, they were under constant sensory observation the entire time they were in the area of the cell blocks.

There were also the friendly sounds—the small, incidental, relatively unimportant noises, such as the rats scurrying throughout the cellblocks at night in their search for food, the chirping of a bird somewhere outside, the rustle of a stiff breeze through the leaves of a tree beyond the courtyard wall, the rushing of the water in the drains or gutters after an afternoon rain storm, the sounds of the food carriers bringing the daily rations into the cell blocks---these noises gave us the feeling of comfort in an odd sort of way. For in this limited world in which we now lived, certain sounds indicated that everything was "normal," as far as life for a POW in North Vietnam went.

And then there were the other sounds---the unfriendly ones. These were the sounds that brought fear and represented real danger. Sounds that brought an empty feeling in the pit of our stomachs and made us break out in a cold sweat. The shuffle of more than one guard's feet marching into our area meant someone was being taken to quiz (interrogation)-- especially if it happened at night, for that meant the urgency on the part of the captors was greater. We all learned to know that awesome, terrible feeling so well as we expectantly wondered . . . "Are they coming for me?"

As the cell door creaked open, there was a mixed emotion of relief to know it wasn't me they were after, and a feeling of gratefulness for being spared one more time. And yet, there was a deep feeling of sorrow for the other man who was being taken out, wondering what they were after this time and how long he would be gone. (During certain periods of our capitivity, men who were taken out for interrogation like this never did return to their cells. Some of them returned to the United States in 1974 in coffins--the North Vietnamese having listed them as having died in Captivity on the dates they were taken to interrogation.)

At times we lived in fear, at other times we lived with the feeling of relative security. But whatever our emotions or our thoughts were pertaining to our prison life--they were primarily generated by the sounds we heard.

III. THE EFFECTS BEGAN TO SHOW

The reason why the North Vietnamese imposed these harsh conditions is obvious. Their purpose was complete control. Our captors isolated us because they wanted to discourage any unified feelings, any united efforts of resistance as a group. Through complete isolation there was a:

> ... psychological impact and transformation that took place which would make the PW's more susceptible to exploitation ...
> (Eastman, page 4)

> ... there is the realization that one is at the mercy of his captors, that the captor has complete physical control over him, that all moral values, protective laws and avenues of recourse or evading the situation have been removed from his environment ...
> (Schein, page 22)

The effects of sensory deprivations soon became obvious to most of us. Many of us began to react in various different ways. Some went into states of prolonged depression, some could not eat, others suffered from nightmares and hallucinations, etc. I, myself, experienced a combination of several of these effects.

Effects of isolation are fairly well known.

Reports of observations by philosophers, mystics, prisoners in solitary confinement, explorers and shipwrecked sailors have drawn attention to the marked changes in behavior of people exposed to isolation. These changes have included deterioration in the ability to think and reason, perceptual distortions, gross disturbances in feeling states, and occurrences of vivid imagery, sometimes in the form of bizarre hallucinations and delusions.
(Heron, page 10)

People confined to dark, quiet chambers often display bizarre stress and anxiety symptoms, including hallucinations, delusions, apathy, and the fear of losing sanity.

... Our earliest prisons were built so that the sinner might have solitude in which to meditate on and repent his sins; but they produced more suicides and psychotics than repentant sinners. ... 'Cabin fever' and 'going stir-crazy' are still potent expressions for the effects of loneliness ...
(Haythorn, page 155)

In fact, we suffered from everything mentioned here. Furthermore, we recognized what these effects were doing to us, both physically and mentally. Besides the dangers of losing our physical and mental balance, we could see that these conditions caused us to be affected to a greater degree to propaganda.

What was probably the greatest realization on the part of the POW's in North Vietnam was the necessity to combat this effort of the North Vietnamese in every way possible, both mentally and physically. We realized the necessity to remain united in our efforts of group resistance to their propaganda and indoctrination attempts. We understood that every man needed the feeling of belonging merely as a matter of survival alone.

> . . . Research shows . . . that man needs a minimum level of stimulation—and a variety of stimulation—to survive and retain his facilities.
>
> Man is a social animal . . . He needs other people; He gets emotional support from them; he understands and tests reality and his feelings and beliefs, in large part through his interactions with them.
> (Haythorn, page 152)

Later on, when groups of two or three were formed, the same basic situations existed. Even though most men now had a roommate, someone to share experiences with, many dangers were still present.

> . . . a variety of psychological strains—apart from any physical dangers—are created when small groups are isolated from their fellows and confined to limited spaces . . .
> (Vernon, McGill)

> . . . Interpersonal conflict becomes exaggerated . . . there is less chance to go outside and blow off steam or to escape from the difficulties of the adjustment . . .
> (Ruff, Long)

It soon became obvious that if we were to survive and if we were to maintain any degree of sanity for a prolonged period of time, we would have to communicate. And communicate we did. Regardless of the risks involved, the dangers present, the threats of punishment by the officers and guards of the camps, we communicated every single chance we had. Anytime an opportunity arose which would enable one to talk to another prisoner that was in solitary, we availed ourselves of the opportunity, even if just to pass the time of day. All day, and well into the night, the lines of communication were going. Mostly it was nothing more than idle chatter, but it did wonders for our morale. And _morale_ was such a key factor. In order to keep one's spirits high, to keep from losing hope, to give each other comforting thoughts, it was so vitally important to be able to communicate with the men in the other cells.

IV. **SOUND -- OUR NEW WEAPON**

Because of the strictness of the camp regulations forbidding communication with men outside of our own cells, we had to find new, covert means in which to talk to our buddies. Basically, these new means evolved on the use of any mode of generating sound that we could possibly get away with.

The most common method was by tapping on the walls of the cells which were brick and mortar. (McGrath, page 18) We soon discovered the brick walls to be excellent conductors of sound. A light tap with the fingernail could be clearly heard if the man on the opposite side of the wall pressed his ear to the wall. And, there was no danger of the noise being heard outside the cell block by a roving guard. Soon a completely new alphabet was devised utilizing the tapping sound (similar to Morse code). The use of it extended to where message traffic was flowing continually from one end of a cell block to another; then later, from cell block to cell block, from building to building.

As time progressed, the men were gradually let out of their cells more often to do odd tasks such as sweeping the courtyards, weeding the yards, planting small gardens, etc. Whenever the opportunity presented itself during the performance of these odd jobs, the POW's almost always sent code;

be it by the noise the brooms made when swept against the concrete yards, by the striking action of a hand sickle cutting weeds or by the noise of a hoe striking the ground. It even developed to the point that some men sent messages to others by the noises made by shaking out their blankets, or by snapping their towels or wet clothing when they washed them out.

This is not to say that the efforts of communicating were always successful. There were countless times that the individuals were caught, and punished. But it wasn't long before they were right back at it. No matter how hard the North Vietnamese tried to stop the men from communicating, they were never successful for very long.

One example of the ingenuity the POW's displayed is shown in the method of communication developed in a couple of maximum security type camps. The cells were separated by doublewalls; i.e., a void space between the two walls so as to cut out communication by tapping. The guards were doubled as a protection against any known noise communications.

In these camps, the means of sending code developed through the use of the "natural" and sometimes gutteral noises a person made; such as a cough, a clearing of the throat, a sneeze, a belch, a burp, a blowing of the nose, and for a couple of prisoners who had the latent talent to do so at will---the passing of gas. Each of these sounds, or combination of some, represented a letter of the alphabet under this system. It was found that through the silent, echoing passageways of the cell block, these noises were conducted quite easily. Of course, it would take a very long time to transmit even the shortest of messages. Sometimes, depending on the conditions, it would take a complete afternoon to send out one sentence. But the POW's had nothing else to do, so it also was a good time occupier.

I heard of one individual living in one of these camps that would feign sleep for a couple of hours each day during the siesta hours, and through his snoring managed to send complete transmissions, telling how everyone was and what was going on in his cell block. These transmissions were readily received by the men living in two other cell blocks. (Incidentally, this was a method the North Vietnamese never caught on to. As soon as conditions permitted, it was dropped because of the difficulty and time needed.)

V. CONCLUSION

I hope I have stressed the point of the importance that was placed on the maximum utilization of the facilities available while making the transition to a new way of life. In adapting ourselves to this new form of existence, it was important to realize what was happening to us, to recognize the effects of the conditions imposed, and to undertake a self styled program to combat these effects.

The transition from the normal way of life to one of deprivation was difficult indeed. To recognize the routes which one could take to be able to cope with the situation wa challenging. And what <u>was</u> a wonderment of surprise to most of us was the manner in which we could exist in this new way of life; the countless joys we received over some exchanges that were transmitted through the walls, the sorrow we all felt to hear some depressing news that came from a message sent from somewhere beyond the walls, and the numerous times our spirits were bolstered by a few well coined phrases tapped out by a friend who somehow knew how we felt at the time.

Men got to know each other extremely well through these conversations through brick walls. We knew all about each other's boyhood, his background, his experiences, his wife and children, his dreams and his ambitions. All this was passed over the long periods one lived next to another, even though the two had never lain eyes on one another.

What was interesting to most of us was the visual impression we had of what a person looked like strictly from the conversations we had. In our own minds we had preconceived ideas of what he should look like just from what he said, or how he said it. Most of the time, years went by before we finally had the chance to actually see the man. And most of the time our impressions were completely wrong. Instead of the tall, dark haired, well built, deep voiced, heavily bearded individual we had imagined for example, we would be deeply surprised to find ourselves seeing a short, paunchy, balding individual with a high, almost falsetto type voice.

Imagine the situation years later, after our return home, at a function or reunion of some sort, as two individuals were being introduced:

"You're Jim Black?? Hi! . . . I'm Tom!! I lived next to you for two years in the Zoo!"

"Tom! . . . No kidding!! You don't look at all like what you're supposed to . . . I mean, not what I thought you should! . . . Holy Cow!!:

And so life went as a POW in North Vietnam.

BIBLIOGRAPHY

1. Eastman, Leonard C., A Comparison of Prisoner of War Treatment, a paper prepared by author for Behavioral Science, MN 2106, Naval Postgraduate School, February, 1974.

2. Gaither, Ralph, With God in a POW Camp, Nashville, Tenn.; Broadman Press, 1973.

3. Haythorn, William W., and Irwin Altman, "Together in Isolation," Social Psychology, October, 1974.

4. Heron, Woodbun, "Cognitive and Physiological Effects of Perceptual Isolation," Sensory Deprivation, Harvard University Press, Cambridge, Massachusetts, 1965.

5. McGrath, J. M., "American POW's: North Vietnam and North Korea," The Management Quarterly, Naval Postgraduate School, June, 1974.

6. Pierce, John R., David, Edward E., Jr., Mans World of Sound, Doubleday and Co., 1958.

7. Risner, Robinson, The Passing of the Night, Random House, 1973.

8. Roster of Returned POW's by Services, Published by Chief of Naval Operations, Department of the Navy, Distributed to returned POW's, 17 April, 1973.

9. Psychology Today, Chapter 14, CRM Books, 1972.

10. Ruff, George E., Long, E. Z., Thaler, Victor H., "Reactions to Reduced Sensory Input," Sensory Deprivation, Harvard University Press, Cambridge, Massachusetts, 1965.

11. Schein, Edgar H., "Reaction Patterns to Severe Chronic Stress in American Army Prisoners of War of the Chinese," Journal of Social Issues, 1957.

12. Vernon, Jack A., McGill, Thomas E., Gulick, W. L., Candlenlod, D. K., "Effects of Human Isolation," Sensory Deprivation, Harvard University Press, Cambridge, Massachusetts, 1965.

13. Wyburn, G. M., Pickford, R. W., Hirst, R. J., Human Senses and Perception, 1964.